PARISH CHURCHES
OF GREATER LONDON:
A GUIDE

by

Michael Hodges

With photographs by the author

Heritage of London Trust
2015

In piam memoriam the Reverend Henry Croyland Thorold,
sometime Squire of Marston Hall, Lincolnshire,
author of *Lincolnshire Churches Revisited*
and many other works.

"Matchless never to be forgotten friend" in the words of the
poet Henry King, sometime Bishop of Chichester.

© Michael J. Hodges, 2015

ISBN 978-0-946694-08-2

Published by The Heritage of London Trust, 34 Grosvenor Gardens,
London SW1W 0DH

Printed by Henry Ling Ltd, Dorchester

Cover photograph of St Mary Magdalene Paddington, by the author

Contents

Boroughs of Greater London

HRH The Duke of Gloucester KG GCVO

KENSINGTON PALACE
LONDON W8 4PU

I am delighted to have the opportunity to write the Foreword to this book, which covers so many of London's fascinating and often over-looked churches. London's parish churches are a vital part of its heritage, telling the story of the city, its people and their faith over many centuries. This book will encourage an appreciation of all they have to offer.

London is a city that has been expanding for many centuries, and for many years faster than any other city. During that time church building has had to keep up with the growing population.

To build a church requires the confidence of its creators to believe they know what is best for their community. Attitudes and tastes change from generation to generation. 'New' architecture may be admired or regretted and it is unlikely that any reader of this volume will appreciate every one of these churches. It requires a very comprehensive education to understand all nuances of each new influence in the design of churches.

For thirty-five years, the Heritage of London Trust has been supporting the restoration of London's historic buildings, monuments and churches across all the city's boroughs. As Patron of the Trust, I am very proud of all it has achieved. The Trust continues to make a major contribution to the preservation of London's wonderful heritage for the benefit of future generations.

I hope that this book will enable many people to understand better the significance of 'their' church and those of other neighbourhoods and appreciate that the role they play in the townscapes reflects the time of their building.

V

The fine red brick exterior of Holy Trinity, Sloane Street, Chelsea

INTRODUCTION, ACKNOWLEDGEMENTS AND BIBLIOGRAPHY

The idea for this book sprang from *The Parish Churches of Wiltshire* by Brian Woodruffe, published by the Wiltshire Historic Churches Trust in 2011. Diana Beattie, then Director of The Heritage of London Trust (HOLT), thought London was in need of a similar work in order to draw the attention of interested people to its rich ecclesiological heritage. Her support has been invaluable as has been that of her successor Nicola Stacey and her colleague Nicholas Bell. Dudley Fishburn, Chairman of HOLT, has maintained a supervisory eye.

Greater London is a considerable area, measuring some 606 square miles and consisting of 32 boroughs, many of which I had never attempted to visit in any detail (or at all) before. The exercise has, however, been fascinating.

The most dramatic element of local government reorganisation in London was the disappearance of the ancient County of Middlesex, in two tranches. In 1889 it lost Camden, Hackney, Hammersmith & Fulham, Islington, Kensington & Chelsea, Tower Hamlets and Westminster to the new County of London. This was followed in 1965 by the total abolition of Middlesex and the transfer of Barnet, Brent, Ealing, Enfield, Haringey, Harrow, Hillingdon, Hounslow, Islington and Richmond (Twickenham) to the new Greater London Council. John Betjeman had a great affection for Middlesex as a county and wrote "a few surviving hedges keep alive our lost Elysium – rural Middlesex again". The hayfields of Perivale and the mayfields of Greenford, which he hymned, are, alas, unlikely to be seen again.

Diana suggested at the start I exclude the City as she felt this had been more than adequately covered by other books. I decided, somewhat reluctantly, for reasons of space, to restrict myself to buildings which are or have been Anglican or Catholic parish churches, thereby excluding four Cathedrals (St Paul's, Westminster and Southwark (x2)), one Royal Peculiar (Westminster Abbey), a large number of extremely interesting chapels and an even vaster number of nonconformist buildings. As it is I cover some 420 buildings; the relevant five volumes of the new(ish) London Pevsner list almost 1200 Anglican and Catholic parish churches so this volume discusses approximately a third of those mentioned.

I appreciate that my list of some 420 churches will not be the list of many others. I am sure I have left out the occasional gem and doubtless will be told so. I can only say *mea culpa*.

The format I have adopted is to cover the Greater London area borough by borough treating firstly Anglican churches and then Catholic churches, both in the main chronologically.

I have written a short introduction to each borough in order to provide a degree of context.

This task would have been impossible without the internet. I decided at the start to do my best to avoid troubling busy incumbents, church wardens, etc. and in the main have managed to look at churches mainly before and after weekday services, although a few Sundays in London have also been necessary. I am however specifically grateful to Canon Andrew Tremlett, Rector of St Margaret's Westminster, for allowing me to photograph that church.

Eoghain Murphy, my former colleague at HSBC, has kindly contributed his technical expertise in setting me up with the appropriate tools for the whole exercise.

As will, I think, be apparent to readers I am by no means a professional photographer and it would have been financially impossible to hire such. I do not think I had previously taken a photograph since I laid down my Brownie 127 at some stage in the late 1960s. Fortunately digital photography has made life considerably easier. I am extremely grateful to Brian Woodruffe who has rendered my raw material more acceptable through what might be described as the light rather than the dark arts of modern photographic techniques. I think I can say no professional photographer would have felt remotely comfortable in photographing churches in the short time I frequently had available to me.

Hugh Synge of Tisbury has kindly designed the book. He has also been very helpful in liasing with Henry Ling Ltd of Dorchester on the printing. I am delighted to have been able to have the book published in Dorchester where the Hodges family were wine merchants for 100 years; my grandfather as a younger son however went off to sea with the Royal Navy in the late 19th century. (His siblings took their full part in the religious vicissitudes of the time, one becoming a Catholic Franciscan, one becoming a Catholic nun and one an Anglican nun. Family gatherings to the extent possible must have been interesting.)

My peregrinations through London have on the whole been solitary ones but I am very grateful to my wife Vron, Gail Turner Mooney and Ian Scott for having accompanied me on one or more excursions. The first named in particular has borne the brunt of the preparation of this book.

Anglican churches in the Greater London area are reasonably well known to those who care about such things. This is not so much the case with Catholic churches and I am very grateful to Father Mark Vickers, then Parish Priest of St Peter, Hatfield and now Parish Priest of the Holy Ghost and St Stephen, Shepherds Bush, and to Monsignor John Armitage, then Vicar General of Brentwood Diocese and now Rector of the Catholic Shrine at Walsingham, for drawing my attention to a number of omissions. The latter was also kind enough to arrange entry to a number of buildings in Newham.

My own London ecclesiastical/spiritual journey has embraced a fair number of churches. I was baptised at St Paul's, Knightsbridge. As a London child I was despatched to St Luke's Chelsea and Chelsea Old Church. I returned to the latter after being educated outside London. The desire for "madder music and for stronger wine" subsequently drove me initially to Holy Trinity Brompton and then after some time to St Mary's Bourne Street. I felt I needed a more sacramental form of worship; I had been intrigued by Barbara Pym's use of the phrase "full Catholic privileges" in an Anglican context; a girl friend lived near St Mary's, in Caroline Terrace, although I doubt she ever entered the doors of that curious but moving building. The turmoil affecting the Church of England in the early 1990s drove me to St Stephen's Gloucester Road and then across the Tiber following Bishop (later Monsignor) Graham Leonard and others, initially to the Holy Redeemer, Chelsea, where the Rt Rev Alan Hopes, currently Bishop of East Anglia and quondam Vicar of St Paul's Tottenham, was Parish Priest. Now I share my favours in London equally between the Brompton Oratory and St James, Spanish Place, both at the time of writing headed by converts from Anglicanism, respectively Fathers Large and Colven, formerly Vicar of St Stephen, Gloucester Road. I am also an occasional visitor to The Assumption, Warwick Street, now in the care of the the Ordinariate of Our Lady of Walsingham.

My head lies firmly across the Tiber in Rome. Part of my heart has undoubtedly been left behind in a now pretty much vanished form of Anglo-Catholicism, the tail end of which, I think, was still detectable as late as the 1980s and which to me then possessed a considerable aesthetic and spiritual beauty. I remain very grateful to the late Father John Gilling, once Chaplain of Christ Church, Oxford and then Vicar of St Mary's Bourne Street, for teaching me the essentials of an Anglo-Papalist catholicism, which I like to think consisted of more than an, in many ways regrettable but still retained, love of birettas, fiddleback chasubles, the asperges, Travers baroque, red brick Victorian churches, Comper screens, altars and glass, "solemn devotions" and billowing clouds of incense, the enjoyable "inessentials of the Faith".

I am grateful to Alan Black, a Balliol contemporary, agnostic Scottish Presbyterian and long time (42 years) English master at Lancing College for initially introducing me in the mid 1970s to the architectural pleasures of Anglo-Catholicism, in his case the wonderful 'Wagner' churches in Brighton. I remain very grateful to Anglo-Catholicism for its robust sense of humour, essential kindliness and some extremely good jokes, shades of which may have crept into the text.

John Martin Robinson, the late Rev Henry Thorold, to whose memory this volume is dedicated, the Rev Anthony Symondson SJ (at one stage Vicar of St Anne's Hoxton and the leading expert on Ninian Comper) and the late Rev Gerard Irvine (Vicar in turn of St Dunstan Cranford, St Cuthbert Philbeach Gardens and St Matthew's Westminster) did much to refine my taste, if such indeed was refinable. Peter Howell, Peter Maplestone (seemingly perpetual churchwarden of St Mary-le-Strand and brief colleague during a secondment at the Department of Trade and Industry) and Michael Hall have also been very encouraging of this venture, the first two kindly reading the text and suggesting the additions of various (usually pretty inaccessible) buildings.

Hilaire Gomer has been very helpful with her thoughts on how to publicise the book.

I have been enormously grateful over the years to the Victorian Society, the Georgian Group, the Ecclesiological Society, the Anglo-Catholic History Society and the Pugin Society for the tours and lectures they have organised – in addition to the already mentioned Fr Anthony Symondson, Peter Howell and Michael Hall I must pay tribute to the much appreciated efforts over the years of Gavin Stamp, Rosemary Hill, Geoffrey Brandwood, Ken Powell, Paul Velluet and many others.

I should perhaps state the rather obvious fact that this book is written in the main from an aesthetic rather than a spiritual view. The intelligent reader may detect a certain irritation with Evangelicals. I am not particularly exercised by their creed which in many ways is more sympathetic to me than liberal Anglicanism. I merely wish they did not generally tend to have such disdain for the church furnishings they have inherited from their more cultivated forebears.

I am also an unashamed "pewbore" (copyright Loyd Grossman); a church with its historic (and by this adjective I mean to include Victorian) woodwork ripped out often seems to me to lack any real devotional feel.

It is slightly ironic that after the depredations following the Second Vatican Council Catholics are now making some effort, at least in some places, to restore their churches as regards aesthetics. This is not necessarily true of Anglicans although the effect to date seems possibly worse outside London than within; historic pews are too frequently ripped out and replaced by "comfy" chairs usually in hideous primary colours (although there are still firms which can provide decent lightweight woodwork), often attractively arranged in a nice circle, presumably on the grounds that the Almighty might be offended by any sense of decorum and order. Betjeman and Piper must be turning (or possibly spinning) in their graves.

I am, as will be immediately apparent to the cognoscenti, no architectural historian. I have been very heavily reliant on the five relevant London Volumes of Pevsner, i.e. excluding Volume 1 on the City. These are:

London 2: South: Bridget Cherry and Nikolaus Pevsner (1983)
London 3: North West: Bridget Cherry and Nikolaus Pevsner (1991)
London 4: North: Bridget Cherry and Nikolaus Pevsner (1998)
London 5: East: Bridget Cherry and Nikolaus Pevsner (2005)
London 6: Westminster: Simon Bradley and Nikolaus Pevsner (2003)

Other relevant works include:-

John Betjeman. *Collins Guide to Parish Churches of England & Wales* (1958)
Mervyn Blatch. *A Guide to London Churches* (1978)
Basil Clarke. *Parish Churches of London* (1966)
Denis Evinson. *Catholic Churches of London* (1998)
Michael Hall. *George Frederick Bodley and the Later Gothic Revival in Britain and America* (2014)
Leigh Hatts. *London's 100 Best Churches* (2010)
Christopher Hibbert. *London's Churches* (1988)
Peter Howell & Ian Sutton. *The Faber Guide to Victorian Churches* (1989)
Stephen Humphreys & James Morris. *Churches and Cathedrals of London* (2000)
Simon Jenkins. *England's Thousand Best Churches* (1999)
John Leonard. *London's Parish Churches* (2011)
Christopher Martin. *A Glimpse of Heaven: Catholic Churches of England* (2009)
Arthur Mee. *London* (1937)
John Martin Robinson. *Treasures of the English Churches* (1995)
Gavin Stamp & Colin Amery. *Victorian Buildings of London 1837–1887* (1982)
Anthony Symondson. *Sir Ninian Comper: An Introduction to the Life and Work, with Complete Gazetteer* (2006)
Elizabeth & Wayland Young. *London's Churches* (1986)

I cannot realistically list the masses of church guides, etc., but I am very grateful for the work that has gone into them. There is also an extremely useful website for Catholic churches which operates under the name of *Taking Stock* and which to date covers all Catholic dioceses in England and Wales save that of East Anglia.

I need to thank Alan Black, Elizabeth Philipps (née Black but unrelated) and my wife specifically for their kind and invaluable assistance in proof reading the text. Peter Howell also kindly cast his eye over this introduction and removed a number of factual errors. It was also read by Diana Beattie and Gail Turner Mooney, the latter in particular trying to improve my doubtless inadequate English. Any errors which remain in the book are mine alone.

It is, I suppose, incumbent on me to attempt a brief survey of church building in Greater London outside the City.

In the Middle Ages the present London area outside Westminster and the City was mainly rural and largely consisted of agricultural land and villages. I have been surprised at how many predominantly medieval churches still survive in the Greater London area. These tend to be fewer in the old LCC area although medieval work survives even there.

NORMAN

Norman work survives in the following churches:

St Helen and St Giles, Rainham

St Mary, East Barnet (Barnet)
St Mary, Hendon (Barnet)
St Paulinus, Crayford (Bexley)
St Mary, Willesden (Brent)
St Martin of Tours, Chelsfield (Bromley)
All Saints, Edmonton (Enfield)
St Mary, Harrow (Harrow)
St Helen and St Giles, Rainham (Havering)
St Mary, Harmondsworth (Hillingdon)
St Peter and St Paul, Harlington (Hillingdon)
St Mary, East Bedfont (Hounslow)
St Mary Magdalen, East Ham (Newham)

MEDIEVAL GOTHIC

Medieval Gothic work can be found in the following churches:

St Margaret of Antioch, Barking (Barking and Dagenham)
St Peter and St Paul, Dagenham (Barking and Dagenham)
St Mary, Hendon (Barnet)
St John the Baptist, High Barnet (Barnet)
St Mary, Monken Hadley (Barnet)
St Mary, Bexley (Bexley)
St John the Baptist, Erith (Bexley)
St Paulinus, Crayford (Bexley)
St Mary, Willesden (Brent)

St Nicholas, Chislehurst (Bromley)
St John the Baptist, West Wickham (Bromley)
Old St Pancras (Camden)
St Etheldreda, Ely Place (Camden)
St Mary, Addington (Croydon)
St John the Evangelist, Coulsdon (Croydon)
St Mary, Norwood (Ealing)
Holy Cross, Greenford (Ealing)
St Andrew, Enfield (Enfield)
All Saints, Edmonton (Enfield)
St Nicholas, Plumstead (Greenwich)
St Augustine, Mare Street (Hackney)
Old St Mary, Stoke Newington (Hackney)
All Saints, Fulham (Hammersmith & Fulham)
St Mary, Hornsey (Haringey)
All Hallows, Tottenham (Haringey)
St Mary, Harrow (Harrow)
St John, Pinner (Harrow)
St Mary Magdalen, North Ockendon (Havering)
St Mary and St Peter, Wennington (Havering)
St Andrew, Hornchurch (Havering)
St Laurence, Upminster (Havering)
St Laurence, Cowley (Hillingdon)
St Mary, Harmsworth (Hillingdon)
St Peter and St Paul, Harlington (Hillingdon)
St Mary, Hayes (Hillingdon)
St Martin, Ruislip (Hillingdon)
St John the Baptist, Hillingdon (Hillingdon)
St Mary, Harefield (Hillingdon)
St Dunstan, Cranford (Hillingdon)
St Mary, East Bedfont (Hounslow)
St Leonard, Heston (Hounslow)
St Nicholas, Chiswick (Hounslow)
The Knights Hospitaller Priory of St John of Jerusalem, Clerkenwell (Islington)
All Saints, Cheyne Row (Kensington and Chelsea)
All Saints, Kingston (Kingston upon Thames)
St Mary, Lambeth (Lambeth)
St Leonard, Streatham (Lambeth)
St Mary, Lewisham (Lewisham)

St Mary, Monken Hadley, Barnet

St Nicholas, Deptford (Lewisham)
St Mary, Merton (Merton)
St Mary, Wimbledon (Merton)
All Saints, West Ham (Newham)
St Peter, Petersham (Richmond upon Thames)
St Mary, Twickenham (Richmond upon Thames)
St Mary Magdalen, Richmond (Richmond upon Thames)
St Mary Magdalen, Bermondsey (Southwark)
St Mary, Beddington (Sutton)
All Saints, Carshalton (Sutton)
Lumley Chapel, Cheam (Sutton)
St Dunstan and All Saints, Stepney (Tower Hamlets)
St Mary Stratford-le-Bow (Tower Hamlets)
All Saints, Chingford (Waltham Forest)
St Mary, Walthamstow (Waltham Forest)
St Mary, Putney Bridge (Wandsworth)
St Margaret, Westminster (Westminster)

All Saints, West Ham, Newham

STUART

From the reign of James I it is possible to detect the work of individual architects. The London churches in which many, but not all of them, were involved are listed beneath their names and very brief biographical details.

Inigo Jones (1573–1652)

Inigo Jones was of Welsh descent. He was heavily influenced by Palladio. He built the Banqueting House in Whitehall and the Queen's Chapel at St James's.

St Paul, Covent Garden (Westminster)

Sir Christopher Wren (1632–1723)

Wren was the son of the Rector of East Knoyle, Wiltshire. He was educated at Wadham College, Oxford and then became a Fellow of All Souls. His greatest ecclesiastical work was the rebuilding of St Paul's Cathedral and some 51 churches in the City after the Great Fire. He became Surveyor of the King's Works and MP for Old Windsor.

All Hallows, Twickenham (tower) (Richmond upon Thames)

St James, Piccadilly (Westminster)
St Clement Danes (Westminster)

GEORGIAN

Nicholas Hawksmoor (1661–1736)

Hawksmoor was born in Nottinghamshire and became Clerk to Sir Christopher Wren. He worked with him on St Paul's, Chelsea and Greenwich Hospitals and Hampton Court. He subsequently worked with John Vanbrugh on Blenheim Palace and Castle Howard. In 1723 he became Surveyor to Westminster Abbey and constructed that edifice's two west towers. He was active at both Oxford and Cambridge Universities. He built a number of churches under the Fifty New Churches Act of 1711.

St George, Bloomsbury (Camden)
St Alfege, Greenwich (Greenwich)
St Luke, Old Street (Islington)
Christ Church, Spitalfields (Tower Hamlets)
St George-in-the-East (Tower Hamlets)
St Anne, Limehouse (Tower Hamlets)

Thomas Archer (1668–1743)

Archer was born in Warwickshire and attended Trinity College, Oxford. Summerson said of his churches they "represented the most advanced Baroque style ever attempted in England".

Christ Church, Spitalfields

St Paul, Deptford (Lewisham)
St John Smith Square (Westminster)

John James (1673–1746)

James was the son of a Hampshire parson and worked closely with Hawksmoor.

St Alfege, Greenwich (tower and spire) (Greenwich)
St Lawrence, Stanmore (Harrow)
St Luke, Old Street (Islington)
St Mary, Twickenham (Richmond upon Thames)
St Mary, Rotherhithe (Southwark)
St Margaret, Westminster (tower) (Westminster)
St George, Hanover Square (Westminster)

James Gibbs (1682–54)

Gibbs was born a Catholic in Scotland, and trained in Rome. He was a follower of Inigo Jones and Christopher Wren. His most famous building is perhaps the Radcliffe Camera in Oxford.

St Clement Danes (steeple) (Westminster)
St Mary-le-Strand (Westminster)
St Martin in the Fields (Westminster)

George Dance the Elder (1695–1768)

Dance was born in London. His major work was the Mansion House in the City. His son George Dance the Younger also became an architect.

St Leonard, Shoreditch (Hackney)
St Matthew, Bethnal Green (Tower Hamlets)

Henry Flitcroft (1697–1769)

Flitcroft came from humble origins. He was discovered by Lord Burlington and eventually became Comptroller of the King's Works. He was a major designer of Palladian country houses including Ditchley, Wimpole and Woburn.

St Giles-in-the-Fields (Camden)

Thomas Hardwick (1752–1829)

Hardwick was born in Brentford . He was the father of Philip Hardwick (qv).

St Mary, Wanstead (Redbridge)
St Paul, Covent Garden (restoration)
    (Westminster)
St Mary, Marylebone (Westminster)

John Nash (1752–1835)

Nash was born in Lambeth and trained under Sir Robert Taylor. He was the architect of Regency London and was also responsible for the Brighton Pavilion.

All Souls, Langham Place (Westminster)

All Souls, Langham Place

Sir John Soane (1753–1837)

Soane was born in Goring-on-Thames and trained under George Dance the Younger and Henry Holland. His best known work was arguably the old Bank of England.

St Peter, Walworth (Southwark)
St John, Bethnal Green (Tower Hamlets)

Henry Hakewill (1771–1830)

Hakewill seems to have been brought up in London. He was appointed architect to Rugby School and did extensive work there.

St John, Bethnal Green

St John of Jerusalem, South Hackney (Hackney)
St Peter, Eaton Square (Westminster)

William Inwood (1771–1843)

Inwood was brought up in Highgate. He was steward to Charles Abbot, later Lord Colchester. He usually worked as an architect with his son William Henry Inwood (1794–1843).

New St Pancras (Camden)

James Savage (1779–1852)

Savage was born in Hoxton. He was mainly an ecclesiastical architect.

St Luke, Chelsea (Kensington and Chelsea)
St James, Bermondsey (Southwark)

Edward Lapidge (1779–1860)

Lapidge was the son of the head gardener at Hampton Court. He built in both Gothic and classical styles.

St Peter, Hammersmith (Hammersmith and Fulham)
St Andrew, Ham (Richmond upon Thames)
St Mary, Hampton (Richmond upon Thames)

Sir Robert Smirke (1780–1867)

Smirke was born in London and was briefly a pupil of Soane's. He is best known for his secular work such as the British Museum, the Oxford and Cambridge Club and Eastnor and Lowther Castles.

St Anne, Wandsworth (Wandsworth)

F.O. Bedford (1784–1858)

Not a great deal seems to be known of Francis Octavius Bedford. He died in Kent.

St John, Waterloo Road (Lambeth)
St Luke, West Norwood (Lambeth)
St George, Camberwell (Southwark)

St Anne, Wandsworth

VICTORIAN AND EDWARDIAN

(As a very general, and not invariably accurate observation, the Victorians were better builders of new churches than restorers of old ones:

> "The Church's Restoration
>   In eighteen-eighty-three
> Has left for contemplation
>   Not what there used to be."

as Betjeman wrote.)

Thomas Cundy II (1790–1867)

Cundy was born in London, the son of the architect Thomas Cundy I. He was primarily the architect of the Grosvenor Estate in London.

St Paul, Wilton Place (Westminster)
St Mark, Hamilton Terrace (Westminster)
St Barnabas, Pimlico (Westminster)
St Gabriel, Warwick Square (Westminster)
St Saviour, Pimlico (Westminster)

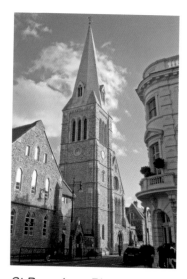

St Barnabas, Pimlico

Lewis Vulliamy (1791–1871)

Vulliamy was born in London, the son of a clockmaker. He was articled to Sir Robert Smirke. His first major work was at Syston Park, Lincolnshire for Sir John Haydon Thorold, Bt.

St Michael, Highgate (Camden)
St Barnabas, Addison Road (Kensington and Chelsea)
The Assumption and All Saints, Ennismore Gardens (Kensington and Chelsea)
St John the Divine, Richmond (Richmond upon Thames)
St Peter, Bethnal Green (Tower Hamlets)

Philip Hardwick (1792–1870)

Hardwick was born in London the son of the architect Thomas Hardwick. He was mainly known for his railway stations such as Euston.

St Clement, King Square (Islington)
St Anne, Limehouse (restoration) (Tower Hamlets)

St Clement, King Square

Sir Charles Barry (1795–1860)

Barry was born in Westminster, the son of a stationer. He was taken up by the Whigs and became part of the Holland House set. He designed numerous country houses such as Cliveden and Highclere as well as clubs, etc. He is best known for his rebuilding of the Palace of Westminster.

Old St Mary, Stoke Newington (brick tower, spire and fittings) (Hackney)
Holy Trinity, Cloudesley Square (Islington)
St John the Evangelist, Holloway Road (Islington)

John Joseph Scoles (1798–63)

Scoles was born in the Midlands and was a Catholic Gothic Revival architect. His sons Canon Scoles (qv) and the Rev Ignatius Scoles SJ were also architects.

St John the Evangelist R.C., Duncan Terrace, Islington (Islington)
The Immaculate Conception R.C., Farm Street (Westminster)

E.B. Lamb (1806–69)

Edward Buckton Lamb born in London, the son of a government official. He was one of Goodhart Rendel's "rogue architects" ie who did not follow medieval precedent, to the particular chagrin of The Ecclesiologist. Pevsner describe him as "the most original though certainly not the most accomplished architect of his day".

St Martin, Gospel Oak

    St Martin, Gospel Oak (Camden)
    St Mary Magdalen, Addiscombe (Croydon)

T.H. Wyatt (1807–80)

Thomas Henry Wyatt was born in County Roscommon. He was a member of the Wyatt architectural dynasty. He became the Salisbury Diocesan architect and built numerous churches in Wiltshire.

    The Garrison Church of St George, Woolwich (Greenwich)

Benjamin Ferrey (1810–80)

Benjamin Ferrey was born in Dorset. He studied under both Pugin and William Wilkins. He designed and restored many Anglican churches. Eastlake wrote of him that he was "one of the earliest, ablest and most zealous pioneers of the modern Gothic school".

    All Saints, Blackheath Common (Lewisham)
    St Stephen, Rochester Row (Westminster)

Sir G.G. Scott (1811–1878)

Sir George Gilbert Scott was born in Gawcott, Buckinghamshire, the son of a cleric. He started his architectural life as a leading designer of workhouses. He was inspired by Pugin. He was a prolific architect and amongst other secular edifices built the Midland Grand Hotel at St Pancras Station, the Foreign and Commonwealth Office and the Albert Memorial. He was the founder of an architectural dynasty. The greatest among them was his son George Gilbert Scott, Jr; educated at Eton and eventually a Catholic convert; his major works in London were All Hallows, Southwark (destroyed in the Blitz save the north aisle) and the original St Agnes, Kennington (destroyed by the Diocese of Southwark after bomb damage). He went mad and died, perhaps appropriately, in his father's Midland Grand Hotel.

St Peter, South Croydon (Croydon)
St John, Shirley (Croydon)
St John the Baptist, Croydon (Croydon)
Christ Church, Ealing (Ealing)
Christ Church, Southgate (Enfield)
St Mary, Stoke Newington (Hackney)
St Mary, Harrow (restoration) (Harrow)
St John the Baptist, Hillingdon (restoration and partial rebuilding)
    (Hillingdon)
St Andrew, Uxbridge (Hillingdon)
St Mary, Abbots, Kensington (Kensington and Chelsea)
St Stephen, Lewisham (Lewisham)
Christ Church, Wanstead (nave and north aisle) (Redbridge)
St Matthias, Richmond (Richmond upon Thames)
St Giles, Camberwell (Southwark)
St Margaret, Westminster (nave restoration) (Westminster)
St Matthew, Westminster (Westminster)

S.W. Daukes (1811–80)

Samuel Whitfield Daukes was born in Gloucestershire and built a number of churches. He was a Low Churchman. From 1841 to 1850 he was in partnership with John R. Hamilton.

St Andrew, Wells Street/ Kingsbury (Brent)

A.W.N. Pugin (1812–42)

Augustus Welby Northmore Pugin was the son of a French draughtsman in whose office he initially worked. He was the pioneer of the Gothic revival and in 1836 (two years after he became a Catholic convert) published the very influential *Contrasts*. He lived in Salisbury and then Ramsgate. His major patron was John Talbot, 16th Earl of Shrewsbury. He was married three times. He was a prolific designer of cathedrals and churches in a short but extremely active life. He worked with Sir Charles Barry on the interior of the Palace of Westminster. He is buried at St Augustine, Ramsgate.

St Peter R.C., Woolwich (Greenwich)

St Thomas of Canterbury RC, Fulham

Our Ladye Star of the Sea R.C., Croom's Hill (fittings) (Greenwich)
St Thomas of Canterbury R.C., Fulham (Hammersmith and Fulham)
The Immaculate Conception R.C., Farm Street (high altar) (Westminster)

R.C. Carpenter (1812–55)

Richard Cromwell Carpenter was educated at Charterhouse and introduced to the Cambridge Camden Society by Pugin. He was responsible for much of Lancing College. He died relatively young from tuberculosis. Eastlake wrote of him that he was "foremost among professional designers for his accurate knowledge of ancient work, his inventive power and his refined treatment of decorative detail".

St Mary Magdalen, Munster Square (Camden)

S.S. Teulon (1812–73)

Samuel Sanders Teulon was of Huguenot descent. He was known for his polychromatic brickwork. He was another of Goodhart-Rendel's "rogue architects".

St Stephen, Rosslyn Hill (Camden)
St Mary, Ealing (Ealing)
Holy Trinity, Northwood (Hillingdon)
St Silas, Pentonville (Islington)
Christ Church, Wimbledon (Merton)
St Mark, Silvertown (Newham)
All Saints, Benhilton (Sutton)

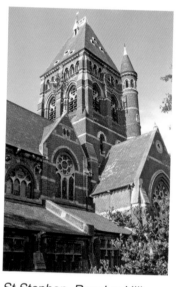

St Stephen, Rosslyn Hill

R.L. Roumieu (1814–77)

Robert Lewis Roumieu was articled to Benjamin Dean Wyatt as was his partner Alexander Dick Gough (1804–71).

Old St Pancras (restoration) (Camden)
St Paul, Hammersmith (Hammersmith and Fulham)
St Cuthbert, Philbeach Gardens (Kensington and Chelsea)

J.W. Wild (1814–92)

James William Wild was born in Lincoln. He was a slightly esoteric architect being responsible for parts of the Victoria and Albert Museum, the chancery buildings of the Legation in Tehran and the brick tower at Grimsby Docks, which used to be described by the late Reverend Henry Thorold, nothing if not a loyal son of

Lincolnshire, as "like Siena, only better". Wild spent the last 14 years of his life as Curator of the Sir John Soane Museum.

Christ Church, Streatham Hill (Lambeth)

Ewan Christian (1814–95)

Christian was born in Marylebone. He was a relation of Fletcher Christian of HMS Bounty fame. He is probably best known for the National Portrait Gallery and as a rather harsh church restorer. He was a determined Evangelical.

Holy Trinity, Dalston (Hackney)
St Stephen, Hounslow (Hounslow)
Christ Church, Spitalfields (restoration) (Tower Hamlets)

William Butterfield (1814–1900)

Butterfield was born a nonconformist in London. He set up a practice in Lincoln's Inn Fields and rapidly became "the architect of the High Church party", as Scott described him. He was a difficult man and Beresford Hope was moved to say "He has the stuff of a heresiarch in him ... stiff, dogmatical and puritanical". He was known for his use of polychromy and red brick. Summerson thought he had a positive love of ugliness. He often worked with Alexander Gibb as his stained glass designer. His only pupil of note was the Old Etonian, Henry Woodyer (1816–96), who did no church work in London. Butterfield's most noted work outside London was Keble College, Oxford. He also built Balliol College Chapel. He remained a bachelor and was buried in Tottenham.

St Mary Magdalen, Enfield

St John the Baptist, Chipping Barnet (Barnet)
St Alban, Holborn (mostly destroyed) (Camden)
St Mary, Dartmouth Park (Camden)
St Mary Magdalen, Enfield (Enfield)
St Matthias, Stoke Newington (Hackney)
St John the Evangelist, Hammersmith
    (Hammersmith and Fulham)
All Hallows, Tottenham (east end and fittings)
    (Haringey)
All Saints, Harrow Weald (Harrow)
St Augustine, Queensgate (Kensington and
    Chelsea)
All Saints, Margaret Street (Westminster)

J.P. St Aubyn (1815–95)

John Piers St Aubyn was of Cornish extraction and is chiefly known for his harsh restorations in that county.

St John, Friern Barnet (Barnet)
Christ Church, Erith (Bexley)

J.L. Pearson (1817–97)

John Loughborough Pearson was articled successively to Ignatius Bonomi and Philip Hardwicke. He built severe churches on an Early English model, frequently with vaulted ceilings. His most famous work is Truro Cathedral. His son Frank Pearson followed him as an architect.

St John, Friern Barnet (Barnet)
St John the Evangelist, Upper Norwood (Croydon)
St Michael, Croydon (Croydon)
St John the Baptist, Pinner (restoration) (Harrow)
St Nicholas, Chiswick (Hounslow)
St Peter, Vauxhall (Lambeth)
St Augustine, Kilburn (Westminster)

Gilbert Blount (1819–76)

Blount was born into an old Catholic family. He initially trained under Brunel as a civil engineer. He was appointed as architect to Cardinal Wiseman.

St Mary R.C., Mortlake (Richmond upon Thames)
St Anne R.C., Underwood Road (Tower
    Hamlets)
Our Lady and St Catherine of Siena R.C., Bow
    (Tower Hamlets)

Joseph Peacock (1823–93)

Peacock was articled in Worthing and then practised in London. He was favoured by the Low Church party. Goodhart-Rendel regarded him as a 'rogue' architect.

Holy Cross, Cromer Street (Camden) (never
    remotely 'Low')
St Stephen, Gloucester Road (Kensington and
    Chelsea)

Holy Cross, Cromer Street

St Simon Zelotes, Chelsea (Kensington and Chelsea)

William Wardell (1823–99)

Wardell was brought up in London and trained as an engineer. Under the influence of Pugin he converted to Catholicism in 1843 and built a number of churches. In 1858 he migrated to Melbourne, Australia for his health.

St Mary R.C., Chislehurst (Bromley)
Our Ladye Star of the Sea R.C., Croom's Hill (Greenwich)
Holy Trinity R.C., Brook Green (Hammersmith and Fulham)
Our Lady of Victories R.C., Clapham (Lambeth)
St Mary and St Michael R.C., Commercial Road (Tower Hamlets)

G.E. Street (1824–81)

George Edmund Street was educated in Mitcham and worked in the office of Sir Giles Gilbert Scott. He was a prolific Gothic revivalist looking to earlier models. He was appointed the architect of the Diocese of Oxford. He used polychromy extensively. He was an active High Churchman and Churchwarden of All Saints, Margaret Street.

St Mary Magdalen, Paddington

St Mary, East Barnet (woodwork) (Barnet)
St Mary, Monken Hadley (Barnet)
Holy Trinity, Eltham, Greenwich (Greenwich)
St John the Divine, Lambeth (Lambeth)
All Saints, Putney (Wandsworth)
St James the Less, Vauxhall Bridge Road
(Westminster)
St James the Less, Sussex Gardens
(Westminster)
St Mary Magdalen, Paddington (Westminster)

R.J.Withers (1824–94)

Robert Jewell Withers was born in Shepton Mallet, Somerset. He mainly built and restored churches in the West country and Wales.

St John, Sidcup (chancel) (Bexley)
St Mary, Bourne Street (Westminster)

Charles Alban Buckler (1824–1905)

Buckler was the son of John Chessell Buckler, anti-quarian writer and church restorer (1793–1894). He became a Catholic in 1844. He was created a Knight of Malta and in 1880 Surrey Herald Extraordinary.

> Our Lady of the Rosary and St Dominic R.C., Haverstock Hill (Camden)
> Our Lady of Mount Carmel and St Joseph R.C., Battersea Park Road (Wandsworth)

William White (1825–1900)

White was the son of clergyman and a nephew of Gilbert White of Selborne. He worked for Sir George Gilbert Scott before setting up on his own.

> St Saviour, Aberdeen Park (Islington)
> All Saints, Talbot Road (Kensington and Chelsea)
> St Mark, Battersea Rise (Wandsworth)

Our Lady of the Rosary and St Dominic R.C., Camden

James Brooks (1825–1901)

Brooks was born in Wantage, the son of a farmer. He was educated at Abingdon School. He was a zealous high churchman and is best known for his urban high churches, especially in the East End.

> St Andrew, Totteridge Village (apse) (Barnet)
> St Paulinus, Crayford (altar table) (Bexley)
> St Andrew, Willesden Green (Brent)
> The Annunciation, Chislehurst (Bromley)
> All Hallows, Gospel Oak (Camden)
> St Michael, Mark Street (Hackney)
> St Chad, Haggerston (Hackney)
> St Columba, Kingsland Road (Hackney)
> Holy Innocents, Hammersmith (Hammersmith and Fulham)
> St John the Baptist, Holland Road (Kensington and Chelsea)
> St Chad and St Andrew, Plaistow (Newham)
> The Ascension, Lavender Hill (Wandsworth)

G.F. Bodley (1827–1907)

George Frederick Bodley was born in Hull and apprenticed to Sir George Gilbert Scott to whom he was related through marriage. From 1869 to 1897 his partner was Thomas Garner (1839–1906) until the latter became a Catholic. Bodley became the leading ecclesiastical architect of his day with his promotion of 14th century Gothic. He often worked with Burlison & Grylls and Kempe on stained glass. Cecil Hare became his partner towards the end of his life.

St Mary, Hendon (reredos) (Barnet)
St Nicholas, Chislehurst (reredos and roof) (Bromley)
St Michael, Camden (Camden)
St Michael, Croydon (font, pulpit, organ case) (Croydon)
Christ Church, Ealing (organ case and roof) (Ealing)
St Peter, Ealing (fittings) (Ealing)
St Mary of Eton, Hackney Wick (Hackney)
St Faith, Brentford (Hounslow)
St Stephen, Gloucester Road (reredos) (Kensington and Chelsea)
Holy Trinity, Prince Consort Road (Kensington and Chelsea)
St Mary Magdalen, Richmond (chancel) (Richmond upon Thames)
St Andrew, Ham (chancel) (Richmond upon Thames)
St Paul, Wilton Place (screen, reredos and organ case) (Westminster)
St Barnabas, Pimlico (reredos and screen) (Westminster)

Sir Arthur Blomfield (1829–99)

Blomfield was the son of the Bishop of London. He was apprenticed to Philip Hardwick. He built a huge number of churches.

All Saints, Fulham (Hammersmith and Fulham)
St Andrew, Surbiton (Kingston upon Thames)
St Mary, Lewisham (restoration) (Lewisham)
St Mary, Hampton (sanctuary) (Richmond upon Thames)
St Mary, Mortlake (Richmond upon Thames)
Christ Church, Kew (Richmond upon Thames)
All Saints, Carshalton (Sutton)

St Andrew, Surbiton

F.H. Pownall (1831–1907)

Frederick Hyde Pownall was educated at Rugby before being apprenticed to Samuel Daukes. He converted to Catholicism at some stage before 1885.

St Peter, London Docks (Tower Hamlets)
Corpus Christi R.C., Maiden Lane (Westminster)

Richard Norman Shaw (1831–1912)

Norman Shaw was born in Edinburgh. He is perhaps best known for his country houses such as Cragside.

St Michael and All Angels, Bedford Park (Hounslow)

E.W. Pugin (1834–75)

Edward Welby Pugin was the son of A.W.N. Pugin and took over his father's practice on the latter's death. E.W. Pugin designed c. 100 Catholic churches.

St Monica R.C., Hoxton (Hackney)
St Anthony of Padua R.C., Forest Gate
   (Newham)
Our Lady of Sorrows R.C., Peckham
   (Southwark)
St Thomas More R.C., Dulwich (high altar)
   (Southwark)
The English Martyrs R.C., Tower Hill (Tower
   Hamlets)

St Monica R.C., Hoxton

Alexander Scoles (1834–96)

Canon Scoles was the son of Joseph John Scoles, also an architect. His Jesuit brother Ignatius Scoles too was an architect .

St Peter in Chains R.C., Stroud Green (Haringey)
St Thomas of Canterbury R.C., Woodford (Redbridge)

Sir T.G. Jackson, Bt (1835–1924)

Thomas Graham Jackson was educated at Wadham College, Oxford. He was articled to Sir George Gilbert Scott. He did much secular work in Oxford.

St John, Wimbledon (Merton)

J.D. Sedding (1838–91)

John Dando Sedding was born at Eton. He was a pupil of G.E. Street. He started work in Cornwall with his brother Edmund but moved first to Bristol and then to London. He was heavily influenced by Ruskin towards the Arts and Crafts movement.

Holy Redeemer, Exmouth Market

>St John, West Wickham (pulpit, screens and
>   organ case) (Bromley)
>St Peter, Ealing (Ealing)
>St Augustine, Archway (Haringey)
>Holy Redeemer, Exmouth Market (Islington)
>Holy Trinity, Sloane Street (Kensington and
>   Chelsea)

J.F. Bentley (1839–1902)

John Francis Bentley was born in Doncaster. He converted to Catholicism in 1862. He is best known for his design of Westminster Cathedral. He died in Clapham and was buried at Mortlake.

>St Francis of Assisi R.C., Pottery Lane (fittings) (Kensington and Chelsea)
>St Mary Cadogan R.C. (Kensington and Chelsea)
>Our Lady of the Holy Souls R.C., Kensal Town (Kensington and Chelsea)
>Our Lady of Victories R.C., Clapham (fittings) (Lambeth)
>Corpus Christi R.C., Brixton (Lambeth)
>St Gabriel, Warwick Square (high altar) (Westminster)
>Assumption and St Gregory R.C., Warwick Street (Westminster)
>St Mary of the Angels R.C., Bayswater (high altar, reredos, chancel stalls)
>   (Westminster)
>St James R.C., Spanish Place (fittings) (Westminster)

J.O. Scott (1841–1913)

John Oldrid Scott was the second son of Sir George Gilbert Scott. He was educated at Bradfield and inherited his father's practice.

>St John, Palmers Green (Enfield)
>St Mary Magdalen, Woolwich (chancel) (Greenwich)
>St Mary, Stoke Newington (spire) (Hackney)

Basil Champneys (1842–1935)

Champneys was the son of the Evangelical Vicar of Whitechapel, subsequently Dean of Lichfield. He was educated at Charterhouse and Trinity College, Cambridge.

St Luke, Kidderpore Avenue

St Mary, Bexley (screen) (Bexley)
St Luke, Kidderpore Avenue (Camden)
St John, Havering-atte-Bower (Havering)
St George, Borough High Street (ceiling) (Southwark)

J.T. Micklethwaite (1843–1906)

John Thomas Micklethwaite was apprenticed to Sir George Gilbert Scott. From 1876 to 1892 he was in partnership with Somers Clarke.

St Paul, Wimbledon Park (Wandsworth)

A.E. Purdie (1843–1920)

Alfred Edward Purdie was articled to Gilbert Blount and took over his practice. He died in Canterbury.

Our Lady Help of Christians R.C., Blackheath (Greenwich)
English Martyrs R.C., Streatham (Lambeth)

Francis William Tasker (1848–1904)

Little seems to be known about Tasker. He was a Catholic.

St Margaret and All Saints R.C., Canning Town (Newham)
The English Martyrs R.C., Southwark (Southwark)
St Patrick R.C., Wapping (Tower Hamlets)

The Rev Ernest Geldart (1848–1929)

Geldart was the rector of Little Braxted in Essex and was a church designer and restorer.

St Helen and St Giles, Rainham (restoration) (Havering)
St Cuthbert, Philbeach Gardens (reredos) (Kensington and Chelsea)

F.A. Walters (1849–1931)

Frederick Arthur Walters was a Scottish architect born in London. He was articled to George Goldie and built many Catholic churches.

St Anthony of Padua R.C., Anerley (Bromley)
St Anselm and St Cecilia R.C., Kingsway (Camden)
Ealing Abbey R.C. (Ealing)
St Anne, Vauxhall R.C., (Lambeth)
Sacred Heart R.C., Wimbledon (Merton)
St Winefride R.C., Wimbledon (Merton)
The Most Precious Blood R.C., Southwark (Southwark)
St Wilfrid R.C., Southwark (Southwark)
St Mary and St Michael R.C., Commercial Road (sanctuary reordering)
    (Tower Hamlets)
The Guardian Angels R.C., Mile End Road (Tower Hamlets)
Sacred Heart R.C., Battersea (Wandsworth)

Arthur Young (1853–1925)

Arthur Young was brought up and educated in Stamford. He converted to Catholicism. He mainly built churches.

St Edward the Confessor R.C., Golders Green (Barnet)
Our Lady and St Thomas of Canterbury R.C., Harrow (Harrow)

George Fellowes Prynne (1853–1927)

Fellowes Prynne was born in Plymouth and built a number of churches. He was known for his screens.

St John, Sidcup (Bexley)
All Saints, West Dulwich (Lambeth)
Holy Trinity, Roehampton (Wandsworth)

E.W. Mountford (1855–1908)

Edward William Mountford was born in Worcestershire. He is mainly known for his Baroque work such as the Old Bailey.

St Anne, Wandsworth (Wandsworth)
St Andrew, Wandsworth (Wandsworth)
St Michael, Battersea (Wandsworth)

St Andrew, Wandsworth

Temple Moore (1856–1920)

Temple Lushington Moore was born in County Offaly and articled to George Gilbert Scott Junior. He was mainly a Gothicist and an ecclesiastical architect. He has a high reputation. In 1928 Beresford Pite said "It seems as if he summed up and completed the theory of the Gothic Revival". His former pupil Sir Giles Gilbert Scott said "I think Temple Moore's work can rank with the finest done in the Gothic Revival". The majority of his churches are to be found in Yorkshire. He was a High Churchman and worshipped initially at St Augustine, Kilburn and subsequently at St Michael, Camden.

> St Mary, Hendon (south aisle) (Barnet)
> St Luke, Eltham (Greenwich)
> St Agnes, Kennington (fittings) (Lambeth)
> All Saints, Tooting (Wandsworth)

Edward Goldie (1856–1921)

Edward Goldie was the son of the architect George Goldie. He was educated at Ushaw before joining his father's practice.

> St Monica R.C., Palmer's Green (Enfield)
> Most Holy Redeemer and St Thomas More R.C., Chelsea (Kensington and Chelsea)
> Our Lady of the Assumption R.C., Bethnal Green (Tower Hamlets)
> St Thomas a Becket RC., Wandsworth (Wandsworth)
> St James Spanish Place R.C. (Westminster)

W.D. Caroe (1857–1938)

William Douglas Caroe was the son of the Danish Consul in Liverpool. He went to Trinity College, Cambridge before becoming a pupil of Pearson's.

> St Aldhelm, Edmonton (Enfield)
> St Bartholomew, Craven Park Road (Haringey)
> St Michael, Chiswick (Hounslow)
> St Margaret, Streatham (fittings) (Lambeth)
> St Barnabas, Walthamstow (Waltham Forest)

Arthur Beresford Pite (1861–1934)

Beresford Pite was born in London. He became Professor of Architecture at the Royal College of Art.

St Barnabas, Walthamstow

Holy Trinity, Clapham Common (chancel) (Lambeth)
Christ Church, Brixton (Lambeth)

Henry Wilson (1864–1934)

Wilson was born in Liverpool. He started as a pupil of John Oldrid Scott before joining John Dando Sedding whose churches he often finished off. He was much associated with the design of metal work eg at St Bartholomew, Brighton.

St Peter, Ealing (Ealing)
St Augustine, Archway (Haringey)
The Most Holy Redeemer, Exmouth Market
    (Islington)
Holy Trinity, Sloane Street (screen) (Kensington
    and Chelsea)

Sir Edward Lutyens (1869–1944)

Lutyens was born in Surrey. He was not primarily an ecclesiastical architect and is best known for his country houses, the Cenotaph and for the government buildings of New Delhi. He married Lady Emily Bulwer-Lytton.

St Jude, Hampstead Garden Suburb (Barnet)

St Jude, Hamstead Garden Suburb

TWENTIETH CENTURY

E.C. Shearman (1859–1939)

Ernest Charles Shearman was an Anglo-Catholic architect known for his variations on the theme of Albi Cathedral. He was apprenticed to Charles Barry.

St Silas, Kentish Town (Camden)
St Barnabas, Pitshanger Lane, Ealing (Ealing)
St Gabriel, Acton (Ealing)
St Francis of Assisi, Osterley (Hounslow)

Sir Walter Tapper (1861–1935)

Tapper was born in Devon. He spent 18 years working for Bodley & Garner before setting up his own practice in 1900. He was Surveyor of Westminster Abbey.

St Stephen, Gloucester Road (rood) (Kensington and Chelsea)
The Annunciation, Marble Arch (Westminster)

Sir Herbert Baker (1862–1946)

Baker was educated at Tonbridge. His reputation was established through his mainly secular work in South Africa.

St Andrew, Ilford (Redbridge)

Edward Doran Webb (1864–1931)

Doran Webb was based in Wiltshire, living at Gaston House, Tisbury. His chief work was the Birmingham Oratory.

The Most Precious Blood and St Edmund R.C., Edmonton (Enfield)

Sir Ninian Comper (1864–1960)

(Because of his enormously long and prolific life Comper could equally be claimed as a Victorian/Edwardian architect.) He was born in Aberdeen where his father was then Rector of St John's Church. He was educated at Glenalmond before being articled to Charles Eamer Kempe and subsequently Bodley & Garner. From 1888 to 1905 he partnered with William Bucknall. He was a prolific designer of beautiful reredoses, English altars, stained glass, etc., as well as churches. He was an advocate of "unity by inclusion", the combining of Gothic and classical elements. He was much derided by Pevsner but, broadly, supported by Betjeman.

St Mark, Regent Park (reredoses) (Camden)
St Mary, Dartmouth Park (reredoses) (Camden)
St Michael, Croydon (Lady Chapel fittings)
    (Croydon)
St Alban, Thornton Heath (Croydon)
All Saints, Talbot Road (reredos) (Kensington
    and Chelsea)
St Helen, Kensington (Kensington and Chelsea)
St Barnabas, Little Ilford (Newham)
St Giles, Camberwell (fittings) (Southwark)
All Saints, Carshalton (reredos, screen, organ
    case, gallery) (Sutton)
Grosvenor Chapel, Mayfair (screen)
    (Westminster)

St Alban, Thornton Heath

St Barnabas, Pimlico (sacrament house, decoration and sculpture)
(Westminster)
St Matthew Westminster (Lady Chapel) (Westminster)
All Saints, Margaret Street (reredos and statues) (Westminster)
St Mary Magdalen, Paddington (chapel of St Sepulchre) (Westminster)
St Cyprian, Clarence Gate Gardens (Westminster)

Sir Charles Nicholson, Bt (1867–1949)

Nicholson was born in London, the son of the first baronet. He trained with John Dando Sedding. He was primarily an ecclesiastical architect.

St Laurence, Upminster (choir and sanctuary)
(Havering)
St John, Lewisham (Lewisham)

The Rev Benedict Williamson (1868–1948)

Willamson was born in London. He was received into the Catholic church in 1896. He was ordained a priest in the Archdiocese of Southwark in 1909. In later life he became a supporter of Mussolini and died in Rome, surviving Il Duce by some three years.

St Ignatius R.C., Stamford Hill (Haringey)
The Lithuanian Church of St Casimir R.C.,
Hackney Road (Tower Hamlets)
St Boniface, R.C., Tooting (Wandsworth)

St Boniface R.C., Tooting

Cecil Hare (1875–1932)

Cecil Greenwood Hare was born in Stamford. He was chief assistant to Bodley in 1906 and took over the practice.

St Benet, Lupton Street (Camden)
St Michael, Croydon (hanging rood and lectern) (Croydon)
St Mildred, Addiscombe (Croydon)
St Thomas, Hanwell (reredos) (Ealing)
All Saints, Talbot Road (reredos) (Kensington and Chelsea)

Harold Gibbons (1878–1958)

Gibbons embraced the modernist idiom in a conventional form.

> St Peter and St Paul, Bromley (Bromley)
> St Mary, Kenton (Harrow)

Sir Giles Gilbert Scott (1880–1960)

A Catholic, Scott was educated at Beaumont College. He was the son of George Gilbert Scott, Jr. He was articled to Temple Moore. His most famous works are Battersea Power Station and Liverpool Anglican Cathedral, where he was buried outside by Ampleforth monks; as a Catholic he could not be buried inside.

> St Alban and St Michael, Golders Green
> (Barnet)
> Our Lady of Mount Carmel R.C., Kensington
> (Kensington and Chelsea)

Our Lady of Mount Carmel R.C., Kensington

Adrian Gilbert Scott (1882–1963)

Also a Catholic, Scott was educated at Beaumont College. He was the son of George Gilbert Scott, Jr and also articled to Temple Moore.

> St Alban, Holborn (Camden)
> St Mary, Holly Place, Hampstead (baldacchino) (Camden)
> St Joseph R.C., Wealdstone (Harrow)
> St Mary and St Joseph R.C., Poplar (Tower Hamlets)

Sir Edward Maufe (1882–1974)

Maufe was born Edward Muff but later changed his name. He is best known as the architect of Guildford Cathedral.

> St Thomas, Hanwell (Ealing)

W.C. Mangan (1884–1968)

Wilfred Clarence Mangan was a prolific Catholic architect. He was born in Preston of Irish extraction and did a lot of work in the Catholic Diocese of Portsmouth.

> St Peter R.C., Dagenham (Barking & Dagenham)

St Francis of Assisi, R.C., Grove Crescent Road (Newham)
Chapel of the Sacred Heart of Jesus R.C., Canning Town (Newham)

Martin Travers (1886–1948)

Travers was born in Margate. He studied briefly under Comper. He worked mainly on Baroque fittings for the Anglo-Catholic movement, although not an Anglo-Catholic himself.

St Mary, Northolt Green (statue of St Stephen) (Ealing)
St Thomas, Clapton Common (high altar and reredos) (Hackney)
St Dunstan, Cranford (fittings) (Hillingdon)
St Augustine, Queensgate (reredos and Lady altar) (Kensington and Chelsea)
Holy Redeemer, Streatham Vale (Lambeth)
The Good Shepherd, Carshalton Beeches (Sutton)
St John, Bethnal Green (aumbry) (Tower Hamlets)
All Saints, Poplar (tabernacle) (Tower Hamlets)
St Mary, Bourne Street (high altar and statue of Our Lady) (Westminster)

Harry Stuart Goodhart-Rendel (1887–1959)

Goodhart-Rendel was educated at Eton and Trinity College, Cambridge. He studied briefly under Sir Charles Nicholson. In 1913 he inherited the Hatchlands estate in Surrey from his maternal grandfather. He fought in the Grenadier Guards during the First World War. He converted to Catholicism in 1936. He was President of RIBA.

The Most Holy Trinity R.C., Bermondsey
   (Southwark)
St Mary, Stratford-le-Bow (restoration) (Tower
   Hamlets)

*The Most Holy Trinity R.C.,
Bermondsey*

Craze and Milner

Craze was Romilly Bernard Craze (1892–1974) and Milner was Sir William Milner, 8th Baronet (1893–1960). Their chief work was the Anglican shrine at Walsingham, Norfolk.

St Alban, Urswick Road (Barking & Dagenham).

N.F. Cachemaille-Day (1896–1976)

Nugent Cachemaille-Day was one of the more imaginative Modernist architects of the 20th century. He embraced the Liturgical Movement. He was in partnership with Felix Lander and Herbert Welch 1929–35.

St Mary, Grafton Road (Barking & Dagenham)
St Saviour, Eltham (Greenwich)
St Thomas, Clapton Common (restoration)
    (Hackney)
St John of Jerusalem, South Hackney (spire)
    (Hackney)
St Michael, London Fields (Hackney)
St Andrew, Belmont (Harrow)
St Paul, South Harrow (Harrow)
St Stephen, Hounslow (tower) (Hounslow)
All Saints, Hanworth (Hounslow)
St James, Clapham Park (Lambeth)

St Saviour, Eltham

F.X. Velarde (1897–1960)

Francis Xavier Velarde was a Liverpudlian whose buildings are almost exclusively in the North West of England.

St Luke R.C., Pinner (Harrow)

Stephen Dykes-Bower (1903–1994)

Dykes-Bower was the last of the great Gothicists. He was educated at Merton College, Oxford. His most lasting work is St Edmundsbury Cathedral. He was Surveyor of Westminster Abbey, where he is buried.

St Nicholas, Plumstead (three altars) (Greenwich)

Anthony Delarue (1959–)

Delarue was educated at Westminster School and Edinburgh University. He went into architectural practice and converted to Catholicism. His ecclesiastical work has invariably been for the Catholic Church and includes the new church of Corpus Christi, Tring. His restoration of the sanctuary of St Joseph, Hertford (open daily) for Father Gladstone Liddle is a work of remarkable beauty. He is currently working at the Oxford Oratory. He is a Knight of Magistral Grace in Obedience of the Order of Malta.

St George R.C., Sudbury (ironwork
and light fittings) (Brent)
St Edward the Confessor R.C.,
Romford (restoration) (Havering)
St John the Evangelist R.C., Brentford
(restoration) (Hounslow)
The Transfiguration R.C., Kensal Rise
(restoration) (Kensington &
Chelsea)
St Mary R.C., Mortlake (restoration)
(Richmond upon Thames)
Corpus Christi R.C., Maiden Lane (restoration) (Westminster)

*Restoration by Anthony Delarue at St
Edward the Confessor R.C., Romford*

One early enthusiasm in my life was church monuments. Good collections of these
are to be found throughout Greater London and a certain bias towards these can
perhaps be noted in the text and photographs.

Some early and much Victorian glass has survived in spite of the best efforts of
the Luftwaffe during the Blitz, as has more recent work by Comper and Travers.

I hope this somewhat jejune work will inspire others to investigate more thor-
oughly the treasures at their doorstep, many of which were certainly unknown to
me three years ago. I have where possible tried to indicate when churches might
be open but openings should if possible be checked as these tend to be in a perma-
nent state of flux. Catholic and some Anglo-Catholic churches often have a daily
Mass with the former often being open in the mornings. Many Anglican churches
have at least one service in the middle of the week. Evangelical churches tend to
be locked except around services on Sunday.

In spite of secularisation and everything else the Church in London in its broad-
est sense seems to me to be in surprisingly good heart. These buildings were built
AMDG – ad maiorem Dei gloriam, to the greater glory of God; long may they
remain outposts, if not everywhere citadels, of the Faith. Much of our history
resides in these buildings and they need not to be demolished as unsatisfactory
'plant' but to be preserved and cherished, preferably for the purpose they were
originally designed, rather than utilised as bars, offices or flats.

Michael Hodges
(michael.jeremyhodges@gmail.com)
September 2015

*The monument of Sir Charles Montague in armour in a tent (1625)
at St Margaret of Antioch, Broadway, Barking*

BARKING AND DAGENHAM

The London Borough of Barking and Dagenham was formed in 1965 out of most of the former municipal boroughs of Barking and Dagenham and moved from Essex to the GLC area.

It is bounded by Havering to the east, Redbridge to the north west, Newham to the west and the River Thames to the south.

The name of Barking derived from Bericingum (Berica's people) and that of Dagenham from Daeccanham (the "ham" or farmstead of a man called Daecca). Both were among the earliest settlements in Essex.

Historically most of the borough was part of the estate of the Abbey of Barking, dedicated to Our Lady and St Ethelburga. The Abbey was founded in 666 by St Erkenwald, Bishop to the East Saxons. It was destroyed in 870 and refounded a century later as a royal foundation with the monarch able to nominate the Abbesses. The Abbess had precedence over all other abbesses in England. William the Conqueror spent his first year as King here. The Abbey was eventually suppressed in 1539. The last Abbess was Dorothy Barley. Fortunately the King's Commissioner appointed to negotiate the Deed of Surrender was Dr William Petre, whose sister-in-law was a nun at the Abbey. Within a fortnight of the Deed of Surrender the Abbess and the 30 nuns were given pensions related to rank and age, and were sent home. The Abbey was the third richest nunnery after Shaftesbury and Sion Abbeys. Some idea of the magnificence of the Abbey can be gleaned from the fact that 3,586 ounces of silver gilt were sent to the King's Treasury. Demolition began in June 1540 and went on for 10 months. Most of the stone was shipped across the Thames to build the King's new manor at Dartford. The lead went to Greenwich Palace. The site of the Abbey then became a farm for 400 years.

Dagenham was not mentioned in Domesday Book but was a recognisable village by the 13th century. Most of its surviving medieval buildings were destroyed in the 1960s and 1970s.

Agriculture gave way in the 19th century to industry. Barking in 1850 was the busiest fishing port in the United Kingdom with 220 smacks operating out of it. The fishing industry however collapsed in the 1860s. In 1857 a fertiliser and sulphuric acid plant was built at Creekmouth where the Roding meets the Thames. In 1866 the largest jute factory in the world opened in Fisher Street. Armaments plants followed. The final fields vanished in the 1920s. The huge Ford car factory was constructed on a 500 acre site from 1929 to 1931. In the latter year the District Line was extended to Upminster.

St Margaret of Antioch, Broadway, Barking (open during daylight hours – entry through the Church Centre) stands on the banks of the River Roding within the former bounds of the Abbey. It became a parish church in the early 14th century. Adjacent to the 15th century Curfew or Fire Bell Gate (1) of the Abbey is the 13th century flint and ragstone church (2). The arcades were lengthened and the tower built in the 15th century. The 13th century chancel has a stuccoed vault of 1772, paid for by Sir Bamber Gascoigne. The pulpit and reredos are 18th century. The church has a large number of monuments and a couple of brasses. Among the former is one of 1625 attributed to Maximilian Colt of Sir Charles Montague in armour in a tent (3) and another of 1737 of Sir Orlando Humfreys

(4). A considerable amount of stained glass can be found including a Crucifixion of 1913 at the east end of the North Chapel (5). Captain James Cook was married in the church in 1762.

St Peter and St Paul, Dagenham, marooned amongst 20th century surroundings, has a 13th century chancel but is otherwise of 1801–5 by William Mason, following the collapse of the tower (6). Pevsner described the new tower as being "of the most ignorant and entertaining Gothic" while Ian Nairn said of the building that it was "marvellous nonsense" and

"pure froth without a care in the world". The altar tomb of Sir Thomas Urswyck, Baron of the Exchequer in 1479 and Recorder of London, a firm Yorkist, has a brass of him in the robes of a judge with wife and nine daughters, the eldest dressed as a nun (7). The monument of another judge, Sir Richard Alibon, and his wife, attributed to Van Nost, lies in the north transept; he was appointed, by James II, the first Roman Catholic judge since the Reformation, fortunately for him dying in August 1688 i.e. just before the 'Glorious Revolution'(8).

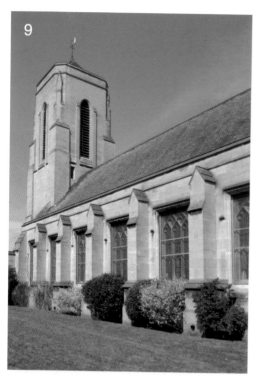

St Alban, Urswick Road, 1933–3, was built by Milner and Craze for Dame Violet Wills of the tobacco family (9). It is neo-Perpendicular and built of ashlar from Jurassic Limestone. It has a long nave with no aisles.

St Mary, Grafton Road, 1934–5 is by Welch, Cachemaille-Day and Lander. The endowments of Ram's Episcopal Chapel in Homerton were transferred together with the organ and communion plate. The curiously Gothic building is rough cast with brick window tracery (10). It consists of nave and north aisle surmounted by the large but uncompleted tower, the base of which is used as the chancel (11). The church is Evangelical with the living held by the Church Pastoral Aid Society.

The Catholic church of **St Peter, Dagenham** was designed in 1926 by Wilfrid Mangan in red brick Lombard style for the La Salette Fathers (12). It was reordered in 1985 but the ceiling collapsed in 2005 and the original internal arrangement was reinstated; "God moves in a mysterious way His wonders to perform" (in the words of Cowper's hymn). There is a deep frieze with golden lettering as well as a good classical baldacchino (13).

Ecclesiastical grants in Barking and Dagenham made by the Heritage of London Trust

2005   £4000 in respect of the Alibon monument at St Peter & St Paul, Dagenham

2005   £3500 for the stonework of the Curfew Tower at St Margaret, Barking

2008   £3000 for the art deco reredos at St Patrick, Barking

St John the Baptist, Wood Street, High Barnet: Butterfield Gothic in a medieval idiom

BARNET

The London Borough of Barnet was formed in 1965 from the Municipal Boroughs of Hendon and Finchley and the Urban Districts of Friern Barnet (formerly Middlesex), East Barnet (formerly Hertfordshire) and Barnet (formerly Hertfordshire). Barnet now has Enfield and Haringey to the east, Camden to the south, Brent and Harrow to the west and Hertfordshire to the north.

The Borough was originally part of a deep forest ("Baernet" means an area cleared by burning). Watling Street once ran through it.

Hendon is the only one of the villages mentioned in Domesday Book. It is today mostly built up, with some industry. The Hendon Aerodrome was famous in its day, and part of its site has become the Metropolitan Police College. Finchley lies on a plateau 300 feet high. It was a manor of the Bishop of London in the Middle Ages.

Friern Barnet was originally a possession of the Hospitaller Knights of St John of Jerusalem, "Friern" being a corruption of "Frá" or "Frère". The village remained rural until the 19th century. Its greatest claim to fame today is that Colney Hatch, the largest lunatic asylum in Europe (Architect – Samuel Daukes), lay within its boundaries; it was open from 1851 to 1991 and at its peak had 3,000 patients. (vide *Right Ho, Jeeves* by P.G. Wodehouse. "It seemed to me what Gussie (Fink-Nottle) needed was not so much the advice of a seasoned man of the world as a padded cell in Colney Hatch"). East Barnet on the other hand is mainly residential.

"Barnet" is actually High Barnet or Chipping Barnet and stands on high ground. In the Middle Ages it was a possession of the great Benedictine Abbey of St Albans. It is claimed that the tower of St John the Baptist Church is the highest point until the Urals (2000 miles east) are reached. In 1471 the sanguinary Battle of Barnet took place at Hadley. Here Edward IV and the Yorkist forces achieved victory over the Lancastrians, led by Richard Neville, the Earl of Warwick, known to history as the Kingmaker; the latter was killed. (This date of 1471 once led to a somewhat surreal conversation between a mutual friend and the Reverend Henry Thorold, to whose memory this book is dedicated. The friend rang Henry, by then slow and crippled, at Marston Hall in Lincolnshire and failed to get an answer. Henry rang back ten minutes later. The friend asked how on earth he knew it was him ringing. Henry portentously replied "1471" (the BT recall number), and added "a date of the greatest significance in English history." "O yes", replied the friend, "What happened then?". Henry airily answered "I haven't the faintest idea ..." Had he lived to read this tome, he would have.)

St Mary, Church Hill Road, East Barnet (open Saturday 10–2) is basically a Norman church. The Patron from the 11th century until the Reformation was the Abbey of St Alban's. It subsequently became a crown living, which it remains. In 1423 the Archbishop of Canterbury passed through Barnet, and the priest was reprimanded for not ringing the bills in his honour. From 1591 to 1601 the pluralist Edward Grant, Head of Westminster, "the most noted Latinist and Grecian of his time", was rector. The ugly yellow brick tower (1, 2) is of 1829. At the time it was reported, "This unpleasant construction absorbed, it is believed, the larger part of the subscription destined to the general improvement of the edifice." The church has some woodwork by Street and stained glass by Clayton & Bell of the crucifixion in the east window (3). An enjoyable series of obelisk tombstones to the Grove family can be found in the churchyard (4).

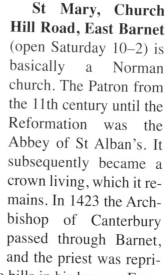

St Mary, Church End, Hendon (Parish Office open Tuesday – Thursday 10 am – 1 pm) is mainly 13th century although the tower (5) with its blue clock (6) is later. The Norman font has arcading. This dates from the time when the church was a possession of Westminster Abbey; it was subsequently transferred to the Bishop of London. The church is enriched with a south arcade by Temple Moore; Pevsner says, "One of the rare cases in which a Gothic revival architect ... has considerably enriched the original effect." Bodley designed the reredos in the north chapel; amongst the Victorian glass is a window of Our Lady, interestingly dressed in red for martyrdom rather than her traditional blue, by Kempe (7). A number of monuments can be found in the church including one of 1703 to Sir William Rawlinson; the glass behind was designed by Henry Holiday for Queen Victoria's Diamond Jubilee (8). A brass plaque in the church commemorates Sir Stamford Raffles, the founder of Singapore, who died in 1826.

9

10

St John the Baptist, Wood Street, High Barnet (open Monday to Friday 10 am – 1 pm and 2 pm – 5 pm / Saturday 9.15 am – 3 pm) was originally 15th century and a chapel of ease to St Mary, East Barnet. The parish only became independent in 1866. In 1871–5 Butterfield was commissioned to expand the old building and added a new loftier nave. The big west tower is his (9), as is the spire (10). The church was re-dedicated in 1875 by the Bishop of Rochester in whose diocese the church then was. The chancel has a prettily decorated roof. Butterfield was responsible for the red and grey marble font. The pulpit boasts a curiously Anglican selection of carved figures: St Augustine of Canterbury, St Aidan, St Hugh of Lincoln, Hugh Latimer, John Wesley and Canon Liddon. Some good woodwork adorns the chancel (11). In the south chapel can be seen a huge canopied tomb of Thomas Ravenscroft who died in 1631 (12). He was a Welshman born in Hawarden who came to seek his fortune in London. He became Clerk of the Hanaper, then the Deputy in the Alienations Office as well as MP for Monmouth.

11

12

St Mary, Hadley Green Road, Monken Hadley (open on the second Sunday in the month 2.30 to 4 pm) is situated in a pleasantly verdant area. The church originally belonged to the Abbey of Walden in Essex, hence the name Monken Hadley. The present church was built in 1494 and consists of nave, two aisles and a

chancel (13). The tower has a copper beacon, repaired in 1779. Street restored the church in 1850. There are many monuments including two busts of Wilbrahams by Nicholas Stone. Sir Roger died in 1616 (14).

St Andrew, Totteridge Village (open daily 9 am to 5 pm) was rebuilt in 1790 (17). It has a brick nave with no aisles and classical windows, and an attractive weatherboarded bell turret (15). The apsed chancel was added by Brooks in 1869 (16). Much Victorian and later glass survives.Cardinal Manning's father, Governor and Director of the Bank of England, and brother are both buried in the churchyard.

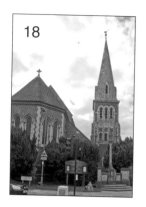

All Saints, Oakleigh Road North was built by Joseph Clarke in 1881–3 for John Miles, a local landowner (18). The iron screen ends with the pulpit (19). Its chief interest lies in the ornate decoration carried out by Gambier-Parry and the Vicar from the 1880s to the 1920s including the prickly gabled reredos, the organ

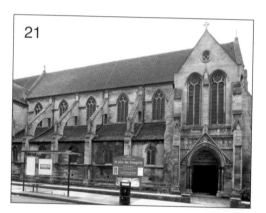

(20), stained glass by Ward & Hughes and wall paintings.

St John, Friern Barnet Road is a late work (1890–1901) by Pearson, completed by his son (21). The interior is stone, with vaulted roofs based on continental precedents (22). A narrow ambulatory surrounds the apse. The stained glass is all by Clayton & Bell, in the north aisle concentrating on various Anglican and earlier worthies (23, 24).

The 20th century has contributed three interesting Anglican churches to Barnet.

St Jude, Hampstead Garden Suburb (open most Sundays from late March to late October 11.45 – 17.30) was built by Lutyens 1909–11 for the Rev Samuel and Dame Henrietta Barnett, the founders of Hampstead Garden Suburb. It is a diverse building of many styles, including Byzantine,

Gothic and Baroque. The vast roof stretches almost to the ground (25). The tall tower looks Byzantine but is surmounted by a Gothic spire. Domes and apses abound (26). The spacious sanctuary has a marbled altar (27). The church is heavily painted (28) and includes Victorian women doing good works in the Lady Chapel, the Risen Christ and angels in the main apse and the Revelation of St John in the south chapel. Evelyn Waugh worshipped here as a child and wrote in *A Little Learning*, "I went to church with my parents who had taken to frequenting St Jude's Hampstead Garden Suburb, a fine Lutyens edifice then in the charge of a highly flamboyant clergyman named Basil Bourchier ... His sermons were dramatic, topical, irrational and totally without theological content. Despite Mr Bourchier's extravagant display I had some glimpse of higher mysteries."

St Alban and St Michael, Golders Green is by Sir Giles Scott in 1932–3. It has a central tower and a good plastered interior (29, 30). The church was originally built as a chapel of ease to All Saints, Childs Hill in 1910. In 1979 St Alban was united with St Michael Golders Green, now the Greek Orthodox Cathedral of the Holy Cross and St Michael.

The John Keble Memorial Church, Deans Lane, Hendon was built in 1935–7 by D.F. Martin-Smith for the then vicar. The dedication was suggested by the Dean of York, Dr Milner-White. The west tower has a certain presence ending in a concrete lantern surmounted by a cross (31). The interior is a large, bright, white square with a blue and gold mosaic baldacchino with a dove in the centre (32). The current vicar Chris Chivers was previously Precentor of Westminster Abbey and the Canon Chancellor of Blackburn Cathedral, and will shortly be President of Westcott House.

33

34

Of Catholic churches **St Edward the Confessor, Finchley Road, Golders Green** (1915 by Arthur Young) is worth mentioning. On a site formerly owned by the Benedictines, it is brick and cruciform Gothic (33), with a good carved reredos inside (34). It has suffered from an arson attack in 1960, and reorderings in the 1970s and 1996.

Ecclesiastical grants in Barnet made by the Heritage of London Trust

2005 £6000 for the roof of St Jude, Hampstead Garden Suburb
2006 £4000 for the rose window of St John the Baptist, Chipping Barnet
2005 £4000 for the stained glass at St Paul's Church, Mill Hill, Barnet

St Mary, Bexley with its rustic shingled spire

BEXLEY

The London Borough of Bexley was formed in 1965 out of the municipal boroughs of Bexley and Erith, Crayford urban district council and parts of the urban districts of Chislehurst and Sidcup. All these formerly were part of the county of Kent.

Bexley is bounded by the River Thames to the north, Greenwich to the west, Bromley to the south and the county of Kent to the east.

The Borough was very thinly populated and predominantly rural up the 20th century. It possesses some high ground at Shooter's Hill on the boundary of Greenwich but most of the rest of the borough is flat. It retains a considerable amount of open space. Of the various villages only Crayford was mentioned in Domesday Book. Lesnes Abbey near Erith was founded as the Abbey of St Mary and St Thomas the Martyr in 1178 by Richard de Luci, the Chief Justiciar of England, possibly in expiation of the murder of "the holy blissful martyr", as Chaucer later called Becket, eight years earlier. It never flourished economically and was suppressed by Cardinal Wolsey as early as 1525. Various ruins of the abbey remain. Hall Place on the outskirts of Crayford dates back to 1540 when it was constructed for Sir John Champneis, Lord Mayor of London. In the 17th century the house was sold to another city merchant, Sir Richard Austen, who added a redbrick second wing. Danson House between Bexleyheath and Welling is a Palladian villa built in 1766 for the St Kitts sugar merchant and slaveowner Sir John Boyd. Nathaniel Richmond, an assistant of Capability Brown, landscaped the estate with a 12-acre lake at its centre. Philip Webb designed the Arts and Crafts Red House in Bexleyheath in 1860 for William Morris, who for financial reasons had to sell it five years later; Burne-Jones described it as "the beautifullest place on earth".

With the coming of the railways, development began although the Borough remains a somewhat confusing mixture of disconnected settlements and green spaces.

Erith (a fairly grim spot) was a small riverside port until the 1850s with a naval dockyard opened by Henry VIII; its pier was was a target for day trippers. In the late 19th century it became known for its heavy industry – armaments (Vickers) and cables (BICC). It was heavily bombed in the Second World War and most of what remained of the past was demolished in 1966.

The Thamesmead "new town" was built on part of the Erith marshes in the borough.

Sir Edward Heath was latterly MP for Old Bexley and Sidcup.

St Mary, Bexley is a 13th century church built of flint. Basil Champneys restored it in 1883. It has a shingled spire (1). The fairly elaborate chancel screen is by Champneys (2). A number of monuments date from the 16th to the 18th centuries including one to Sir John Champneis (3). He was the son of Robert Champneis of Chew Magna, Somerset, a Skinner who became Lord Mayor. He was also a Skinner and became Lord Mayor in 1534. John Stow attributed his blindness in later life to having built a high tower of brick at his house in Mincing Lane – "the first I ever heard of in any private man's house, to overlook his neighbours in the city". He died in 1556.

Some Victorian angels are painted on the sedilia (5). The Victorian glass is good (4). Several neo-classical tombs are to be found in the churchyard (6).

7

St John the Baptist, Erith lies near the southern bank of the Thames, surrounded by housing and industrial estates. It is mainly 13th century, albeit heavily restored in 1877 (7). Its chief interest is the recumbent effigy of Elizabeth, Countess of Shrewsbury, who died in 1567 (9); Pevsner says "It might almost be in Westminster Abbey". She was the second wife of George Earl of Shrewsbury, Lord Steward to both Henry VII and Henry VIII and the daughter of Sir Richard Walden of Erith. Her husband is buried in the south chapel of Sheffield Cathedral, surrounded by his first wife Anne (daughter of Lord Hastings) and herself. Her will stated

8

"Within one year next after my decease there will be a tomb made over me with a flat stone of marble having the picture of mine arms graven therein." The manor of Erith passed to her daughter Anne, Countess of Pembroke. Chantrey designed a monument of 1826 to Lord Eardley (previously Sir Samuel Gideon, Bt) and his brother (8).

9

10

11

12

St Paulinus, Crayford (parish office open Mon – Tues / Thur – Fri, 9 am – 11 am; last Tuesday of month instead 7 pm – 9 pm) is mainly Perpendicular although with some earlier Norman work (10). The vestry and south porch were added in the 16th century. It has a number of 17th and 18th century monuments including ones to William and Mary Draper of 1650–2 (11) and the widow of Admiral Sir Cloudesley Shovel who died in 1732. The altar table of the four evangelists is c. 1895 and by James Brooks (12).

Christ Church, Bexleyheath (normally open Monday to Friday 12 noon – 1pm) was built by a William Knight of Nottingham in 1872–3 (14). It is an extraordinary, spiralling church in grand French Gothic style with rose windows in the transepts (13). It lacks decent fittings. (12)

13

14

Christ Church, Victoria Road, Erith is by J.P. St Aubyn, the harsh restorer of so many Cornish churches. Here he built a substantial brick church with tower and spire in 1874 (15). It has a rich interior with nave and chancel walls covered with early 20th century wall paintings (16). Much of the glass is by Hardman, contemporaneous with the date of construction; there is also a window of the coronation of Edward VII and Queen Alexandria (17).

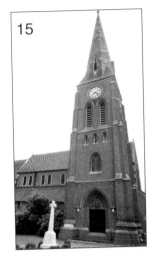

St John, Church Road, Sidcup (open Monday to Saturday 9 am – 2 pm) is another large brick church, this time by Fellowes Prynne of 1899–1901 (18), absorbing an earlier chancel and Lady Chapel by Withers. Pevsner is dismissive of the architecture but the church is rather appealing. The stone screen has statues of saints on either side (19). Comper designed some glass (20).

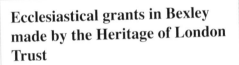

Ecclesiastical grants in Bexley made by the Heritage of London Trust

1986 £5000 for the tower of St Paulinus, Crayford
2001 £4000 for the spire of St John the Evangelist, Bexley

The High Church interior, St Andrew, Willesden Green

BRENT

The London Borough of Brent consists of the former boroughs of Wembley and Willesden, both until 1965 in the County of Middlesex.

It is neighboured by Hammersmith and Fulham, Kensington and Chelsea and Westminster to the south, by Camden and Barnet to the east, by Barnet and Harrow to the north and by Ealing to the west.

The Borough takes its name from the river Brent, a tributary of the Thames. The Borough is mainly low-lying with some higher ground to the north. Until the 19th century the Borough was primarily agricultural but with the coming of the railways there was a great deal of both industrial and residential development, the latter of course being the commencement of 'Metroland'. As the late Laureate hymned "Gentle Brent I used to know you, Wandering Wembley-wards at will, Now what change your waters show you, In the meadowlands you fill."

Wembley was originally a manor of the Archbishop of Canterbury, its name deriving from Wemba Lea, meaning Wemba's meadow. It was joined with Kingsbury and Sudbury for municipal purposes and also incorporated the former villages of Alperton, Preston, and South Kenton. It has become best known for its Stadium originally opened in 1924 for the British Empire Exhibition. The original stadium was demolished against considerable opposition in 2003 and replaced by the new one in 2007.

Most of Willesden was owned by St Paul's Cathedral up to the Reformation with All Souls College, Oxford owning the more southerly areas. It was a major centre of Marian pilgrimage, second only to Walsingham in the Middle Ages, deriving originally from a holy well. The cult was well established by 1249 and reached its zenith in the early 16th century when, for example, the shrine was visited by Elizabeth of York, the wife of Henry VII, and St Thomas More. The Black Madonna of Willesden was burnt by the wretched Thomas Cromwell at Chelsea in 1538.

Willesden also incorporated a number of former villages such as Brondesbury, Cricklewood, Dollis Hill, Harlesden, Kilburn and Neasden. The Prime Minister Earl of Aberdeen (when not at Haddo) lived at the now demolished Dollis Hill House; Mark Twain subsequently lived there. Neasden obtained a degree of notoriety from *Private Eye* with its famous football club managed by "ashen-faced Ron Knee". Kensal Green Cemetery was opened in 1832; G.K. Chesterton concluded his poem "The Rolling English Road" with the following words: "For there is good news yet to hear and fine things to be seen, Before we go to paradise by way of Kensal Green"; I trust he is right.

The bulk of **St Mary, Willesden** (open daily) is ragstone, 13th – 14th century. It was much restored by the Victorians (Thomas Little and E.J. Tarver in particular). It has an attractive large churchyard (1). Various brasses and monuments lie inside. The font is Norman, of Purbeck marble (2). In the south east chapel is to be found a black Virgin of 1972 by Catherine Stern (3). Charles Read, the fiery author of *The Cloister and the Hearth*, lies in the churchyard.

St Andrew, Church Lane, Kingsbury is a curiosity. It was originally erected in Wells Street, Marylebone by Daukes & Hamilton in 1847 and rapidly became a centre of Anglo-Catholicism especially under Benjamin Webb, Vicar from 1862 to 1885, and co-founder of the Cambridge Camden Society and Editor of *The Ecclesiologist*. The church was re-erected in Kingsbury in 1934 (4). The building is Perpendicular rather than the approved Middle Pointed, and has a narrow chancel. Eastlake described "the selection of so late a type of Gothic a mistake" in his *Gothic Revival* (1872). The fittings are a goldmine of Victoriana and everybody who was anybody seems to have contributed – altar (Pugin), chancel screen, reredos, font and pulpit (Street), sanctuary arcading, sedilia and font cover (Pearson), litany desk (Burges), wall painting (Clayton & Bell), lectern (Butterfield), etc. (5–8). The stained glass by Hardman was destroyed in the Second World War. Some Clayton & Bell glass from the 1860s remains. The old 12–13th century church survives in the churchyard. By 1248 the church had been appropriated to the Hospital of St John of Jerusalem.

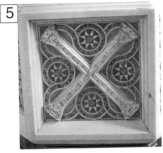

All Souls, Station Road, Harlesden was built by E.J. Tarver in 1875–6 and consists now of a large brick octagon (9), the nave having been demolished in 1978. The timber roof is dramatic (10). A plethora of Victorian glass, some of it by Heaton, Butler & Bayne survives. The white altar and baldacchino are modern.

St Andrew, High Road, Willesden Green is by James Brooks, 1886–7 (11). Pevsner describes it as "impressive in scale and more elaborately detailed than his East End churches. Large and ambitious ... it displays a stately if somewhat dull E.E. [Early English]" The interior is lofty, brick with stone facings (13). The church has lavish furnishings, especially a dramatic high altar with reredos with painting by Westlake. Victorian glass by Lavers, Barraud and Westlake and by Kempe can be found. The modern glass of 1963 is by John Hayward (12). The church is traditionally Anglo-Catholic. At least one vicar, Father David Irwin, has "poped" in living memory.

St Gabriel, Walm Lane, Cricklewood is by Basset Smith and Day, 1897–1903. It has a saddleback tower and is Decorated in style (15). The

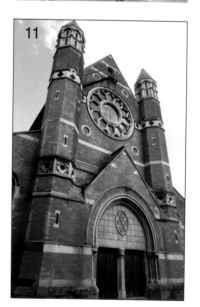

fittings are costly, notably a huge carved reredos with painted wings (16). Kempe contributed some good glass (14). The pews have been removed and replaced by orange chairs, but the reordering feels less oppressive here than in some other churches.

Of Catholic churches in the Borough, **St George, Harrow Road, Sudbury** is worth a mention. It is a neo-Perpendicular church, of grey brick and stone, built in 1926 by Leonard Williams for Father Clement Lloyd Russell, a convert clergyman (17, 18). Anthony Delarue has recently provided new ironwork and light fittings.

Ecclesiastical grants in Brent made by the Heritage of London Trust

2008 £3000 for repairs to west end window of St Andrew, Sudbury

2010 £2000 for restoration of clock at St Gabriel, Walm Lane, Cricklewood

Stained glass window by Freeth at St George,
Beckenham

BROMLEY

The London Borough of Bromley was formed in 1965 out of the municipal boroughs of Bromley and Beckenham, the urban districts of Orpington and Penge and part of the urban districts of Chislehurst and Sidcup. Bromley is bounded to the north by Southwark, Lewisham, Greenwich and Bexley, by Croydon to the west and by Surrey and Kent to the south and east.

Bromley is the largest borough in the GLC area, and the least densely populated. Most of its settlements (i.e. Beckenham and Bromley) lie to the north. Sydenham Hill is in the north, and Westerham Heights on its southern boundary is at 245 metres the highest point in the GLC area. The area of the Borough was predominantly rural until the railways arrived in the 1850s and 1860s. These brought increasing residential development in the middle which speeded up after the First World War. St Mary Cray was sacrificed to industrial development. Alphabetically:

The Manor of Beckenham was purchased by John Cator in 1773 and developed by his heirs. In Bromley, Bromley College was founded by John Warner, Bishop of Rochester, under his will in 1666 for "twenty poore widowes (of orthodox and loyall clergymen)". Sundridge Park (now a golf hotel) by Nash and Repton lies outside. Biggin Hill was a famous RAF Aerodrome in the Second World War.

Chislehurst, still a green oasis, is perhaps the most interesting settlement. Sir Francis Walsingham, the notorious Protestant Principal Secretary under Queen Elizabeth I, and his son Sir Thomas, the patron of Christopher Marlowe, lived at Scadbury Park. The admirable antiquary William Camden lived in the village from 1609 to 1623. Charles Pratt, the Attorney General, bought the site to build Camden Place and by 1786 had been created Earl Camden. From 1871 to 1873 Napoleon III lived at Camden Place, which Empress Eugenie (who amazingly survived until 1920) did not sell until 1885. The Tiarks banking family built there the neo-Jacobean Foxbury by David Brandon (often an imaginative architect) in 1875–6; it is regrettably described by Pevsner as "All in all a poor effort".

Crystal Palace was moved in 1852 from Hyde Park to Sydenham Hill and finally succumbed to fire in 1936. Charles Darwin lived at the 17th century Downe House outside Downe in the south of the borough. Outside Keston William Pitt the Younger as Prime Minister bought the estate of Holwood. Orpington is notorious for the Liberal victory by Eric Lubbock in the 1962 by-election. Penge had a couple of nasty murders in the late 19th century and Horace Rumpole of course established his reputation with the Penge Bungalow Murders... Sir Henry Heydon from Baconsthorpe in Norfolk built the Court in West Wickham in the late 15th century.

St Martin of Tours, Chelsfield (open daily) has an early Norman nave and Early English chancel, much restored (1,2). The tower and chapel were added in the 13th century. The church is situated in countryside and comes under the Diocese of Rochester. The roof is of wood (3). Peter Collet, alderman and merchant of London, who died in 1607 and his wife have a good pendent monument (4). A number of brasses lie around. The pews date from 1886. The church was hit by a flying bomb in the Second World War, which destroyed all the existing stained glass, and which Moira Forsyth was commissioned to replace in the 1950s.

St Nicholas, Chislehurst (parish office open Monday – Friday, 9 am – 1 pm (or 3 pm on Wednesdays and Thursdays)) is approached by a yew avenue (6). It is mainly 15th century although partly rebuilt in the 19th century. The reredos is by Bodley & Garner in 1896 (5), as is the chancel roof (7). Many monuments from the 15th century onwards including works by Rysbrack, Cheere and Chantry are to be found in the church.. The reclining effigy of Earl Sydney (sometime Lord Chamberlain) in Garter robes of 1890 is by Boehm, completed by Gilbert (9). A monument to Henry Frederic Tiarks (1832–1911), partner of Schroders for 40 years, and who lived at Foxbury House nearby, lies in the churchyard (8). The famous Father Lowder of St Peter's, London Docks is also buried here.

St John the Baptist, West Wickham
(parish office open Monday – Tuesday /
Thursday – Friday, 9.15 am – 12.15 pm) is
engulfed in suburbia but protected to a degree
by playing fields and farmland (10, 11). The
church was in the main built by Sir Henry
Heydon c. 1490, although it has been much
restored subsequently. J.D. Sedding was responsible for the pulpit, screens (12, 13) and
organ case. Some medieval glass including a
window of St Katharine (14) can be found,
and also a number of monuments (15).

The first Victorian church of note is **St George, Bickley Park Road, Bickley** (open daily). This is by F. Barnes in 1863–5. It is of Kentish rag and the style is Decorated (16). It is a large, handsome church (18) with clerestories and a hammer-beam roof. The tower and spire date from 1905–6. The church suffered a bad fire in 1989 (19) and has been rebuilt subsequently so that it is now light and airy. High church fittings are much in evidence (17). The church is "under the pastoral care of the Bishop of Fulham", i.e. traditional Anglo-Catholic.

St John the Evangelist, Bromley is full of character in an ugly way. It is by an architect called Truefitt of 1879–80 and built in a mixture of Kentish rag and brick (21). Beatrice Elizabeth Barker, the wife of the first Vicar has a memorial at the west end (20). Francis Spear designed the stained glass of 1951 in the north transept (described by Pevsner as "brash") (22). The east end is apsidal (23).

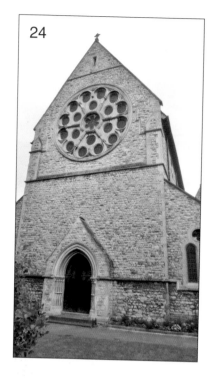

More exciting architecturally is the **Annunciation, High Street, Chislehurst**. This is by Brooks of 1868–70 for Canon Francis Murray, Rector of Chislehurst, and one of his best churches (24, 25). The nave has a high clerestory and low aisles. The reredos is by Brooks. The mosaic of the Last Judgement above the chancel arch is by Salviati (27). The wall paintings are by Westlake (26, 28). It is a very satisfying church. This is another traditional Anglo-Catholic parish.

29

30

St George, Beckenham

(open 8.30 am – 4.00 pm weekdays / all day Sunday) was rebuilt in 1885–7 by W. Gibbs Bartleet, a local architect, in Perpendicular style (30); Pevsner describes it as a "confident town church". The church retains a number of monuments from the earlier church including one to Hugo Raymond, who died in 1737, by Thomas Adye (29). Flaxman and Chantrey also designed monuments. William Lord Auckland (1745–1814) was buried in the graveyard (sometime Envoy to France and President of the Board of Trade). Comper designed some of the glass (31), while Thomas Freeth contributed more in 1963–1966 (32).

31

32

34

J·HAROLD GIBBONS
ARCHITECT OF THIS CHURCH
DIED DEC·30 1957
SI·MONUMENTUM
VIS·CIRCUMSPICE

Only the medieval tower of **St Peter and Paul, Bromley** survived the bombing of 1941 (33). A new Gothic-style church by Harold Gibbons was joined to it in 1948–57 (35). The architect is commemorated in the church (34). A number of brasses (36) come from the old building.

The most interesting Catholic church in the borough is **St Mary, Hawkwood Lane, Chislehurst**, which is a ragstone building by Wardell (38). Napoleon III, the Empress Eugenie and the Prince Imperial lived at nearby Camden Place (now Camden Golf Club) in exile after 1870. In 1874 a mortuary chapel to the church's south was

added by Clutton (37). This was intended for the body of Napoleon III but in the end all three eventually lay in the more magnificent surroundings of Farnborough Abbey. A monument to the Prince Imperial showing him fully armed remains; he died in the Zulu War of 1879 (39). From 1900 to at least 1925 the Tiarks family of Foxbury House contributed £200 pa to the

upkeep of the church, Frank Tiarks having married a Catholic, Emma Maria Franziska of Hamburg, in 1899.

St Anthony of Padua, Anerley is a late Gothic revival church built by F.A. Walters in 1929 (40) for his son Father James Walters who was Parish Priest. The reredos and other fittings survive (41).

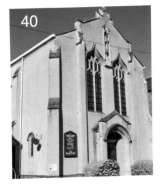

Ecclesiastical grants in Bromley made by the Heritage of London Trust

1990   £5000 for the murals of St Mary
       Plaistow, Bromley
1999   £3000 for the restoration of stencilling of
       St Paul, Beckenham
2010   £3000 to restore the clock of St John the
       Evangelist, Penge

An Altar at Our Lady of the Rosary and St Dominic, Southampton Road, Haverstock Hill

CAMDEN

The London Borough of Camden was formed in 1965 from the boroughs of Holborn, St Pancras and Hampstead. It takes its name from Charles Pratt, Earl Camden, (cf Chislehurst in Bromley) who had an estate in St Pancras.

Barnet and Haringey lie to the north, Brent to the west, the Cities of London and Westminster to the south and Islington to the east.

For some centuries the Borough consisted of a number of small farming hamlets, the inhabitants of which kept pigs in the forest. In 959 King Edgar gave land in the south to Westminster Abbey.

Holborn was already expanding by the 16th century. The lawyers had colonised Gray's Inn and Lincoln's Inn by then. The Bishop of Ely had his palace by Smithfield. In the 17th century the Earl of Southampton started developing the area round his manor of Bloomsbury (the name deriving from the 12th century William de Blemund). The Foundling Hospital was set up in 1742 by Captain Coram and the Bedford Estate further developed Bloomsbury, e.g. with Bedford Square of 1775. South of this region, notorious slums grew up around St Giles and Seven Dials. The building of the neo-classical British Museum by Sir Robert Smirke commenced in 1823. London University arrived subsequently.

St Pancras takes its name from the ancient parish church. Highgate on its hill became a small town by the 18th century. Highgate School was founded by Sir Richard Cholmeley in 1568. In the 18th century James Thompson wrote "Heavens! What a goodly prospect spreads around, of hills, and dales, and woods, and lawns, and spires and glittering towns, and gilded streams." Highgate Cemetery opened in 1839 and various luminaries lie there – George Eliot, John Galsworthy, Radcliffe Hall, Karl Marx, Ralph Richardson and Christina Rosetti. Betjeman was brought up at 31, West Hill "safe in a world of trains and buttered toast". Camden Town to the south was developed by Earl Camden from 1791 and Somers Town by Earl Somers. The southern part of St Pancras was transformed by the arrival of the three railway termini: Euston (1838), King's Cross (which derived its name from a short-lived statue of George IV) (1851) and St Pancras (1868). There was an industrial area north of the station consisting of goods and marshalling yards, canals and gasworks. Slums spread in Somers Town, extending into Camden Town and Kentish Town.

Hampstead on its hill became a spa village in the early 18th century, protected by its heath and other green spaces. The Earl of Mansfield bought Kenwood House in 1754 and set Robert Adam to work on it. Leigh Hunt sang "With balmy fields in front and sloping green, Dear Hampstead is thy southern face serene." John Keats lived near Downshire Hill.

There is one surviving Anglican church with medieval work. This is **Old St Pancras Church** (open Monday to Friday noon to 3 pm). St Pancras was the orphan son of a Phrygian aristocrat who was brought up at the Emperor's Court in Rome. At the age of 14 he was beheaded on the Aurelian Way in 304 AD for refusing to burn incense to the Emperor Diocletian. The church is to be found in Somers Town, behind the station later named after it, on top of the Fleet River. It is one of the earliest churches established in London; it has a 7th century altar stone to prove it. Some 12–13th century work survives but the church was brutally Normanised in 1848 by

Roumieu and Gough (1, NB the porch 2) and further restored later on by Blomfield. The church has a number of monuments including a 17th century wall monument to William and Mary Platt (3), originally in Highgate School Chapel. The churchmanship is now fairly high (4). There was considerable bomb damage in the Second World War. A number of monuments are in the large churchyard, including one by Sir John Soane to his wife. Certain French emigres after the Revolution were also buried there, as was the proto-feminist Mary Woolstonecraft.

One of the first fruits of the Fifty New Churches Act of 1711 was **St George, Blooms-bury Way** (usually open 1–4 pm) by Nicholas Hawksmoor, begun in 1716 and completed in 1731. It has a six-column Corinthian portico on the south side and a spire on top based on the Mausoleum of Halicarnassus, crowned by a figure of George I with lion and unicorn supporters; the latter were removed by Street in 1871 but have been reinstated (5). The church itself is a square, originally with north and south galleries respectively for the Dukes of Bedford and Manchester. It has good mahogany fittings (6). The whole has recently been splendidly restored. The East India Company erected a monument to its sometime Chairman, Charles Grant MP (7) by Bacon and Manning. Horace Walpole thought the church "a masterpiece of absurdity"; tastes change over the centuries. Anthony Trollope was baptised in the church in 1824.

TO THE MEMORY OF CHARLES GRANT

8

9

10

Another 18th century church is **St Giles-in-the-Fields** (open Monday to Friday, 9 am to 4 pm), once aptly so named. There was originally the chapel of a leper hospital founded in 1101 by Queen Matilda on the site. In 1542 it became a parish church. Henry VIII gave the hospital itself to John Dudley, consecutively Lord Lisle, Earl of Warwick and Duke of Northumberland; he was the Protector of Edward VI and executed by Queen Mary on her accession in 1553. The earlier church was rebuilt in 1731–3 by Henry Flitcroft. In the 18th and 19th centuries the parish became notorious for its poverty and squalor and was known as the St Giles Rookery. The church is plain and classical outside, with a pleasing square then octagonal tower surmounted by a spire with gilt ball and cross (8). The interior is airy and vaulted with galleries (9). It was restored in the 19th century. The chandeliers are worth noting as is the earlier pulpit of 1676. An interesting monument commemorates Duchess Dudley (10). She was Alice Leigh who in 1594 married Sir Robert Dudley, 'base born' son of Robert Dudley, Earl of Leicester. In 1644 she was made a Duchess of the Holy Roman Empire. Charles I made her "Duchess Dudley for her life, in England,... with such precedencies as she might have had if she had lived in the dominions of the Sacred Empire as a mark of our favour to her". She died in 1669.

St Oliver Plunkett, Archbishop of Armagh, was originally buried here after his execution in 1681; his body was subsequently moved to Lamspring Abbey in Germany and thence to Downside Abbey in Somerset.

A third 18th century church of interest is **St John, Hampstead** (open daily). It was in fact only in 1917 that the Bishop of London decided that the dedication was to St John the Evangelist rather than St John the Baptist. In the Middle Ages the benefice belonged to Westminster Abbey. On the Dissolution of the Monasteries the Abbey was replaced by the Bishop of Westminster. The see was short-lived and abolished by Edward VI in 1551. The existing church was built in 1754–7 by Henry Flitcroft and John Sanderson. It is a strong broad church with a sturdy tower and a small castellated spire at the east end (11). The exterior is built in plain brown brick. Cupids adorn the drain pipes. The interior is 18th century with high Ionic columns (12). The building was extended 30 feet westwards in 1843. Temple Moore built the choir and the vestry. The church has many minor monuments, including a memorial of Keats. The churchyard with its wrought iron gates from Canons Park, Stanmore has a number of monuments. John Constable, Temple Moore, Gerald du Maurier, Evelyn Underhill, Hugh Gaitskell, Kay Kendall and Peter Cook are all buried there (13, 14).

St Pancras New Church, Euston Road ("often open during the daytime") was built 1819–23 by William and Henry Inwood. Its most striking feature is the six column portico with Ionian columns on the model of the Erectheum in Athens; terracotta caryatids hold ewers and reversed torches as symbols of mortality (15, 18). The tower is modelled on the Temple of the Winds (17). The church at the time cost £77,000 and was the most expensive church built in London since St Paul's Cathedral. The interior with its uncoffered ceiling is dominated by the six green scagliola columns in the apse (16). Clayton & Bell and others provided the glass (19). Sir John Summerson wrote of the church "St Pancras is the Queen of early 19th century churches; its architecture earns it the title as much as its size and its cost".

St John, Downshire Hill, Hampstead was originally a proprietary chapel and was built 1818–23. The pretty exterior is stuccoed. The west front has a porch with Doric columns and a cupola (20). In 1832 the copyhold was purchased by an Evangelical admirer of George Whitefield, who fell foul of the incumbent of St John, Hampstead leading to a temporary closure of the church. It is now in modern Evangelical hands and the interior has received the customary treatment (21).

St Michael, South Grove, Highgate was built in 1830 by Lewis Vulliamy. The building was constructed by Cubitt. It has a brick front with spired steeple and is the highest (by altitude rather than liturgy) church in London (22). The east window of 1954 is by Evie Hone (24) and the decoration of the Four Doctors of the church by Temple Moore (23). Samuel Coleridge is buried here.

The Gothic Revival and Tractarianism hit Camden with considerable vigour.

St Mary Magdalene, Munster Square is an early example being built 1849–52 by R.C. Carpenter. It is a Decorated hall church with broad aisles in Kentish ragstone (25). There is no clerestory. It was founded by the Rev Edward Stuart, previously curate of Christ Church, Albany Street, who asked Carpenter for "a church as near perfection as the handicraft of man, the skill of architects, and the experience and ingenuity of ecclesiastical art could make it." Stuart died in 1877 and was succeeded by the Rev F. Ponsonby until his death in 1894. He was Treasurer-General of the Confraternity of the Blessed Sacrament and sat on the Council of the English Church Union;

Queen Victoria rather surprisingly sent a wreath to his funeral but he was, of course, a Ponsonby. The church was decorated in a high church style from the late 1870s to the 1930s, with painting by Clayton & Bell and others (26). The east window was designed by Pugin (27), and the rood by Micklethwaite (28). (The stained glass in the crypt by Margaret Rope comes from St Augustine, Haggerston).

St Mark, Prince Albert Road, Regents Park (1851–2) was built by Thomas Little for Canon Dale, the Evangelical Vicar of St Pancras, who was gravely concerned by the increase in population of the area. The church was consecrated in 1853 by Bishop Blomfield of London. The first (Evangelical) Vicar for 40 years was William Galloway. The second Vicar was a high churchman, Dr William Sparrow-Simpson, who wrote the hymn 'All for Jesus' as part of the text of Stainer's 'Crucifixion'. In 1902 Charles Booth mentioned St Mark's "to which many people are drawn from a distance, attracted by the extreme High Church practices adopted". The third Vicar, Maurice Bell, helped write the English Hymnal and eventually "crossed the Tiber". The church has a rag-stone exterior and a white nave (29). The 1890 chancel is by Blomfield. The reredoses for the high altar and the north chapel are by Comper, as is much of the glass (30–32). The church suffered badly in the Blitz but Comper was fortunately still around to supervise the reconstruction.

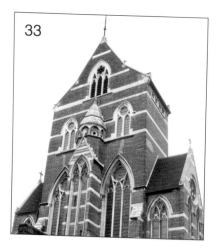

St Alban, Brooke Street, Holborn (open lunchtimes Monday to Friday) is one of the shrine churches of Anglo-Catholicism. The church was built by Butterfield in 1856–62 in a terrible, very crowded slum (described by Dickens in *Oliver Twist* as "one of the lowest and worst that improvement has left in the heart of London") and paid for by Lord Addington, sometime Governor of the Bank of England. It was however seriously damaged by bombing in 1941 and rebuilt by Adrian Scott in 1959–61. Butterfield's powerful west saddleback tower in red brick with stone bands survives (33), as does the entrance (34). The rebuilt church is dominated by a huge mural on the east wall by Hans Feibusch of 1966 (35). Most of the elaborate Anglo-Catholic furnishings were lost in the bombing but the Mackonochie chapel in the south west with its carved reredos and stained glass by Kempe gives something of the flavour of what was lost (36). It contains a recumbent marble effigy of Father Alexander Mackonochie. Father Arthur Stanton who died in 1913 after half a century as a curate is remembered with a fine recumbent bronze effigy by Hamo Thornycroft (37); alas the chantry chapel by Ninian Comper in which it originally stood is no more although glass by the latter can still be found in the church.

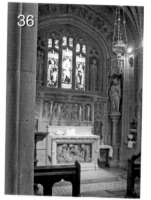

St Mary Brookfield, Dartmouth Park Hill (1869–75) is also by Butterfield but is not one of his more distinguished works although it illustrates his favoured pattern of red and yellow bricks (38–41). Various of the furnishings are by Comper.

St Mary, Primrose Hill (open Monday to Friday 9 am to 2 pm) is by M.P. Manning and was built 1870–2 on a site given by the Eton College Estate. It is a red brick French Gothic basilica (42). Percy Dearmer, author of *The Parson's Handbook*, was Vicar here 1901–15 and simplified the furnishings (mainly by Bodley & Garner). He whitewashed the walls in his pursuit of the "English Use"(43) (derided as "British Museum religion" by his liturgical enemies.)

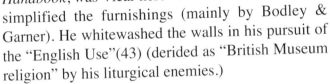

St Michael, Camden Road (open Tuesday to Friday afternoons) is an imposing work by Bodley & Garner built between 1880 and 1894 (45). It has a tall interior of bare stone (44). Furnishings are sparse (46) but there is a brass to the first vicar, Father Edward Penfold (47).

Holy Cross, Cromer Street is of 1887 by Joseph Peacock and is a brick building with lancet windows built in memory of Commander James Goodenough, who was speared to death in the Solomon Islands (48). Peacock was asked to design a church fit "for the more "advanced" kind of religion". It has a stately tall interior with polychromatic brick work. The font is by Pearson (49). The Anglo-Catholic fittings are early 20th century (50) and include a Pieta made at Malling Abbey for Father Maryon-Wilson (51). Father Hope-Patten of Walsingham fame was a curate here.

All Hallows, Shirlock Road, Gospel Oak was built 1892–1901 by James Brooks as originally the Church of the Good Shepherd. (The Diocese of London subsequently demolished the Wren Church of All Hallows the Great, Lombard Street; part of the proceeds of the sale of the site were allocated to this church provided the name was changed). The foundation stone was laid by the Duchess of Teck, mother of Queen Mary, in 1892. It is a long, lofty, aisled, towerless church, and is magnificent, rising up from the surrounding red brick Victorian villas (52). Basil Clark described it as "certainly Brooks's best church and a most impressive example of the ambition of later 19th century church builders". Sadly the vaulted roof was never built. The chancel was designed by Giles Gilbert Scott in 1914. Anglo-Catholic fittings are in evidence (53). The capitals are unfinished (54, 55). The Stations of the Cross come from St Alban's, Holborn. A series of rather aggressive buttresses lie on the north side of the church.

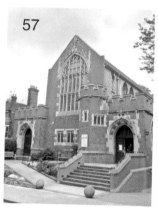

St Luke, Kidderpore Avenue on its hillside is of 1897–9 by Basil Champneys (57). The parish was carved out of St John Hampstead in 1896. The church has a picturesque west front and is built in red brick and stone. It has a tall and impressive interior, with no chancel arch (56). Some glass is by Morris.

St Benet and All Saints, Lupton Street, Kentish Town (1908) has a chancel by Bodley's later partner, Cecil Hare, and is very much in the tradition (60). A mission church of 1881 predated the building. The interior is white-plastered and certain furnishings such as the rood (59) and baroque painted statue of the Virgin survive. Archbishop Laud, "the meddling hocus pocus" is commemorated in glass (58).

St Silas, Prince of Wales Road, Kentish Town was built by Shearman in 1911–12, resembling Albi Cathedral. It is surrounded by council estates. The interior furnishings are quite extraordinary, to all intents and purposes looking like a Catholic church prior to the Second Vatican Council. T.S. Eliot used to come here for confession. (61–64).

Standing apart from this broadly high church tradition are two churches.

The first is **St Martin, Vicars Road, Gospel Oak**, which was built by E.B. Lamb, one of Goodhart-Rendel's "rogue architects", in 1864–5. The inoffensive exterior of Kentish rag with its tall and unusual tower (66) fails to prepare the visitor for the craziness of the hammerbeam roof. There is a low church emphasis on preaching and visibility, and low church fittings to match (65).

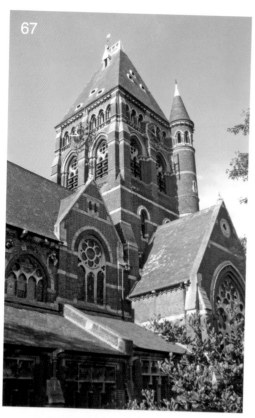

The other is **St Stephen, Rosslyn Hill** 1869–73 by S.S. Teulon, who called it his "mighty church". It held 1200 worshippers at its peak. The exterior is of red brick with stone dressings, dominated by a big heavy tower with a pyramid roof (67). The interior has slanting arches (68). Thomas Earp carved the luxuriant capitals with their foliage. Declared redundant in 1977, it has finally been rescued by the St Stephen's Restoration and Preservation Trust, which has raised £4 million for its restoration. It has good glass (69).

The borough is relatively well off for interesting Catholic churches.

St Etheldreda, Ely Place (open daily) is a rarity in being a medieval building in Catholic hands. It was originally built in the late 13th century as the chapel of the town house of the Bishops of Ely (70). In 1570 Bishop Cox was forced to lease the buildings to Sir Christopher Hatton after Queen Elizabeth wrote to him in the following words, "Proud Prelate, I understand you are backward in complying but I would have you understand that I who made you what you are can unmake you", a forthright example of Erastianism. The Spanish Ambassador lived in the buildings in the 1620s. In 1873 it was ruinous and acquired at auction

by the Oxford convert, Father William Lockhart, for the Rosminians, who are still here. It is two-storeyed, and the interior is dominated by modern glass (71). The screen is by Bentley. A medieval wall painting adorns the crypt (72).

St Mary, Holly Place, Hampstead is a tiny church of 1816 in the centre of a recessed terrace of cottages (73). It was built in 1816 by the emigre priest Abbe Morel (75). The stuccoed front was added by Wardell in 1850. There is a statue of the Virgin in a niche above. The baldacchino over the high altar was erected by Adrian Gilbert Scott in 1935 (74). Graham Greene was married in the church in 1927 and General de Gaulle attended Mass here during the Second World War.

St Peter, Clerkenwell Road was a mission church built for the poor Italian community living round there by Sir John Miller Bryson in 1862–3 for the Pallottine Order (76). The partly painted interior is spacious and imposing (77) with a baldacchino with black marble columns. It remains the Italian church.

Our Lady of the Rosary and St Dominic, Southampton Road, Haverstock Hill (open daily) was built for the Dominicans by Charles Alban Buckler in 1874–83 (78). In 1861 Cardinal Wiseman had invited the Dominicans to take over the mission in Kentish Town. A gentleman called Thomas Walmsley from Tunbridge Wells dreamt of building a church in honour of Our Lady of Lourdes "to mark the gratitude of the Catholics of the United Kingdom for the many graces and blessings received through Our Lady of Lourdes". The building is 299 feet long and is one of the largest Catholic churches in London. It has an uninterrupted roof line. The church lacks a tower. The style is Early English in yellow brick. The church cost £40,000. Fourteen side chapels with altars, all dedicated to a mystery of the Rosary, line the church (79); the final 15th mystery, the Crowning of Our Lady as Queen of Heaven, is commemorated in the stained glass above the high altar (80). It has elaborate contemporaneous furnishings and a column from the pre-Reformation Dominican church at Blackfriars. The grotto of Our Lady of Lourdes was built by Westlake in 1914 (81).

St Anselm and St Cecilia, Kingsway (open daily) is the successor of the Sardinian Chapel. During the reign of James II there was a chapel at 54 Lincolns Inn Fields occupied by Franciscans. This chapel was destroyed in 1688 following the flight of that monarch. By 1700 the restored building was occupied by the Portuguese Embassy. In 1715 a Sicilian Embassy Chapel was recorded there. Following a swap of islands this became the Sardinian Chapel by 1722. The 18th century Catholic Bishop Richard Challoner frequently preached there and called it "the chief support of religion in London". The Chapel was wrecked in the Gordon Riots of 1780 but restored. In 1798 the Apostolic Visitor of the London District John Douglass acquired the property which however remained under the protection of the King of Sardinia until 1858. In 1853 the dedication was changed to that of St Anselm who was born in Savoy, part of the Kingdom of Sardinia. In 1902 the church was demolished to create Kingsway. Cardinal Vaughan commissioned a new church (82, 83), which was designed by F.A. Walters and opened in 1909 (800 years after the death of St Anselm). The interior is neo-Renaissance. The square-ended sanctuary is the most striking architectural feature; the reredos has a finely carved depiction of the Coronation of the Virgin (84). The painting of the Deposition after Corregio, the Sardinian Royal Arms, the organ (on whose predecessor Thomas Arne had composed the tune for "Rule Britannia"), the altar in the Lady Chapel and the font were all brought here from the old Sardinian Chapel. In September 1941 the building was badly damaged by bombing. It was also damaged by fire in 1992 and was reopened two years later by Cardinal Hume. A tablet in the church commemorates Monsignor Francis Bartlett, uncle of the late 'Fat Lady', Jennifer Paterson.

Ecclesiastical grants in Camden made by the Heritage of London Trust

1990 £433.55 for repairs to the reredos at St Saviour, South Hampstead

1991 £5000 for work on the façade of St Mary R.C. Church, Holly Walk, Hampstead

1993 £2500 for columns on the tower of St Saviour, South Hampstead

1995 £3000 to restore the tomb of Sir John Soane at Old St Pancras Church

2001 £3172.50 for St Alban the Martyr, Holborn

2002 £3000 for the tomb of Beerbohm Tree at St John, Hampstead

2003 £2500 for the clock tower at Old St Pancras Church

2003 £2500 for St George Church, Bloomsbury

2005 £4000 for St Anne Brookfield, Highgate

2006 £1500 for stained glass at St Mary Church, Kilburn

2008 £35000 for restoration of caryatids at New St Pancras Church

2009 £2000 for restoration of tower clock at St George, Bloomsbury

2010 £3000 for limewash restoration at the Greek Orthodox Cathedral of All Saints

2014 £1000 for stained glass window at St Saviour, Hampstead

2014 £2500 for stone angel at St Mary with All Souls, Kilburn

2014 £5000 for pinnacle at St Martin, Gospel Oak

The atmospheric churchyard at St John, Shirley

CROYDON

The London Borough of Croydon was formed in 1965 out of the County Borough of Croydon and the Urban Districts of Coulsdon and Purley. It was historically in Surrey. It has the highest population of any borough in the Greater London area.

It is bounded by Lambeth and Southwark to the north, Bromley to the east, Surrey to the south and Sutton and Merton to the west.

Croydon itself lies in a valley between the heights of Upper Northwood in the north and the edges of the North Downs in the south. Open country survives in the latter around Addington, Coulsdon and Sanderstead. The name "Croydon" means apparently "The Valley of the Crocus", i.e. it was originally a centre of saffron growing like Saffron Walden in Essex.

Croydon was an estate of the Archbishops of Canterbury from Saxon times. Domesday Book mentions that the manor was held by Archbishop Lanfranc. An archepiscopal palace was built and used until 1781 when, somewhat ruinous, it was sold. Archbishop Whitgift liked it in the late 16th century for "the sweetness of the place" although Sir Francis Bacon found it "an obscure and darke place". The building is now the Old Palace School. A new Palladian palace was built at Addington, a few miles to the east. Six archbishops lived there from 1807 until 1898 when it was sold. From 1953 to 1996 the building was the Royal School of Church Music.

Whitgift School was founded by the eponymous Archbishop in 1596, originally north of the town although now situated to the south on the Haling Park estate once belonging to Lord Howard of Effingham, the Catholic commander of Queen Elizabeth's fleet against the Armada.

Croydon was a quiet market town for most of its existence. The London and Brighton Railway came to East Croydon in 1841 and brought development. There was a major rebuild in 1883. The 20th century brought industrial development with car manufacture and metal working. Croydon Airport in the West was London's main airport from 1920 to 1958 when Heathrow took over. The town suffered badly from the V-1 flying bombs and the V-2 rockets in the Second World War. It is now a slightly depressing centre full of tall office buildings.

Norbury, South Norwood and Thornton Heath in the north were rural until the 19th century. In 1831 a spa was set up to exploit a spring of chalybeate water at Beulah Hill on the south east slopes of Upper Norwood with buildings by Decimus Burton; Sir Ninian Comper lived at the Priory. The rest of the area is now suburban sprawl. Both Sir Arthur Conan Doyle and D.H. Lawrence lived in Norwood at various times.

The chancel of **St Mary, Addington** (open May to September on the 2nd and 4th Sundays of the month, 2.30 pm to 6 pm) dates back to the 12th century, and the rest of the church is restored medieval. In the 15th Century Lord Bardolf acquired the manor house; after his death it was bought by the Leigh family who lived there for 300 years. In 1808 the manor became the property of the Archbishops of Canterbury to replace the Old Palace in Croydon as a summer residence. Six Archbishops resided there until 1896 when Archbishop Benson died and his successor Frederick Temple decided to move to Canterbury. In the churchyard a cross was erected by Archbishop Randall Davidson to various of his predecessors (1). Inside many monuments can be found including semi-reclining effigies of Sir Olliphe Leigh (obit 1612) and his wife (3). The chancel was richly gilded and stencilled in the 19th century in memory of Archbishop Benson (who is buried in Canterbury Cathedral) (2). Five Archbishops lie in the churchyard – Manners-Sutton, Howley, Sumner, Longley and Tait. Kempe designed some of the glass. (4).

St John the Evangelist, Coulsdon (usually open Monday, Wednesday and Friday, 10 am to noon and 2–4 pm) is well situated on the village green. It is mainly 13th and 15th century (5). The south aisle is J.S. Comper in 1958. He added glass (6) and a baldacchino (7). Kempe designed windows commemorating various Archbishops such as St Augustine and Lanfranc.

St Peter, St Peter's Road, South Croydon, with soaring tower and later spire, is a flint church by Sir George Gilbert Scott in 1849–51 in Middle Pointed style (8). It has a good reredos (9) and glass (10).

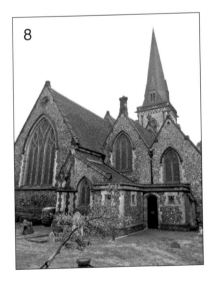

Another church by Sir George Gilbert Scott is **St John the Evangelist, Shirley** of 1854–6 in flint and stone with bell turret and spike (11). It has rather an atmospheric graveyard (12). A tomb to the parents of John Ruskin lies in the churchyard with the following inscription, "John Ruskin, son of John James Ruskin and Margaret his wife who wrote thus of his parents and ever spoke truth was born in London Feb 8th 1819. Died at Brantwood, Jany 20th 1900, and rests in Coriston churchyard". The church itself has an attractive reredos with mosaics (13). The chapel on the south side of the chancel was built in 1955 by Caroe and Partner.

Sir George Gilbert Scott was also responsible for rebuilding **St John the Baptist, Croydon** (open Monday – Wednesday and Friday, 10 am – 4 pm / Saturday, 10 am – 12 noon) after a bad fire in 1867. The exterior is of flint and stone (14); Queen Victoria appears in a boss (17). It has a fine reredos (15) and good glass. A 15th Century brass lectern survives. The Archbishops of Canterbury had a palace in Croydon from the 13th to the 19th centuries. The tomb of Archbishop Whitgift shows him as a recumbent effigy in prayer (18). Whitgift became Bishop of Worcester in 1577 and Archbishop of Canterbury 1583–1604. He disliked the Puritans and insisted on religious uniformity. The damaged tomb to Archbishop Sheldon (died 1677) is by Jasper Latham and shows him in a lounging position (16). Sheldon was Warden of All Souls College, Oxford, 1626–48. At the Restoration he was made Bishop of London before becoming Archbishop of Canterbury in 1663. He criticised the philandering of Charles II. He died in 1677. Since 2011 the church has been known as Croydon Minster.

St Mary Magdalen, Canning Road, Addiscombe was built by E.B. Lamb in 1868–70 for the Reverend Maxwell M. Ben Oliel, a former rabbi, whose non-conformist enterprise failed in 1874 after the adoption of ritualistic services. The church was then sold to the rival establishment of the Church of England (19). The building is distinctly eccentric. It has a most extraordinary wooden roof with vast beams and an elaborately carved chancel (20).

As a counterpoise to this, Croydon is fortunate in having two works by Pearson. The first is **St John the Evangelist, Sylvan Road, Upper Norwood**, 1878–87, red brick and Early English (21). The inside is dominated by screen and rib vaulting (22, 23). Comper designed the glass for a rose window and Travers the statue of Our Lady (24).

St Michael, Poplar Walk, Croydon (open Monday to Friday, 9.30 am to 3 pm), 1880–83, is one of his finest churches (25), again red brick outside and brick vaulted throughout. Of it Pearson said "This is a place for real worship". The first vicar appointed in 1871 was the Rev. Richard Hoare; he remained for 47 years. The church cost £16,000. The foundation stone was laid by Earl Nelson in 1880. Lavish fittings abound – the font, pulpit and organ case by Bodley, the hanging rood

(26) and lectern by Cecil Hare and the Lady Chapel fittings by Comper. The high altar is very satisfactory (28). Queen Victoria looks mildly unamused by the high church goings-on (27). The stained glass is by Clayton & Bell, Lavers & Barraud, and Kempe.

St Alban, Grange Road, Thornton Heath, 1889–91, is Sir Ninian Comper's first church (29). It is red brick. The chancel has three bays and the aisles six (30). The church is austere and slightly depressing with none of the envisaged fittings, save the rood (32), ever executed. The roof, however, is quite pleasing (31).

St Mildred, Addiscombe (open 9.30 – 12.30 daily) is by Cecil Hare, 1931–2. It is a tall brick church with stone facings (33). The sanctuary is painted pink, somewhat clashing with the purple seating (34). There is a font, a pulpit (35) and some interesting glass (37, 38). Cecil Hare is memorialised here (36).

Ecclesiastical grants in Croydon made by the Heritage of London Trust

1992 £5000 for St Mary Magdalene, Addiscombe

1992 £4000 for the spirelet of St Andrew, Southbridge Road, Croydon

1992 £5000 for Christ Church, Sumner Road, Croydon

1992 £4000 for the apse stonework of St Mark, South Norwood

1994 £3000 for the church tower of St Peter, Croydon

1995 £3000 for stone and brick work repairs at St Alban, Thornton Heath

1996 £1200 for the tower clock face of St Peter, Croydon

1997 £5000 for the stone chancel screen of St John the Evangelist, Upper Norwood

1997 £844 for the grave of Admiral Fitzroy at All Saints, Upper Norwood

1997 £2000 for the tower of St John Congregational Church, Thornton Heath

1999 £3000 for the parapet wall of St Peter, Croydon

2000 £1250 for railings at St Mark, South Norwood

2001 £3500 for St John the Evangelist, Shirley

2001 £2000 for St Mary Magdalene, Addiscombe

2001 £3000 for St Augustine, South Croydon

2007 £4000 for St John the Baptist, Croydon

2007 £2000 for cast iron gate pier at All Saints, Upper Norwood

2009 £2000 for stonework on the tower of St Mary Magdalene, Addiscombe

2010 £500 for restoration of stone work at St John the Baptist, Croydon

The interior at Christ the Saviour, New Broadway, Ealing

EALING

The London Borough of Ealing consists of the former boroughs of Ealing, Acton and Southall. Its boundaries are Fulham & Hammersmith to the east, Hounslow to the south, Hillingdon to the west and Harrow and Brent to the north.

There is higher ground to the north of the borough but it is otherwise flat.

Ealing was originally known as Gilling, i.e. in Anglo-Saxon the people associated with Gilla. Both Ealing and Acton formed part of the Bishop of London's manor of Fulham in the Middle Ages although the countryside at that stage was primarily forested. The passing of turnpike acts in the early 18th century led to the development of the Uxbridge Road to Oxford through the borough and this in its turn led to the growth of market gardens for the benefit of London.

Great Ealing School was founded in the rectory of St Mary's Church in 1698 and in its day was very well known as a private school; W.S.Gilbert, Thomas Huxley, Captain Marryat, Cardinal Newman, Bishop George Augustus Selwyn and Thackeray were amongst those educated there.

In the late 18th and early 19th century a number of country houses were built. The most famous of these is Pitzhanger Manor which was bought by the architect Sir John Soane in 1800 and where he lived for a decade, rebuilding the central bloc of the house during the period of his ownership. It has been made over to a trust, chaired by Sir Sherard Cowper-Coles, a local resident, which is in the process of raising funds for its restoration. Edward, Duke of Kent, son of George III and father of Queen Victoria, lived at Castle Hill Lodge, now the site of Ealing Abbey.

The Great West Railway arrived in 1830 and Ealing Station opened eight years later. This opened the way to large scale residential development and Ealing became known in the late 19th century as the "Queen of Suburbs". In the 20th century it was famous for the Ealing Studios where *Kind Hearts and Coronets*, *Passport to Pimlico* and *The Lavender Hill Mob* were filmed. As late as 1961 Betjeman could write "Return, return to Ealing... Regain your boyhood feeling of uninvaded calm!... In Ealing on a Sunday bell-haunted quiet falls... No lorries grind in bottom gear up steep and narrow lanes nor constant here offend the ear low-flying planes."

Acton (originally 'Oak Farm'), famous in the 18th century for its 600 laundries, became known in the 20th century as a major industrial centre – engines, soap, Walls ice cream, etc. The original Waitrose (Waite, Rose and Taylor) was founded here before the First World War.

Southall (the 'South Corner') was again a major industrial centre – brick factories, flour mills, chemical plants, ceramics, margarine, Walls sausages. It suffered from the V-1 flying bombs during the Second World War.

St Mary, **Northolt Green** is mainly c. 1300 with white walls and wooden western turret (1). The chancel (now cleared of furnishings) is 16th century. An early 18th century wooden galley dominates the west end (2). Martin Travers provided a statue of St Stephen.

St Mary, Tentelow Lane, Norwood retains its 13th century chancel but most of it dates from a 15th century rebuilding by Archbishop Chichele (5). Its greatest treasure is an imported 16th century glass window of Our Lady and the Christ Child with the latter holding a toy windmill (3). It has a number of good monuments (4). The pews have been ripped out and replaced by blue chairs; those in the nave have slightly curiously been placed facing north.

Holy Cross, Greenford dates from 1157 but is primarily 15th century (6, 9). It is situated not far from the roar of the A40. It has some fine mainly heraldic glass from the Provost's Lodgings of King's College, Cambridge (8). The new adjacent barn-like church of 1939 by Sir Albert Richardson is now mainly used as a church hall. A monument in the old church commemorates Simon Coston, a local benefactor (7). A couple of brasses to priests can be found on the north wall – John Hart (15th century) and Thomas Symons (16th century). Edward Terry was rector here from 1624 to 1660. In an earlier incarnation he had been chaplain to the British Ambassador at the court of the Grand Moghul in India. He published an account of his travels. Anthony a Wood was unusually obliging about him: "He was an ingenious and polite man of a pious and exemplary conversation, a good preacher and much respected by the neighbourhood".

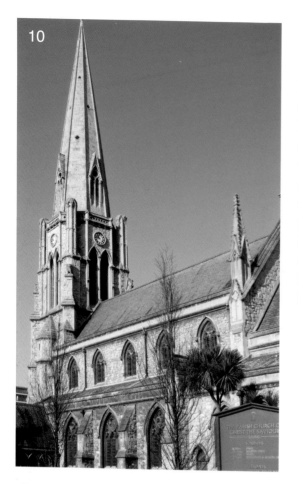

The 19th century hit Ealing with some degree of vigour.

Christ the Saviour, New Broadway, Ealing (open daily) is by G.G. Scott in 1852 in Middle Pointed style (10). It has a tall interior (illus., p.104). The best things inside date from the Bodley restoration of 1906, which provided the organ cases (12) and the prettily painted roofs (13) and much else besides (11). The stained glass in the east window is by Hugh Easton (14).

St Mary, St Mary's Road, Ealing (open most mornings) is the old medieval-Georgian parish church, dramatically remodelled by Teulon in 1866–74. The medieval church suffered badly in the Civil War and in 1650 was described as "ruinated and lying open since the plundering". A new Georgian building was opened in 1740. By 1860 the church was too small and "did not call forth feelings of reverence". The Teulon remodelling was reconsecrated by Bishop Tait in 1866 who commented "St Mary's has been transformed from a Georgian monstrosity into a Constantinopolitan basilica". A huge tower was built (15) and the interior was completely altered by brickwork, horseshoe arches, traceried roof and iron columns (16). The church was reordered in 2002–3 with new furniture by Luke Hughes. It has excellent glass, mainly by Heaton, Butler & Bayne (17, 18).

Numerous tablets by Westmacott and others survive from the previous church. The chancel is painted a pretty blue (19). It is all in all an amazing building. The Old Etonian radical politician, the Rev. John Horne Tooke (1736–1812), is buried in the churchyard.

St Peter, Mount Park Road, Ealing (open 9.30 am – 4pm daily) was designed in 1889 by J.D. Sedding. *The Builder* commented "The whole thing is a piece of real originality in design which is refreshing to come across after seeing so many repetitions of old forms, Classic and Gothic". It was completed by Sedding's partner, Henry Wilson, and is built in late Gothic style with a west front distantly similar to that of Holy Trinity, Sloane Street (20). It has chaste early 20th century fittings by Bodley and Hare (21) and glass by Kempe.

The 20th century also provided Ealing with three Anglican churches of interest. Two of these are by Shearman – **St Barnabas, Pitshanger Lane, Ealing** and **St Gabriel, Noel Road, Acton**.

St Barnabas of 1914–16 looms over the neighbouring cottages, built mainly in brick (24) with a spacious interior. It was consecrated in 1916 by the

Bishop of London. It has an apse at the east end and a large rose window to the south (22). The sanctuary has a mural of 1917 by James Clark (23). The church since 2007 has had a magnificent 1877 William Hill organ transported from St Jude's, Southsea.

St Gabriel of 1929-31 is similar (25) with another rose window. It has a severe red brick interior (26). It possesses a modern painting of the Annunciation by John Pelling (born Hove 1930) (27).

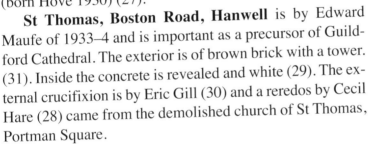

St Thomas, Boston Road, Hanwell is by Edward Maufe of 1933–4 and is important as a precursor of Guildford Cathedral. The exterior is of brown brick with a tower. (31). Inside the concrete is revealed and white (29). The external crucifixion is by Eric Gill (30) and a reredos by Cecil Hare (28) came from the demolished church of St Thomas, Portman Square.

The only Catholic church of major architectural interest in Ealing is **St Benedict's Abbey, Charlbury Grove, Ealing**. It started life in 1897 as a priory of Downside Abbey, becoming an Abbey in its own right in 1955. It is a long medieval building by F.A. Walters in 1895–7 and by E.J. Walters in 1905. The west front is rather uninspiring Perpendicular (33). The somewhat austere interior is dominated by a modern font (35). The church boasts a good hammerbeam roof (32). Comper worked here as well as at Downside (34). Dom David Knowles, author of *The Monastic Orders in Britain* and subsequently Regius Professor of Modern History at Cambridge, was resident 1937–9.

Ecclesiastical grants in Ealing made by the Heritage of London Trust

1998 £2000 for the restoration of a tomb at St Mary, Perivale

1999 £2264 for restoration of a tomb at St Mary, Tentelow Lane, Norwood

2001 £3000 for the clock at St Mary, Acton

2008 £4000 for the organ case at St George, Southall

2014 £4000 for stone arch on roof at St Peter, Ealing

Reclining effigies of Sir Nicholas Raynton and his wife, attributed to Thomas Burman, at St Andrew, Enfield

ENFIELD

Enfield was formed in 1965 out of the former boroughs of Enfield, Edmonton and Southgate. It is bounded by Barnet to the west, Haringey to the south, Waltham Forest to the east, Hertfordshire to the north and Essex to the north east.

The villages of both Enfield and Edmonton were mentioned in Domesday Book. Enfield Chase was a forest famous for its hunting in the Middle Ages. In the 15th century the Manor became part of the Duchy of Lancaster, and thus the Crown.

Enfield was the second largest parish in Middlesex in the Middle Ages. Queen Elizabeth I spent a portion of her youth at the now vanished Enfield Palace. Enfield Grammar School (now a comprehensive) was founded in 1558. Forty Hall was built in 1629–33 for Sir Nicholas Raynton, Lord Mayor of London; it is now maintained as a museum by the council.

The Royal Small Arms Factory at Enfield Lock, on a marshy island in the River Lea, originally opened in 1818. From 1895 until 1957 it produced the Lee Enfield .303 rifle which was standard issue for the British Army. In 1935 it started production of the bren .303 machine gun (the word a combination of Brno and Enfield) and in 1941 the sten 9mm sub machine gun (the word a combination of Shepherd, Turpin and Enfield). The factory was privatised in 1984 as part of Royal Ordnance, bought by British Aerospace and closed in 1988. The east of the borough is industrialised and the first mass-produced dishwasher came from the Hotpoint factory there. Reg Varney opened the first ATM machine at Barclays in 1967.

Edmonton lay on the route of Ermine Street from London to Lincoln. Pymms Park (now vanished) was owned by Robert Cecil, 1st Earl of Salisbury. John Gilpin in Cowper's *Diverting History* of the same set out in vain for the Bell Inn in Edmonton. It subsequently became very industrialised thanks to, among others, British Oxygen and Ever Ready batteries.

Southgate (for which Michael Portillo once sat as MP) is a respectable green settlement. Until the start of the 20th century and later it was the site of a number of estates. The most interesting of these is perhaps Trent Park, now a teacher training establishment under the aegis of Middlesex University. It was originally built in 1777 by Sir William Chambers for Sir Richard Jebb, a doctor who had saved the life of the Duke of Gloucester in Trento. Repton designed the park. From 1926 to 1939 it was lived in by Sir Philip Sassoon, Bt, a very rich aesthete. After education at Eton and Christ Church, he was private secretary to Haig, 1915–18. MP for Hythe from 1912, he was Lloyd George's PPS. He entertained generously here, and at Port Lympne in Kent, individuals as varied as the Duke of York, Winston Churchill, Arthur Balfour, George Bernard Shaw and Rex Whistler.

St Andrew, Enfield (open 9 am – 3pm except Tuesday) has a 12th century tower but mainly dates from the 13th and 14th centuries (1, 3). The wall painting of the Crucifixion is a war memorial of 1923 (2). The church has various monuments of interest, including a brass of 1446 of Joyce, Lady Tiptoft, surmounted by a carved and painted stone canopy. Some reclining effigies are attributed to Thomas Burman and are of Sir Nicholas Raynton, and his wife; he was Lord Mayor and died in 1646 (illus., p.114).

All Saints, Edmonton is a 15th century church (4) although heavily restored in both 1772 and 1889. Some fragments remain from the Norman church (5) built by Geoffrey de Mandeville in 1136. The church has a decorated Victorian chancel and a number of interesting monuments including Gothic tablets of 1888 to Charles Lamb and William Cowper.

Christ Church, Southgate (open 9 am – 1 pm weekdays) was built in the 1860s by Sir Giles Gilbert Scott in stone in a spacious Early English style. It was built on the site of the Weld Chapel, demolished in 1861. The church has a tower with a broached spire (6). The new church was consecrated on 17th July 1862 by Dr Tait, the Bishop of London. The reredos has Salviati mosaics of the Last Supper of 1869 (8); the design is similar to one in Westminster Abbey. The original encaustic tiles can be found at the east end. Much good glass by Clayton & Bell (7), Morris, Burne-Jones, etc. (9, 10, 11), can be found here.

St Mary Magdalene, Windmill Hill, Enfield was built in Kentish rag by Butterfield in 1883. It is cruciform with western tower and spire (12). Its chief glory is the recently restored rich polychrome chancel decoration with ceiling angels by Buckeridge, 1897–8 (15). Heaton, Butler & Bayne provided glass (13) and Butterfield the font (14).

St Aldhelm, Silver Street, Edmonton is by W.D. Caroe, 1903; brick with a western turret, fleche on the crossing and low aisles (16). The reredos with its painting of the Ascension is by Walter Percival Starmer (17).

St John, Dysons Road, Edmonton is by C.H.B. Quennell (father of Peter) of 1905–6. It is a large, idiosyncratic brick building, hidden away in a back street by the North Circular Road (19). The church is tall with a narrow chancel and slim passages, with a simple wooden screen (20). It was closed in 2007 but re-opened in 2012.

St John the Evangelist, Green Lane and Bourne Hill, Palmers Green, Southgate (parish office open 9 am – 1pm, Tuesday, Wednesday and Friday) is by John Oldrid Scott, 1903–9, and is one of the most imposing buildings in Palmers Green. It has a lively red brick and flint exterior with twin turrets (21). Inside the church is red brick supported by stone pillars (23). Morris & Co. provided much post World War I glass. The east window is by J.H. Dearle (22). The church also has glass of 1918 by Frank Salisbury and more recent glass by Goddard & Gibbs.

Of Catholic churches, **The Most Precious Blood and St Edmund, Hertford Road, Edmonton** was built in a simple Gothic style in 1903 for the Redemptorists by Doran Webb (24, 25). It has retained the reredos and there is glass by Kempe, unusually for a Catholic church (27).

St Monica, Palmers Green was built in 1914 by Edward Goldie in Perpendicular style (26). The Sacred Heart chapel at the east end of the north aisle has rich decoration do-nated by Theodore Singer (28). The aisle windows have stained glass of 1930 by Mayer of Munich.

Ecclesiastical grants in Enfield made by the Heritage of London Trust

1990 £350 for restoration of the triptych at St Matthew, Ponders End

1993 £5000 for the restora-tion of monuments at St Andrew, Enfield

2012 £2500 for fleche restoration at St John the Baptist and St Luke, Clay Hill

The later tower and spire of Hawksmoor's church of St Alfege,
Greenwich High Road

GREENWICH

The Royal Borough of Greenwich was formed in 1965 out of the two old boroughs of Greenwich and Woolwich.

It is surrounded by Southwark and Lewisham to the west, Bromley to the south, Bexley to the east and the River Thames to the north.

In Anglo-Saxon Greenwich meant the Green Place on the Bay. The borough is flat by the Thames but rises towards Shooters Hill in the east and Blackheath in the west. The scrubland of Erith lay to the east and the plateau of Blackheath to the south. The way to Dover lay by Watling Street. From 1011 for three years the Danish fleet anchored at Greenwich during the reign of Ethelred the Unready and in 1012 beat to death with ox bones St Alphege, the Archbishop of Canterbury. In Domesday Book the manor was held by Odo of Bayeux.

In the Middle Ages Greenwich, Plumstead and Woolwich were fishing villages. Wat Tyler in 1381 and Jack Cade in 1450 both set up camp on Blackheath. Eltham Palace became a royal establishment in the early 14th century; the great hall has been incorporated into the Art Deco house built by the Courtaulds in the 1930s.

The Palace of Placentia or Pleasaunce (subsequently Greenwich Palace) was originally built by Duke Humphrey of Gloucester in the 15th century. Henry VIII and Elizabeth I were both born there. Anne of Denmark commissioned Inigo Jones to build the Queen's House. The Palace fell into disrepair during the Civil War, and Wren assisted by Hawksmoor after the Restoration built the Royal Naval Hospital for Sailors. In 1873 this became the Royal Naval College before becoming in part the University of Greenwich in the 1990s.

West Greenwich was a popular place in which to live in the 18th century. In the east Charlton House was originally built for Prince Henry who died in 1612. The part of Charlton towards the Thames became heavily industrialised with e.g. the Siemens Telegraphic Works. Charlton Athletic football team was founded in 1905.

Woolwich had had a naval dockyard as early as 1512. The Arsenal was built in 1717, probably by Vanburgh. Some of the later buildings are by James Wyatt who also built the Old Royal Military Academy. The Royal Artillery Barracks with its 1000 foot facade is late 18th century. An interesting building is the Rotunda by Nash which was originally built in St James's Park in 1814; once a museum its future is not at present clear.

The rest of Woolwich became heavily industrialised in the wake of the Arsenal and is not today a particularly attractive place. In the east it shares with Bexley the huge Thamesmead estate.

The only church in the borough to retain vestiges of the Middle Ages is **St Nicholas, High Street, Plumstead** with 12th and 13th century work in the south aisle and a 15th century nave rebuilt in 1818 (1). The red brick tower dates from just after the Restoration. The church was aggressively restored by the Victorian C.C.H. Cooke, enlarged by the Edwardians (Greenaway and Newberry) and subsequently suffered bomb damage. Dykes-Bower contributed three altars (4). The east window has stained glass by Martin Travers. The church is now a firm redoubt of traditional Anglo-Catholicism (2). St Martin de Porres was a Dominican mixed race saint who died in Peru in 1639 (3).

St Luke, The Village, Charlton (open for coffee Wednesday 10 am – 12 noon) is an attractive red brick church of 1630 with a Victorian east end, situated near the entrance of Charlton House (5). It has some 17th century fittings. Chantrey sculpted a monument to the Prime Minster Spencer Perceval assassinated in 1812 (6). The inscription states, "His noblest epitaph is the regret of his sovereign and his country, his most splendid monument the glory of England by his counsels maintained, exalted, amplified." The church has many other monuments including one to Michael Richards, Surveyor General of the Ordnance to George I (7), a 17th century pulpit and Victorian glass. The reredos has some attractive painted Victorian angels (8).

St Alfege, Greenwich High Road
(usually open Monday – Wednesday
and Friday 11 am – 3.30 pm, Thursday
11 am – 2 pm, Saturday 10 am – 4 pm
and Sunday 12 noon – 4 pm) was originally erected to commemorate the
martyrdom of St Alfege, Archbishop of
Canterbury, by drunken Danes in 1012.
He was successively Abbot of Bath and
Bishop of Winchester before succeed-
ing Aelfric as Archbishop of Canterbury in 1006. He travelled to Rome to
receive his pallium from Pope John
XVIII in 1007. He was the first Archbishop of Canterbury to die a violent
death. The church now standing was
built by Hawksmoor in 1711–14 under
the Fifty New Churches Act. It is a substantial building in Portland stone. The
west façade has a large pediment on
Doric columns with an arch in the cen-
tre (11). Four 'Roman' altars lie in front of the portico. The somewhat irrelevant
tower and spire of 1730 are by John James (9) The interior is less interesting and
the original fittings were destroyed by bombing (10); Henry VIII was baptised in
the earlier church and General Gordon in the later. Thomas Tallis and General
Wolfe were buried here.

St Mary Magdalene, St Mary Street, Wool-wich was also built under the Fifty New Churches Act, this time in 1727–39 by Matthew Spray. It is built in brick with a small west tower (12). The chancel is by John Oldrid Scott in 1894 (13). The galleries and aisles were closed off in 1961 to make offices and a cafe. Thomas Cribb, the famous boxer who died in 1848, is buried in the churchyard.

St Michael, Blackheath Park was built of brick with Bath stone dressings as an Evangelical church by G. Smith in 1828–9. It has a thin east spire and an eccentric east window (14); "a crazy assembly of motifs utterly unworried by consider-ations of antiquarian accuracy" (Pevsner). Inside it possesses a good organ case and roof (15).

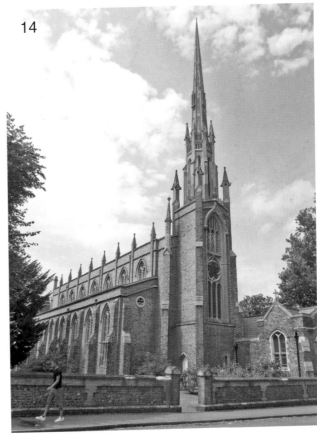

The Garrison Church of St George, Grand Depot Road, Woolwich was built in 1863 by T.H. Wyatt as an early Christian basilica for Lord Herbert of Lea as Secretary of State for War, on the model of Wilton Church outside Salisbury. Not much besides some mosaics in the chancel survived the bombing in the Second World War (16, 17) but a degree of restoration is under way under the auspices of the Heritage of London Trust.

Holy Trinity, Southend Crescent, Eltham (open 10 am – 12 noon Saturday) is by Street of 1868–9 (18). Inside the church has pretty detailing and decoration and glass by Kempe. On the south of the chancel a

chapel has been commemorated to remember those who died at Gallipoli (19), particularly the men of the 29th Division. Henry Hall (Vicar 1907 –1942) was their Chaplain.

Two interesting Anglican twentieth century churches survive in Greenwich.

St Luke, Westmount Road, Eltham (usually open 10 am – 12 noon Saturday) was built in 1906–7 by Temple Moore (20). It has a spacious interior with a good wagon roof (21).

St Saviour, Middle Park, Eltham is in a different idiom. It was built in 1932–3 by Welch & Lander and Cachemaille-Day in brick modern style. The exterior is interesting but not particularly prepossessing (25). Donald Hastings carved the figure of Christ on the reredos (23, 24). The pulpit is brick. The blue glass is fairly dramatic (22).

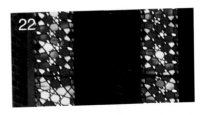

The Catholics have four churches of interest.

The first is **St Peter, Woolwich New Road** by A.W.N. Pugin, which was begun in 1842 (27). The subscription list included the names of David O'Connell, the Countess of Shrewsbury and the Earl of Arundel. The interior of the church is painted green (26). The chancel and side chapel are later, by Walters in 1887–9. Because of shortage of funds the tower was never built. The church suffered from bombing in the Second World War, and was modestly reordered in the 1970s.

Our Ladye Star of the Sea, Croom's Hill (usually open from 8.30 am) was built in 1851 by Wardell for the 500 Catholic pensioners of the Royal Naval Hospital. The church has a good tower and spire (30). The nave and aisles have six bays. Many of the decent fittings are by Pugin (29 on previous page, 33) including a lovely statue of the Virgin holding a ship (32). He was also responsible for the design of the glass (28 on previous page, 34). The first incumbent, Father Richard North (1808–60), has a tomb next to the chancel (31). The church was opened in 1851 by Bishop Grant of Southwark. It was substantially reordered in the 1960s (flat roof, organ case, confessional) but the recently appointed enthusiastic, convert priest, Father Kevin Robinson, hopes to raise funds to remedy this.

30

31

32

33

34

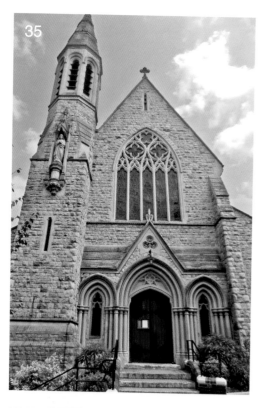

Our Lady Help of Christians, Cresswell Park, Blackheath is by Purdie 1890–1. The exterior has a square clock tower with an octagonal bell turret on top (35). The nave and aisles have four bays. The chancel boasts a polygonal apse and retains its original fittings (36).

Our Lady of Grace, Charlton (38 next page) was founded by a group of Oblate Sisters of the Assumption from Bordeaux after their eviction from France under the Association Law. The Sisters chose the dedication because of a shrine situated there before the Reformation. The church of 1905–6 was designed by Eugene-Jacques Gervais. It has a colourful interior (37). It was restored in 1959 when a new aisle was added.

38

Ecclesiastical grants in Greenwich made by the Heritage of London Trust

1989   £500 to restore 18th century Coat of Arms at St Mary Magdalene, Woolwich

1992   £7500 for the south aisle doorway at St Peter Church, Woolwich (R.C.)

2001   £2500 for restoration of a bell at Our Ladye Star of the Sea, Greenwich (R.C.)

2004   £3000 for restoration of narthex ceiling at Holy Trinity, Greenwich

2008   £5000 for Garrison church of St George, Woolwich

2010   £2000 to restore Creed monument at St Alfege, Greenwich

2011   £5000 for the tower of St Luke, Charlton

2013   £2000 for roof urns for St Alfege, Greenwich

2014   £1000 additional grant for St Luke, Charlton

The 16th century tower of St Augustine, Mare Street, Hackney

HACKNEY

The London Borough of Hackney was formed in 1965 out of the boroughs of Hackney, Shoreditch and South Newington.

It is bounded to the south by Tower Hamlets, to the east by Newham and Waltham Forest, to the north by Haringey and to the west by Islington.

Shoreditch, on the edge of the City in the south, has for many centuries been fairly urban. In the Middle Ages there was a house of Augustinian nuns at Halliwell Priory, now entirely vanished. In the late 16th century James Burbage set up a couple of theatres. The Huguenots brought the silk industry to Spitalfields, and furniture making followed in Haggerston and Hoxton. A group of almshouses was built for Ironmongers Company in 1712-14; this was converted into the Geffrye Museum in the early 20th century. In the 19th and early 20th century Shoreditch was home to a number of musical halls. The area declined in the first half of the 20th century and by 1938 Dr Mallon of Toynbee Hall could write of "the widespread squalor ... ill health and poverty" of Shoreditch.

In the late Middle Ages Hackney itself was dominated by the Hospitaller Knights of St John. The Templars owned the Manor and St Augustine, Mare Street until their dissolution in 1308, when the property was transferred to the former. The Hospitallers had their own separate house near Well Street further south. The influence of the Knights Hospitaller is commemorated by the Maltese cross on the coat of arms of the London Borough of Hackney. Hackney became a retreat for the nobility after the Reformation. Sutton House (now owned by the National Trust) was built for Sir Ralph Sadleir, Cromwell's henchman, in 1535. Hackney consisted of various villages (including Clapton, Homerton, Shacklewell and Stamford Hill as well as Hackney itself) and remained a pleasant rural area dependent on agriculture and market gardening until 1840 when rapid suburbanisation began to occur. Pepys used to go out to Hackney to "take the ayre". The area still remains surprisingly green with Hackney Marshes, London Fields and Victoria Park. However industry spread north from Bethnal Green and Shoreditch. A huge amount of council housing was built in Hackney in the 20th century.

Stoke Newington remained quite rural until the late 19th and early 20th centuries. The manor in the Middle Ages belonged to St Paul's Cathedral. Stoke Newington was a strong centre of nonconformity in the 18th century with, for instance, the hymn writer Isaac Watts educated and living there. Edgar Allen Poe was able to describe Stoke Newington where he was at school as "a misty looking village of England". It is the site of two substantial reservoirs.

Little medieval work survives in Hackney.

The tower of St Augustine, Mare Street, Hackney is early 16th century (1). The body of the church itself was demolished in 1798.

The Old Church of St Mary, Stoke Newington, is mainly a rebuilding in red brick of 1563, a rather unusual date (2). The brick tower and spire are of 1828 by Barry, who also provided much of the furnishing. The current intention is to remove the pews and turn the building into an arts venue.

The medieval church of **St Leonard, Shoreditch** (open 12 noon to 2 pm Monday to Friday) (immortalised in the nursery rhyme "Oranges and Lemons", "When I grow rich, says the bells of Shoreditch") was rebuilt in 1736–40 by George Dance the Elder. It has a 192-feet high spire surmounting an elegant stone cupola (4). The four column portico is fine. The front is of Portland stone, the rest red brick. The interior is dominated by large Doric columns. A rood was inserted in the 1920s. The font, pulpit and communion table date from 1740 and and a fine organ gallery clock of 1757 survives. The interior could at present do with a lick of paint (3). The church was used as "St Saviour" in the BBC TV comedy "Rev".

St Thomas, Oldhill Street, Clapton Common was built in 1774 (with a tower of 1829) (5), as a proprietary chapel (the Stamford Hill Independent Chapel). In 1827 it was purchased and became a Chapel of Ease for the Parish of Hackney. It was badly bombed in the Second World War, and then restored in the 1960s by Cachemaille Day. The gilded apse at the east end survives as does the high altar and reredos by Martin Travers (6).

St John, Mare Street, Hackney started life as a Templar church before being passed to the Hospitaller Order of St John of Jerusalem in the 14th century. James Spiller rebuilt the church in 1791–4 in the shape of a vast Greek cross with an odd tower – a massive square, then a bell storey and finally a fantastically decorated top stage. It is all built in yellow brick (7). The shallow-vaulted roofs have no interior supports. There is considerable evidence of damp in the ceiling. The original pews are now stacked at the back and replaced by modern chairs. The tombs include one to Lucye Lady Latimer of 1583 with an alabaster effigy of high quality (9) and one to "Lieutenant Harry Bingley Sedgewick of the 5th Regiment of Foot whose active military career was suddenly terminated on the 2nd of June 1811 by a Cannon Shot from the Castle of Badajos in Spain while besieged by British troops under the command of the illustrious Wellington, in the plenitude of Youth, Health and Spirit. He was totally unconscious of his near approach to Eternity ... when his country lost a gallant Defender at the early age of 23 years" (8). The church was gutted by fire in 1955.

In 1824–6 **St John the Baptist, New North Road, Hoxton** (open 8.30 am – 5.30 pm Monday to Friday) was built as a Commissioners Church in classical style by F. Edwards, a pupil of Sloane (10). The excitement here is the ceiling decorated in 1902–1914 by J.A. Reeve – angels of the Apocalypse – and restored in 1993–94 (11).

The Gothic Revival hit Hackney with vigour.

The first church in this style was **St John of Jerusalem, South Hackney** built on an island site by Hakewill as a high church. The dedication again commemorates the link between the Hospitallers and the neighbourhood. The walls are of Kentish rag with stone dressings. It is Early English on a vast scale and can seat 2000 people (12, 13). Inside the black and white mosaic floor of 1893 should be noted (14). The original broach spire was lost in the war and replaced with one by Cachemaille Day. The stained glass is all post-war.

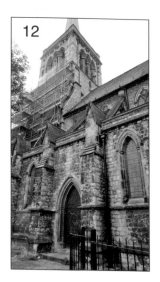

Holy Trinity, Shepherdess Walk, Hoxton was built in 1848 by W. Railton in a simple lancet style. It is flanked by vicarage and school. The south-west tower has a broach spire (15). The inside is whitened and has many Anglo-Catholic fittings (17, 19) including slightly unusually for an Anglican church a statue of the Infant Jesus of Prague (18); the confessional with its tall Corinthian pillars is by Travers (16). The church has a pulpit of 1686 from St Mary Somerset in the City. The late Brian Masters, subsequently Bishop of Edmonton and nicknamed by some "Beryl the Dalek" for his esoteric style of blessing, was once Vicar here. Holy Trinity Hoxton is the heir to some extent of the vanished "extreme" church of St Saviour's, Hoxton by Brooks; from 1919 to 1927 Father Kilburn only celebrated Mass in Latin, again unusual in the Church of England.

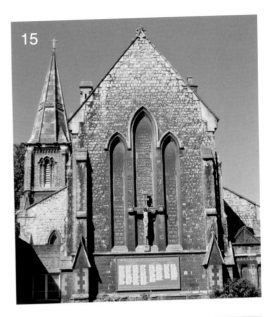

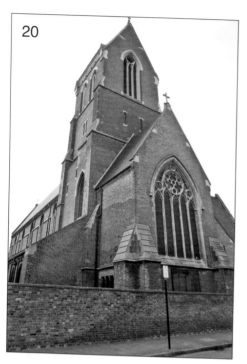

William Butterfield built **St Matthias, Stoke Newington** in 1849–53 as a high church in response to a campaign led by one Robert Brett, a local resident. Its chief feature is the tall saddle back tower over the chancel (20). The church is of stock brick. It was bombed in the war and its rich Victorian fittings were destroyed, hence its rather austere internal appearance. The pews, choir stalls and pulpit from St John, Hammersmith (another Butterfield church) are however in the process of being installed as funds allow. The church has a number of more modern Anglo-Catholic fittings (21) and a dramatic roof (22).

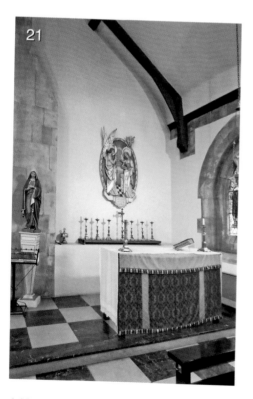

Hackney does have a number of Gothic Revival churches not in the Tractarian tradition.

The New Church of St Mary, Stoke Newington was built in 1858 by George Gilbert Scott. It is a hall church in Decorated style, cruciform, of rubble stone. The church was repaired by Cachemaille Day after war damage. The landmark spire is by John Oldrid Scott and completed in 1890 (23). Good carving (24, 25) and fittings (26) can be found.

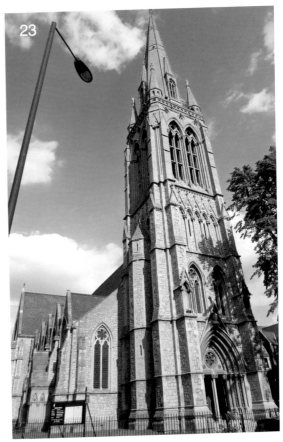

St Mark, Sandringham Road, Dalston is by Chester Cheston Junior and is huge and Early English in style. The exterior is somewhat dull although redeemed by the striking west tower completed by E.L. Blackburne in 1879–80 (27). It is apparently the biggest parish church in London. The low

church interior full of pews is brought to life by the rich glass by Lavers & Barraud (29), the prettily painted organ and the reredos. It has an interesting pulpit (28) and font (30). The politically incorrect Donald Pateman was vicar here for 42 years until 2006. A conservative evangelical, he always used the Book of Common Prayer and was a firm supporter of corporal punishment.

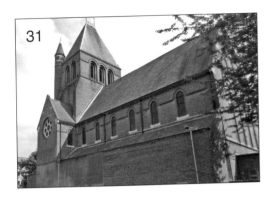

Ewan Christian built **Holy Trinity, Beechwood Road, Dalston**, cruciform, red brick with lancets. The interior has been whitened following a fire in 1985 (32). The exterior is dominated by the large central tower (31). It is known as the 'Clowns' Church' because of an annual service on the first Sunday in February for their benefit and that of Joseph Grimaldi (who was presumably a Catholic). Until recently the vicar was Rose Hudson Wilkin, who holds the role of Speaker's Chaplain in the House of Commons.

Reverting to the high church side of the equation, James Brooks built three churches under the "Haggerston Church Scheme", only one of which remains in Anglican use.

The first was **St Michael, Mark Street** in 1863–5. This was sadly closed in 1964 and is now accessible through the good offices of the London Architectural Salvage and Supply Company. It is brick with stone bands (33). The interior is plain and has an east window by Clayton & Bell.

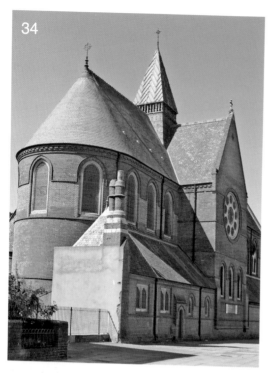

St Chad, Dunloe Street (1867–9) continues to function as a church. It is red brick early Gothic, lacking both tower and polychromy (34). The interior is lofty with whitened columns against a brick backdrop with a reredos carved by Earp (35). Clayton & Bell provide much of the glass. Statues abound (36). The church was described by Sir John Betjeman as "one of the best examples of an East End Anglo-Catholic church".

The third is of 1867–71, **St Columba, Kingsland Road** (now the Christ Apostolic Church). It is again lofty early Gothic of red brick; Eastlake described it as "an exceedingly picturesque composition" (37). It has a tall interior but suffered in the 1960s when among other outrages the walls were whitewashed. A mortuary chapel of 1903–5 was designed by the Rev. Ernest Geldart. The church is not easy of access outside services.

St Mary of Eton, Eastway, Hackney Wick was founded by Eton College in 1880 as the church of the Eton Mission, which survived until 1967, when it was sadly swept away by the climate of the times. Hackney Wick in 1880 was a very poor area. The church was built in 1890–2 by Bodley & Garner. The foundation stone was laid by Princess Christian, Queen Victoria's third daughter. The church is of red brick and has Bath dressings (38, 40). The large north-east gate tower leads to an attractive courtyard with the buildings of the Eton Mission (39). The two west bays of the church were added in 1911–12 by Cecil Hare, who became Bodley's partner after Garner 'poped'. The interior is broad and square with tall piers lacking capitals (41). The wagon roof is painted pink. The church at present has a slightly desolate feel but it is apparently to be refurbished shortly. The area has changed in relatively recent living memory through the building of the Olympic Stadium and the dynamiting of various nearby tower blocks.

St Barnabas, Shacklewell Lane, Hackney is by Reilly in 1909–11. It was set up as a mission church by the Merchant Taylors' School. It is hidden by high buildings and is built in yellow brick (43). The style is Byzantine with large chancel and apse (42). The vaulting is of concrete. The Victorian pulpit, which is not in style, came from another church.

St Michael and All Angels, London Fields was built by Cachemaille-Day in 1959–60 to replace a

47

Victorian church destroyed in the Blitz (47). It is an example of the influence of the Liturgical Movement built as a square with a free standing altar. John Hayward (1929–2007) was responsible for the sculpture of St Michael killing the dragon on the outside of the church (46), the Apostles's Windows of St Paul and others (48, 49) and nine murals (44 The Annunciation, 45 The Empty Tomb). Hayward was rarely allowed to create whole church interiors, as he was here.

48

49

Of Catholic churches, **St Monica's Priory, Hoxton Square** is worth a mention. The church was built for the Augustinians by E.W. Pugin in 1864–5. It is a brick Gothic building (50) with a nave eight bays long with an unusual timber arcade (52). The altar and reredos are by Mayer of Munich (51). The church has a considerable amount of stained glass including a window of the Sacred Heart at the end of the north aisle (53).

Ecclesiastical grants in Hackney made by the Heritage of London Trust

1988   £6700 for the reredos of St Chad, Haggerston
1992   £5000 for brick / stone restoration at St Columba, Hackney
1994   £10,000 for the ceiling paintings at St John the Baptist, Hoxton
1996   £5000 for the Round Chapel, Lower Clapton Street, Hackney
1997   £4000 for Old St Mary, Stoke Newington
1998   £5000 for the west door of St John of Jerusalem, South Hackney
2000   £2500 for the reinstatement of the gable cross at Holy Trinity, Dalston
2001   £3000 for wall paintings restoration at St John the Baptist, Hoxton
2002   £3000 for the fleche of St Bartholomew the Apostle, Stamford Hill
2002   £4000 for restoration of sanctuary metal screen at St Chad, Haggerston
2002   £2000 for six metal gates for St Columba, Haggerston
2004   £3000 for a clock at St Leonard, Shoreditch
2005   £3000 for restoration of painting of crucifixion at St Barnabas, Hommerton
2006   £3000 for a clock at St Mark, Dalston
2007   £4000 for the clock of St Augustine, Mare Street, Hackney
2008   £3000 for monuments at St John, Hackney
2008   £4000 for restoration of paintings at St Michael and All Angels, London Fields
2008   £4000 for stonework on tower of St John of Jerusalem, South Hackney
2008   £5000 for the roof of Downs Road Baptist Church
2009   £4000 for the railings of St Leonard, Shoreditch
2010   £2000 to St Mary's, Stoke Newington for repair of tombs
2011   £500 for the clock of St John of Jerusalem, South Hackney

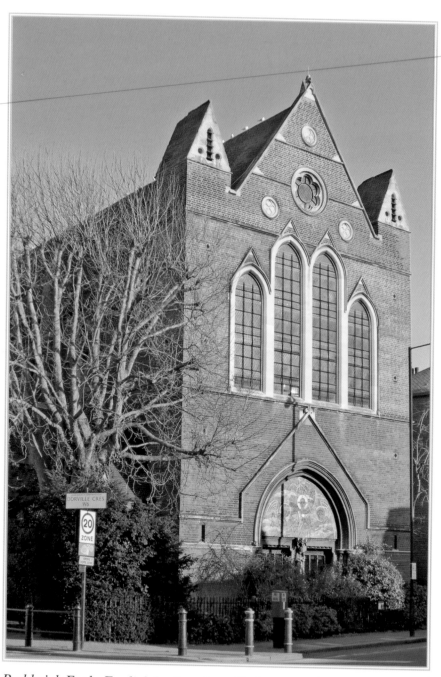

Red brick Early English by Brooks at Holy Trinity, Hammersmith

HAMMERSMITH AND FULHAM

The London Borough of Hammersmith and Fulham was created in 1965 from the Boroughs of Hammersmith and Fulham.

Kensington and Chelsea lies to the east, Brent to the north, Ealing and Hounslow to the west and the River Thames to the south and the south west.

The Manor of Fulhanham (i.e. Fulham) was purchased by Bishop Waldhere of the East Saxons around 704AD and remained in the possession of the successor Bishops of London until 1973, Robert Stopford being the last Bishop to be resident. The Palace was substantially rebuilt in the 18th century when it became the main residence of the Bishops of London but some earlier work such as the 15th century Great Hall survives. The Hon Henry Compton, second son of the 2nd Earl of Northampton, was Bishop from 1675 to 1713 and did much to improve the gardens, which were praised by John Evelyn. Fulham Palace is now run by a trust.

Fulham was also the site of various other Georgian country houses. Hurlingham House is the only one to survive. It was originally built in 1760 and the grounds were designed by Repton. The Hurlingham Club was set up in 1869 for pigeon shooting but later became famous for polo; the polo grounds suffered compulsory purchase by the LCC after World War II. Craven Cottage was built in 1780 for William Craven, 6th Baron Craven; Edward Bulwer-Lytton who wrote *The Last Days of Pompeii* lived there in the 19th century. It was destroyed by fire in 1888 and subsequently became the site of Fulham FC football ground, which it remains to this day. Brandenburgh House was lived in by the Margrave and Margravine of Brandenburg and subsequently by Caroline of Brunswick, wife to George IV.

Until the middle of the 19th century Fulham was given over to market gardens to supply vegetables to London. In the second half of the 19th century streets of houses were built to house the workers in the various industries that were springing up. Fulham in particular was famous for its pottery. These houses built originally for industrial workers have now become expensive residences.

Hammersmith lying to the north of the borough was also historically part of the Bishop of London's Manor of Fulham and equally given over to market gardening and agriculture. In the 18th century malls were built at Chiswick. St Peter's Square is an attractive development of the 1820s. To the north are the more gritty regions of the Goldhawk and Uxbridge Roads and further north still can be found the even more gritty regions of White City with its LCC estates and Wormwood Scrubs with its prison of 1874 by Sir Edward du Cane. Industry arrived at the end of the 19th century. In 1899 Joseph Lyons set up the largest food factory in the UK at Cadby Hall off the Hammersmith Road employing some 30,000 workers.

All Saints, Church Gate, Fulham (open Monday to Friday 10 am to 3 pm) was the medieval church for the borough and is adjacent to Putney Bridge. The west tower is of 1440. The rest of the church was rebuilt in 1880–81 by Sir Arthur Blomfield (1). The church has a large collection of monuments, the most notable being that of 1675 to Viscount Mordaunt by Bushnell; it shows him as a swaggering figure in classical dress (2). Another one is an upright one of Margaret Legh (died 1605) holding a baby in swaddling clothes with another erect beside her (3). Ten Bishops of London are buried in the adjacent churchyard. The architect Henry Holland (*inter alia* the designer of Brooks's Club) is buried outside the vestry door.

St Peter, Black Lion Lane, Hammersmith, visible from the A4, is a Commissioners' Church, of 1827–9, by Edward Lapidge. It is a rectangle of brick with an Ionic portico and a west tower topped by a tiny plastered cupola (6). *The Gentleman's Magazine* commented in 1831 "Taken as a whole this Church presents a very fair specimen of modern Grecian architecture. The tower has considerable merit. The design is modern and pleasing, and the proportions are harmonious. The interior is however chaste and formal, displaying even a presbyterian nakedness, the dullness of which is increased by the purple furnishing of the altar". The murals were added in 1932 (5).

The borough has a number of Anglican Gothic Revival churches, none in the first league.

St John the Evangelist, Glenthorne Road, Hammersmith is by Butterfield in 1857–9 with a later tower. It is large and built mainly in yellow and red brick (7) and has now been converted as the concert hall of Latimer Girls School; certain of the furnishings have been moved to St Matthias, Stoke Newington.

St Paul, Queen Caroline Street, Hammersmith (open 12 noon – 1.45 pm, Monday and Tuesday) is visible from the Hammersmith flyover. It was rebuilt in 1882 by Roumieu, Gough and Seddon. The tower is tall with pinnacles (8). The church is Early English, with lancet windows. The church is in Evangelical hands and the pews have all gone (9). Some furnishings do however survive (10, 12) as does much glass. The church possesses a number of monuments from an earlier 17th century predecessor including one to Sir Nicholas Crisp (died 1665), surmounted by a bust to commemorate "that Glorious Martyr King Charles the First of Blessed Memory" (11).

Holy Innocents, Paddenswick Road, Hammersmith (parish office open 9.45 am – 1.30 pm, Monday to Friday) was designed by James Brooks in an austere and lofty brick style, and most of it was built 1889–91 (13). The huge Gothic baldacchino is possibly by Geldart.

St Alban, Margravine Road is by Sir Aston Webb and Ingress Bell, 1896, in an Arts and Crafts red Gothic style (14). Once notorious for its altars, confessionals and statues (including one of the Infant Christ of Prague), it closed in 2004 and has now re-opened as a 'plant' by Holy Trinity Brompton. An external crucifix is pretty much the only evidence of the Anglo-Catholic past (15).

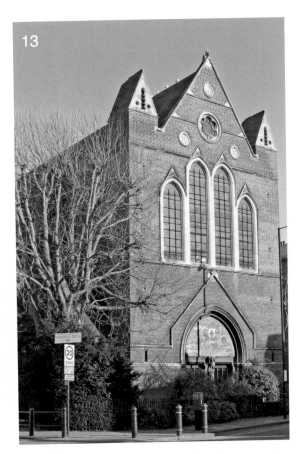

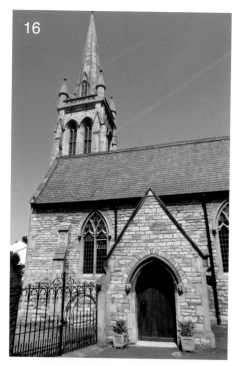

The Catholics possess three churches of interest.

The first of these is **St Thomas of Canterbury, Rylston Road, Fulham** (1847–8), which is Pugin's only complete church in London. The style is Middle Pointed (i.e. Decorated) (16). The church suffered a drastic re-ordering in 1969 although the fittings (altar frontals, reredoses, font, etc.) in the main survived (17). In the last few years the church has been attractively refurbished in a Puginian spirit (18, 19). There is glass by Hardman (20). Various people of note such as the Catholic architects Gribble and Hansom are buried in the churchyard.

The second is **Holy Trinity, Brook Green, Fulham**, 1851–3 by Wardell. It has a spire of the late 1860s by Hansom (22). It is another Middle Pointed church, rather larger with a Decorated east window and a good hammerbeam roof adorned by later angels (21). It has been reordered and quite a lot of the original fittings have gone; some however survive (23, 24). The church has glass by Hardman and Mayer (25).

St Aidan, Old Oak Common Lane, Hammersmith is by John Newton of Burles, Newton & Partners of 1961, of red brick and concrete (26). Inside there is a rich collection of contemporary works of art commissioned by Father James Etherington. Graham Sutherland was responsible for the Crucifixion above the altar (27). Adam Kossowski designed the ceramic mural for the Baptistery (28). The engraved glass screen is by Arthur Fleischmann. Bright modern glass (29, p.159) abounds.

29

Ecclesiastical grants in Hammersmith and Fulham made by the Heritage of London Trust

1986 £1000 for restoration of tombstones at All Saints, Fulham
1989 £3000 for stained glass at St Simon, Rockley Road, Hammersmith
1994 £550 for stained glass restoration at Christchurch, Studdridge Street, Fulham
1994 £6000 for the restoration of the Legh monument at All Saints, Fulham
2002 £2750 for the organ case of All Saints, Fulham
2010 £2500 for the restoration of the memorial window at St Andrew, Fulham
2015 £3000 for the restoration and interpretation of ten tombs of Bishops of London in the churchyard of All Saints Fulham, Bishop's Park.

The spectacular towers of St Ignatius R.C. Church, Tottenham High Road

HARINGEY

The London Borough of Haringey was formed in 1965 out of the former boroughs of Hornsey, Wood Green and Tottenham.

Haringey is bounded to the east by Waltham Forest, to the south by Hackney, Islington and Camden, to the west by Barnet and to the north by Enfield.

There is high ground to the west, and plain and marshes to the east.

Hornsey in the west was a manor of the Bishop of London in the Middle Ages. The Great Northern Railway arrived in 1850 and, thereafter for the next seventy odd years, numerous middle class suburbs were built. Superior housing was to be found in Muswell Hill, the name deriving from a holy well. Some will recall Hilaire Belloc's irritating Charles Augustus Fortescue who "thus became immensely Rich and built the Splendid Mansion which is called The Cedars, Muswell Hill, where he resides in affluence still ...". The first Lotus Car factory was set up in Hornsey in 1954.

Wood Green was originally a parish within Tottenham and has maintained a certain middle class respectability. Alexandra Palace to the west was completed in 1873 as a huge exhibition centre in Italianate style. It has suffered from major fires in 1873 and 1980. The building now belongs to the borough although the BBC signed a long lease for part in 1934. The western part of the park incorporates the site of a house called The Grove, which belonged to Dr Johnson's friend, Topham Beauclerk.

Tottenham lay on the route of Ermine Street. A number of Georgian houses survive as well as one mansion, Bruce Castle, originally built for Sir William Compton in 1514, Groom of the Stool to Henry VIII (an intimate if possibly not a very pleasant role); this was remodelled in 1684 for Henry Hare, second Lord Coleraine.

Middle class villas in Tottenham were however swamped by the boom in working class housing following the introduction of workmen's fares on the Great Eastern Railway in 1872. Numerous factories were built in the 19th century for the productions of such items as crape and india rubber. Many such factories were built along the River Lea in the east. Among the more famous businesses were Ever Ready batteries, Harris Lebus furniture, Gestetner duplicators and William Press engineering. Tottenham has suffered badly from the deindustrialisation of the later 20th century. Tottenham Hotspur Football Club ('Spurs') has its stadium in White Hart Lane. The unloved Broadwater Farm council estate was completed in 1971; Pevsner talks of "the bleakness and artificiality of the original concept". Tottenham is undoubtedly faced with considerable social problems as evidenced by the 2011 London riots which started there.

St Mary, Hornsey has a medieval tower (1). The neo-Perpendicular church of 1889 by Brooks has been demolished.

All Hallows, Church Lane, Tottenham, set in surprisingly green surroundings, has a 14th century brick tower, a porch of c. 1500 and an aisle of roughly the same date (4). The east end is by Butterfield of 1875–7 in red brick. The Butterfield furnishings survive and include glass by Gibbs. Some late 16th century French glass, presented in 1807, shows David, Isaiah and Jeremiah (3). The monument of Sir Robert Barkham and his wife dates from the 1640s and is by Edward Marshall; the detail shows three male children and a baby (2). Butterfield is buried in Tottenham Cemetery.

St Augustine, Armoury Road, Haringey is by John Dando Sedding of 1884–7, completed by Henry Wilson. The brick west front with stone porch is by Harold Gibbons in 1916 (5, 7) and has a small turret. The church itself is built of ragstone with Bath stone facings. The nave by Sedding is austere and Gothic; the piers have no capitals. Good High Church fittings can be found, including the baroque altar of 1938 by Adrian Scott (6). The glass in the north aisle is by Westlake. St Augustine's maintains a robust High Church tradition.

St Bartholomew, Craven Park Road is red brick Art Nouveau Perpendicular Gothic by Caroe of 1904 (9). The small spireover the crossing is shingled. It has a good High Church interior (8). The 17th century furnishings (font, font cover and pulpit) come from St Bartholomew, Exchange, via St Bartholomew, Moor Lane.

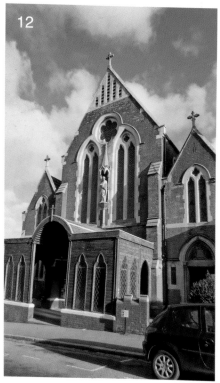

St Paul, Wightman Road, Haringey was built in 1984, to replace a burnt Victorian church, by Peter Jenkins. It is constructed of red brick with horizontal stone dressings. One enters through two vertical columns with wider stone bands (11). The roof is grey and triangular. The inside has white walls and black chairs (10). The brass lectern survives from the previous church.

There are two Catholic churches of architectural interest in the borough. Canon Scoles built **St Peter in Chains, Stroud Green** for the Canons Regular of the Lateran 1902–8.

The church is built in simple red brick Gothic style. St Peter stands above the 1960s wooden narthex (12). The inside has been reordered and the furnishings are simple apart from the reredos (13).

The Jesuits were invited to Stamford Hill by Cardinal Vaughan in the early 1890s. **St Ignatius, Tottenham High Road** is a large cruciform red brick building with twin towers built by the convert Benedict Williamson (who became a priest in 1909) for the Jesuits 1902–11 (14, 15 and p.116). The style is Transitional Romanesque-Gothic, based on Rhineland precedents. The interior is simple and painted white. The high altar and reredos completed in 1923 are however lavish (16). Both Alfred Hitchcock and Cardinal Heenan were educated at what was the adjacent school.

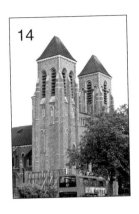

Ecclesiastical grants in Haringey made by the Heritage of London Trust

1990   £5000 for the tower of St Mary, Hornsey

2000   £2000 for tower and tomb in churchyard of St Mary, Hornsey

2004   £3000 for roof of the Church of the Cherubim and Seraphim, Crouch Hill

2004   £7000 for turrets and brick restoration of Holy Trinity, Tottenham

2006   £1800 for the tower of St Mary, Hornsey

2009   £4000 for St Anne, Highgate

The interior of St Lawrence, Whitchurch Lane, with carvings by Grinling Gibbons

HARROW

The boundaries of the London Borough of Harrow remained unchanged in 1965. The Borough is bounded by Hertfordshire to the north, Hillingdon to the west, Ealing and Brent to the west and Barnet to the east.

Harrow has a very visible natural landmark in its 406 feet high hill. Until the Reformation the manor was owned by the Archbishop of Canterbury. The borough remained pretty much agricultural until the coming of the coming of the Railway in 1837 and the Metropolitan Line in 1880–5.

Harrow-on-the-Hill remains a recognisable village in its centre. It possesses a public school, founded by John Lyons in 1572, with some 800 pupils. The school has produced seven British prime ministers (Perceval, Goderich, Peel, Aberdeen, Palmerston, Baldwin and Churchill), on a par with Westminster, considerably less than Eton with its nineteen, but better than Charterhouse with one (Liverpool) and Winchester with one (Addington). The School Chapel is by Giles Gilbert Scott and described by Pevsner as "uncompromisingly Gothic". It was the gift of Dr Vaughan, the headmaster. The Speech Room is by Burges at the probable recommendation of the Catholic convert 3rd Marquess of Bute, who had been at the school.

Pinner equally remains a recognisable village in its centre but became the archetypal 'Metroland' after the First World War when a series of great estates were built, stimulated by the Metropolitan Railway, some with Art Deco houses. Screaming Lord Sutch is buried in South Pinner Cemetery.

Stanmore is famous for the now vanished Canons built in 1713–20 for James Brydges, Duke of Chandos, at a cost of £200,000, by various architects. Defoe described it as "the most magnificent house in England". Handel was in charge of the chapel for a period and wrote both *Esther* and *Acis and Galatea* there. The Duke died in 1744 and the house was demolished three years later. Pope wrote "Another age shall see the golden ear imbrown the slope, and nod on the parterre, deep harvests bury all his pride had planned, and laughing Ceres reassume the land."

Elsewhere in the Borough, Bentley Priory was the Headquarters of Fighter Command during the Second World War and has work by Soane; Edgware is unattractive; Harrow Weald possesses Grim's Dyke, a house of 1870–2 by Norman Shaw and subsequently owned by W.S. Gilbert; Hatch End is a residential suburb; Headstone Manor has a 14th century interior built as a residence for the Archbishop of Canterbury together with an early 16th century great barn; Kenton is mainly 1930s amorphous suburbia; Wealdstone possesses such industry as Harrow has.

St Mary, Church Hill, Harrow (open daily), set with its spire on the hill, was founded by Lanfranc and consecrated by St Anselm. The earliest stonework is from 1130–40 and the rest is 12th/13th century (1). The church has a 15th century timber roof. It was heavily restored by Scott in 1846–9, who, *inter alia*, added the parapet to the nave and aisle roofs. The church has a Purbeck font of 1200, a 17th century wooden pulpit, a number of brasses and monuments (2) and glass by Kempe and Comper (3). Lord Byron wrote "Lines written beneath an Elm in the Churchyard of Harrow"; "Spot of my youth! Whose hoary branches sigh ...". Byron's daughter, Allegra Byron, is buried in an unmarked grave near the south porch.

St John the Baptist, High Street, Pinner
was originally a chapel of St Mary's, Harrow,
forming part of the deanery of Croydon, which
came under the jurisdiction of the Archbishop
of Canterbury. Only in 1766 did Pinner become
an independent parish and in 1836 the parish
became part of the Diocese of London. The
bulk of the church is 14th century with a tower
of the next century (4). Pevsner describes it as
"one more of the all round typical minor Middlesex churches". The church was restored by
Pearson. The stained glass includes some again
by Comper; the window illustrated shows a
splendidly firm Queen Bertha of Kent, a Christian Frankish princess, who welcomed St Augustine to Canterbury in 597 AD in spite of her
husband Æthelbert being a pagan at the time
(5). A number of monuments can be found.

St Lawrence, Whitchurch Lane, Stanmore (open Sunday, 2 to 4 pm or 5 pm in the summer) has a medieval tower. The rest of the church was rebuilt by John James for James Brydges, the 1st Duke of Chandos, who lived in the now vanished Canons nearby, in 1715 in brick and stone (6). The wooden decoration was carved by Grinling Gibbons (7) and the frescoes are by Laguerre (10). The Chandos Mausoleum is attached to the church and contains the monument of the Duke carved by Gibbons; he stands in Roman costume with his kneeling wives on either side (8, also 9 nearby).

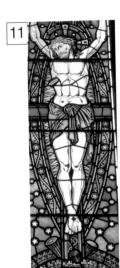

Harrow has a number of Victorian churches. The Parish of Harrow Weald was created in 1845. **All Saints, Uxbridge Road, Harrow Weald** (parish office open weekdays, 9.30 am – 12.30 pm) is mainly by William Butterfield in 1849–52 in stone (13). It is set in a pleasantly overgrown churchyard (16). Much of Butterfield's decoration survives (12, 14, 15). The mosaic in the chancel above the altar represents the Tree of Life; it has been recently restored having been whitewashed in the 1950s. Much Victorian glass can be found (11). The earliest stained glass windows are by C.E.

Kempe. There is a window in the south aisle by Morris & Co of Faith, Hope and Charity, designed by Burne-Jones. W.S. Gilbert of Gilbert and Sullivan fame is commemorated in the church by an ornate wall relief memorial. In the churchyard and its extension there are the graves of William Leefe Robinson VC, who shot down a Zeppelin in September 1916, and Edmund Crosse and Thomas Blackwell of tinned soup fame.

St John the Evangelist, Church and Uxbridge Roads, Great Stanmore was built by Henry Clutton (not the RC convert) in 1849 (17). Its chief interest lies in the various monuments moved from the adjacent, ruined, old church (18). The new church was consecrated by the Bishop of Salisbury in 1850 in the presence of Queen Adelaide in her last public appearance. Sir John Wolstenholme, obit 1638, has a recumbent effigy by Nicholas Stone; he was responsible for the red brick church consecrated by Archbishop Laud in 1632. A huge monument to his son Sir John, obit 1670, is to be found in the tower room. George Gordon, 4th Earl of Aberdeen and Prime Minister 1852–55 during the Crimean War, who died in 1860, and whose son, the Hon. and Rev. Douglas Gordon, was rector here, also has a recumbent effigy (20). Willement and Burne-Jones designed the glass (19). Lord Halsbury, three times Lord Chancellor, is buried in the churchyard.

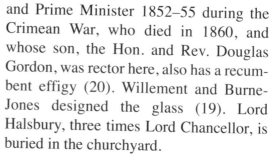

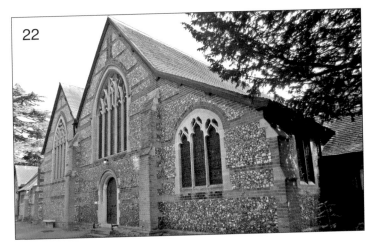

St Anselm, Westfield Park, Hatch End was designed in flint by F.E. Jones in 1895–1905 (22). Its interior is dominated by Charles Spooner's rood screen of 1901, erected after overcoming considerable Protestant opposition through an appeal to the Dean of Arches (21). It was eventually dedicated by Arthur Winning-ton-Ingram, the high church Bishop of London 1901–46, known as 'Uncle Arthur' to his disobedient Anglo-Catholic priests who appreciated his laxity in administrative matters.

Harrow is also reasonably well-endowed with interesting 20th century churches.

St John, Sheepcote Road, Greenhill (open Monday/Friday, 12 noon – 2pm / Saturday 10 am – 12 noon) was built by J.S. Alder in 1904 (23, 24). It has fittings and stained glass by Martin Travers. Joost de Blank was Vicar here before eventually becoming Archbishop of Cape Town.

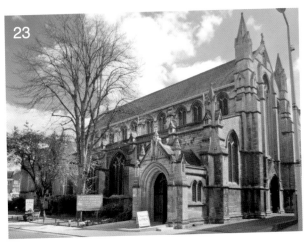

The parish of Kenton was created in 1927 as a mission district out of the territory of a number of other parishes. The missioner and first vicar, Fr F.R. Johnson, known locally as 'Pop', came in 1927 and remained until 1964. **St Mary, Kenton Road** is by J.H. Gibbons (1936) in brown brick Gothic (25). The west front has a Virgin and Child between two lancet windows (28). The good contemporary interior fittings survive (26, 27). The figure of Christ the King above the high altar is interestingly modelled on that of George

V. Queen Mary later reciprocated the compliment by presenting the church with an icon. It maintains a distinct Anglo-Catholic tradition.

Cachemaille-Day built two churches in the borough during the 1930s.

The first is **St Anselm, Uppingham Avenue, Belmont**, a large brick church (29, 30). It has neo-Byzantine fittings moved from St Anselm, Davies Street, Mayfair. It was one of the '45 Churches' ordered to be built between the wars by the then Bishop of London.

The second is **St Paul, Corbins Lane, South Harrow**, in a very modernist idiom with tower and chancel in one, towering above the surrounding houses (31). Its chief internal feature is the fairly dramatic stained glass above the high altar (32).

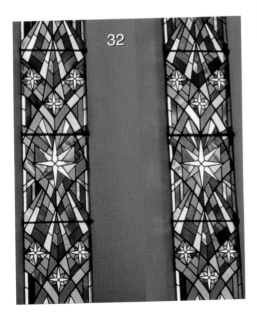

St Alban, Church Drive, Harrow (open Monday & Saturday 10 am – 12 noon / Thursday 3 pm – 5 pm) is a church of 1936–7 by Kenyon (33). It is yellow brick with a high tower. The interior is simple, with a barrel roof.

There are three interesting Catholic churches in the borough.

Our Lady and St Thomas of Canterbury, Roxborough Park was built by Arthur Young in 1894 in simple Arts and Crafts Perpendicular style (36). The interior has a wagon roof (34) and is attractively cluttered with

statues (35). The church has glass by Lavers & Westlake, Mayer, Nuttgens (who lived locally) and Eleanor Bird, the latter of Our Lady, in the 1990s (37).

The original Catholic mission was served by the Salvatorians (Society of the Divine Saviour) from 1901. **St Joseph, High Street, Wealdstone** was built in warm-coloured stone by Adrian G. Scott in 1931 (39). It has good original and more recent fittings (38).

St Luke, Love Lane, Pinner with its twin towers was erected in 1957 by F.X. Velarde

in the neo-Romanesque style he pioneered in Bootle twenty years earlier (41). The exterior has statues of St Luke painting Our Lady (by David John 1957) (40). The roof and the sanctuary are blue in decoration and the roof is supported by concrete columns enclosed in gold mosaic (42, 43).

Ecclesiastical grants in Harrow made by the Heritage of London Trust

1984 £19000 for restoration of painting at St Lawrence, Whitchurch

2010 £2000 for stonework at the ruined church of St John the Evangelist, Stanmore.

2012 £3000 for mosaic restoration at All Saints, Harrow Weald

The Victorian tower of St John, Havering-atte-Bower

HAVERING

The London Borough of Havering was formed in 1965 out of the borough of Romford and the urban district of Hornchurch, both formerly in Essex.

It is bounded in the west by Barking, in the north by Redbridge, in the east by Essex and in the south by the River Thames.

Havering is the furthest east of the London boroughs. It is hilly in the north towards Havering-atte-Bower but flat towards the Thames.

Havering-atte-Bower became a royal hunting lodge at the time of Edward the Confessor and remained so until the 17th century when it became derelict. It has been completely demolished as has the later Pyrgo Park by Salvin. The village itself remains fairly rural.

The 'Liberty' of Havering-atte-Bower was historically coterminous with the parish of Hornchurch further to the south. Hornchurch was a rural village until the 20th century. The Hornchurch Brewery flourished from 1789 to 1930 but has vanished as has the iron foundry.

Until the 19th century Romford was subservient to Hornchurch but its situation on the London-Colchester road gave it a certain importance as a market town. It was historically dominated by Gidea Hall on its outskirts. Sir Thomas Cooke, a Lord Mayor of London, was given a licence to crenellate in 1466. His descendant Sir Anthony Cooke, a confirmed Protestant, was tutor to Edward VI and Lady Jane Grey. The house was visited in 1568 by Queen Elizabeth and in 1637 or 1638 by Marie de Medici, mother-in-law of Charles I and Queen of France. In 1745 it was bought by Richard Benyon, sometime Governor of Fort St George (Madras), who built a new brick mansion. The house was finally demolished for suburban housing in 1930. In earlier centuries Romford was known for the number of its inns. The Eastern Counties Railway came to Romford in 1839 and led to the town becoming a commuter suburb. Romford is now a major retail centre. Humphrey Repton once lived in the area.

The villages in the south and the east have a less suburban feel. Rainham near the Thames once had a wharf on the creek. Rainham Hall, a red brick 18th century building, survives and is quite grand. Wennington is a fairly remote marshland village with a bird sanctuary to the south. The actual villages of North Ockendon and Cranham could both be in Essex as they once were, although suburban development is of course never that far away. Upminster lies at the far eastern end of the District Line. There was much expansion here in the middle of the 20th century but that came to an end with the Second World War and the imposition of the Green Belt.

An avenue of beeches leads to the Norman doorway (2) of **St Mary Magdalen, North Ockendon** (1). This rather wonderful church is remotely and rurally situated and feels more part of Essex than London. The main body of the church is of 1170 although this was added to during the rest of the medieval period. The church has a fine nave roof and in the north chapel there is 15th century glass of St Mary Magdalen (3). The east window also has medieval glass. The church was much restored in the 19th century. A collection of monuments commemorates the Poyntz family; one of 1606 to Sir Gabriel Poyntz and his wife Aethelreda is attributed to Gerard Johnson (4). The tester is charmingly painted with sun, moon, clouds and stars (5). William Jackson, Rector 1619–57, was suspended for "flippancy" in 1636.

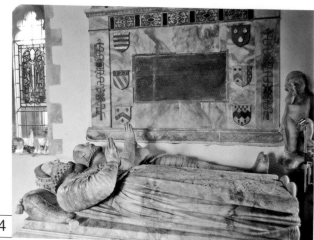

St Helen and St Giles, Rainham is a complete Norman church, built c. 1178 by Richard de Lucy, now marooned in rather a grim urban setting (6). It was sensitively restored in 1897–1910 by the Reverend Ernest Geldart. The south door is Norman. It has a squat tower and inside three bays with unmoulded arches and scalloped capitals. The Norman chancel arch has chevron ornamentation (7). The church has much Victorian glass (8). Charles Churchill, poet and satirist, was curate here in 1756; of his preaching he observed "Sleep at my bidding crept from pew to pew".

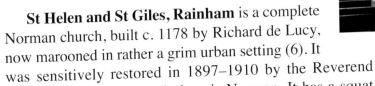

St Mary and St Peter, Wennington is situated in the marshes (now rather urbanised) and is essentially a rural church with a flint and stone exterior (10). It has a 13th century chancel and a 14th century north aisle. The furnishings are 17th century. A monument commemorates Henry Bust (†1624) and his son (9). Good Victorian glass can be found in the east window.

St Andrew, Hornchurch (open
Monday to Friday 10 am – 12.30 pm /
1.30 pm – 4 pm) is a large town church
on a hill (11). It is 13th century in origin
but has a Perpendicular appearance. The
church was an 'alien priory' until 1390
when it was purchased by William of
Wykeham for New College, Oxford. It
has a bull's head with horns at the east
end, there by 1610 (12). Monuments
abound including a curious one to
Thomas Withrings († 1651), the first
post-master general (14). His monument
records he was "second to none for un-
fathom'd poilicy unparraileld sagacious
& diving genious". There are medieval
stained glass fragments of a crucifixion
(13).

15

16

St Laurence, Upminster (open daily 9 am – 5 pm) has a broached and shingled spire on a robust 13th century tower (15). The church was founded by St Cedd in the 7th century. The nave arcade dates from the 13th century but was much altered in the 18th and 19th centuries. The 1928 choir and sanctuary are by Sir Charles Nicholson. A collection of brasses and good armorial glass of 1630 (16) can be found. The oldest bell has "Sancte Gabriel, ora pro nobis" inscribed upon it.

Romford is the major urban centre of the Borough of Havering. Its main church is that of **St Edward the Confessor** (open during daylight hours) built in 1849–50 by John Johnson. It is large and built out of ragstone with a 162-foot spire (17).

17

The nave has five bays, and detailed Decorated tracery. The monument to Sir Anthony Cooke of Gidea Hall is possibly by William Cuer; Sir Anthony died in 1576 and had been tutor to Edward VI (18).

18

All Saints, Cranham was built by Richard Armstrong for the local squire, Richard Benyon, in 1873 and it is a 19th century Tractarian rural church (19). It has a well-carved reredos (21) and brightly coloured stained glass by Hardman (20). General James Oglethorpe († 1785), the founder of Georgia, USA, is buried in the church.

Basil Champneys built **St John, Havering-atte-Bower** in 1878. It is situated by a large green. The church is flint with stone dressings (23). The windows are Decorated. The tower has an elaborate porch (22, see also p.178). Inside can be found a 12th century Purbeck marble font and a number of monuments from the earlier church. The church is now in modern Evangelical hands.

Only one Catholic church is worth recording. This is in **Romford**, and also dedicated to **St Edward the Confessor**. It is by Daniel Cubit Nichols of 1856 (24). The site was dedicated by Cardinal Wiseman in the same year. The 12th Lord Petre was a major donor. It is ragstone with "late 13th century" tracery. The carved stone reredos is by Boulton & Harris. A shrine to Our Lady of Walsingham can be found in the north chapel (25). The church was reordered by Williams & Winkley in the mid 1980s and refurbished by Anthony Delarue in 2000.

Ecclesiastical grants in Havering made by the Heritage of London Trust

2001   £4000 for St Edward The Confessor (C of E) Church, Romford for monuments
2006   £2000 to St Mary Magdalen, North Ockendon for stained glass repairs
2011   £2000 for stone repairs to the spire at St Thomas, Noak Hill, Romford

The 17th century tower and cupola of St John the Baptist, Hillingdon

HILLINGDON

The London Borough of Hillingdon consists of the former borough of Uxbridge and the three urban districts of Hayes & Harlington, Ruislip & Northwood and Yiewsley & West Drayton.

It is bounded to the north by Hertfordshire, to the east by Harrow, Ealing and Hounslow, and to the south and west by Buckinghamshire.

The southern plain of the borough is dominated by Heathrow Airport and the M4. South of the M4, Heathrow takes its name from a now totally obliterated hamlet. Harmondsworth was granted by Offa to Aeldred in 780 and is mentioned in Domesday Book. Its chief claim to fame is its huge early 15th century tithe barn built for when the manor was owned by Winchester College. Lord Bolingbroke lived at Dawley House in Harlington. Cranford's name derives from a ford frequented by cranes (i.e. herons). It is also mentioned in Domesday Book. Part of the manor was owned by the Knights Templar in the 14th century and transferred after their dissolution to the Knights Hospitaller of St John of Jerusalem. The large house belonged to the family of the Earls of Berkeley from 1618 until it was demolished in 1939, apart from the stables.

There are a number of suburbanised former villages between the M4 and the A40. Hayes is an unattractive mixture of inter-war housing and office blocks. West Drayton at least has the red brick Tudor gatehouse and walls of the mansion granted to Sir William Paget in 1547. Uxbridge was an important market town by the 16th century and outstripped its larger neighbour of Hillingdon. Brunel University is situated in West Hillingdon.

The area north of the A40 is more green belt than suburbia. Ickenham has an old village centre but is engulfed in suburbia; the 17th century red brick Swakeleys House survives. Ruislip was mentioned in Domesday Book and the name apparently means "leaping pace on the river where the rushes grow". It has a 14th century barn at Manor Farm. Suburban development followed the arrival of the railways – "Gaily into Ruislip Gardens runs the electric train" in Betjeman's words. Harefield in the north east is still predominantly rural. The great house of the Newdigates who came here in the 14th century has vanished although a lesser 17th century house, Breakspears, belonging to the Ashby family, survives. The Knights Hospitaller of St John of Jerusalem had a cell at Moor Hall in the village. Northwood in the north east of the borough is hilly and became developed after the arrival of the Metropolitan Line in 1887. The great house of the village is in fact Moor Park, a Palladian mansion, just in Hertfordshire. It is by Giacomo Leoni with frescoes by Thornhill.

Hillingdon is rather odd among London boroughs in that virtually all of its interesting churches are medieval, at least in origin. Twelfth century work can be found in three churches.

St Lawrence, Church Road, Cowley is a very small primitive 12th century building, founded by Westminster Abbey, built of flint rubble with a 13th century chancel and a wooded bellcote of 1780 (2). It has a double decker west gallery and a generally simple interior (1). William Dodd, the King's chaplain hanged for forgery in 1777 and brother of the then rector, is buried here.

St Mary, Harmondsworth near Heathrow has a remarkable Norman south doorway with three orders (4). In 1069 the living was given to Holy Trinity, Rouen; in 1391 it passed to Winchester College. Most of the rest of the church is 13th and 15th century. The brick tower is of c. 1500 (3). The church is under threat from a third Heathrow runway (as is the village).

St Peter and St Paul, Harlington (5), 100 yards from the M4, has an even more remarkable Norman doorway with four deep bands of carving, one an arc of 25 observant cats (6). It has a good roof (7) and a Norman font (8). The nave is 12th century, the chancel 14th century, the tower and porch 16th century and the north arcade and aisle of 1880. The Easter sepulchre is 14th century. Sir John Bennet, Earl of Arlington, Charles II's Secretary of State has a monument in the nave. His residence, Dawley House, passed to Bolingbroke and then the De Salis's, several of whom are buried in the church (9).

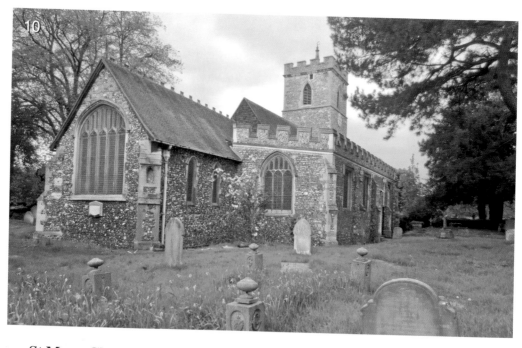

St Mary, Church Road, Hayes (open Sunday 7.45 am – 12 noon / Wednesday 8.45 am – 10 am / Saturday 11.30 am – 12.45 pm) was originally a 'peculiar' of the Archbishop of Canterbury. It has a 13th century chancel and north aisle. There is also 15th and 16th century work (10). In particular the nave and chancel roofs, the former with flat bosses of passion emblems, flowers and Tudor badges, survived the Scott restoration of 1873. On the north wall a 15th century wall painting depicts St Christopher wading across a stream filled with crabs, eels and a mermaid; a little boy in red sits fishing by the stream (12). Sir Edward Fenner, a judge who died in 1612, is commemorated by an elaborate effigy (11). He was MP for Lewes in 1571 and subsequently sat for Shoreham. A high church tradition is still maintained.

St Martin, Ruislip (open daily 8.30 am to 4 pm) lies protected by cottages and almshouses (13). The arcades and chancel arch are 13th century, the rest later. Vestiges of 13th century wall paintings (15) of a crowned Madonna, St Lawrence and St Michael remain as do a 12th century font, 16th and 17th century Hawtrey monuments and Victorian glass including some by Lavers, Barraud & Westlake and Kempe (14). A

number of hatchments line the inside of the tower. The church was restored in 1870 by Gilbert Scott and Ewan Christian. The living belonged to the 'alien priory' of Bec Hellouin until the 14th century, and thereafter to the Dean and Canons of Windsor. A high church tradition is also maintained here.

16

17

St John the Baptist, Hillingdon is situated on a hill and its rebuilt tower of 1629 commands the view (16). The chancel arch is 13th century and the nave and aisles 14th century. Sir George Gilbert Scott restored the church in 1847–8 and rebuilt the eastern half.

18

Lord L'Estrange (obit. 1509), who married Edward IV's sister-in-law, is commemorated by a huge brass. A monument in the chancel to Henry Paget, Earl of Uxbridge, (died 1743) shows him in Roman garb, reclining on a tomb chest (17). The font is medieval (18).

St Giles, Ickenham is a modest 14th century building with a pretty timber porch of 1500 (20). Robert, the infant son of Sir Robert Clayton, who died just after his birth in 1665, is pathetically portrayed in marble as a swaddled, shrouded baby (19). Kempe designed some glass here.

19

20

St Mary, Church Hill, Harefield is mainly 14th century. It was owned by the Hospitaller Order of St John of Jerusalem until the Reformation and is extremely picturesque, set away from the village (21). The essentially 18th century nave and chancel roofs are barrel-shaped and plastered. The woodwork includes a Georgian three decker pulpit, box pews and 17th century altar rails and reredos, probably from a Flemish monastery. The church is rich in monuments, mainly to the Newdigates (including one by Grinling Gibbons) (22) and the Ashbys (23). The most famous monument is however that of Alice Spencer, Countess of Derby who died in 1637. She lies on a tomb chest under a domed and curtained canopy supported on Corinthian columns, wearing a red dress and ermine cloak, her golden hair spread out over the two pillows that support her head, with her three pretty daughters (all eventually countesses) kneeling (24, 25, 26).

St Dunstan, Cranford is a small (in origin) 15th century aisleless building with traffic roaring past on the M4 (27). The 18th century mansion of the Berkeleys was demolished in 1939 with only part of the stables remaining. The church once belonged to the Knights Templar (and subsequently Hospitaller). The nave was rebuilt in brick after a fire in 1710. The church was restored by Pearson in 1895 but is now dominated by the 1930s high church ('Back to the Baroque') fittings provided by Martin Travers for Father Maurice Child (31). Like Harefield, Cranford has many monuments. The earliest is to Sir Roger Aston and his wife of 1611–13 by William Cure II, Master Mason to the King. It

has painted alabaster figures (28). The Berkeleys, to whom the estate long belonged, have numerous tombs (29, 30). Thomas Fuller, the author of *The Worthies of England*, has an alabaster tablet in the chancel; he was rector here at the end of the Protectorate. The monument to Sir Charles Scarbrough, royal physician, says he died in 1693 of "a gentle and easy decay"; may all our ends be so pleasant.

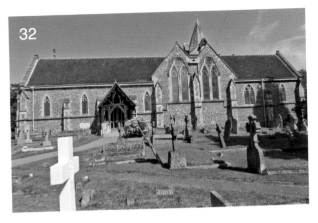

There are two Anglican 19th century churches worth mentioning.

Holy Trinity, Rickmansworth Road, Northwood was designed in 1854 by Teulon for Lord Robert Grosvenor, First Lord Ebury. The church has a flint and stone exterior (32). It was extended subsequently by Cutts as the population grew after the arrival of the railway. Much glass (33) including a memorial window to the Grosvenors by Morris & Co and a baptistery window by Comper can be found. The striking glass of an angel in the north aisle is by Whitefriars (34).

St Andrew, Hillingdon Road, Uxbridge is by Sir George Gilbert Scott in red and yellow brick of 1865 (35). It has later wall paintings and some woodwork on top of the earlier screen by Lethaby (36).

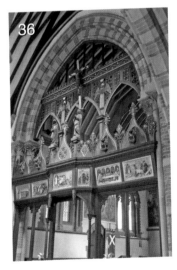

Of Catholic churches, **St Catherine, The Green, West Drayton** was built in 1869, for Irish immigrants, by Willson and Nicholl in brick Gothic (37). The church faces north. The intended spire was never built. Inside it has an elaborate reredos (38). There is glass by Lavers, Barraud & Westlake.

The Immaculate Heart of Mary, Botwell Lane, Hayes was built for the Claretian fathers in 1961 by Burles, Newton & Partners in brick. The exterior is dominated by a tall bell tower (39). The interior is light with modern fittings. The baroque statue of Our Lady looks a little marooned against the modern stained glass (40).

Ecclesiastical grants in Hillingdon made by the Heritage of London Trust

1995 £1000 for a memorial at St Giles, Ickenham
1995 £2500 for Kempe east window at St Peter and St Paul, Harlington
2007 £3000 for the tower clock of St Martin, West Drayton
2008 £5000 for the west window of St Paul, Ruislip Manor
2008 £4000 for the 15th century lynch gate of St Mary, Hayes

*The unusual Arts and Crafts interior of St Michael and All Angels,
Bedford Park*

HOUNSLOW

Hounslow was formed in 1965 from the former boroughs of Brentford, Chiswick, Heston and Isleworth, and the former urban district of Feltham.

It is bounded by Ealing to the north, Hillingdon to the west, Surrey to the south west, Richmond and the Thames to the south and Hammersmith & Fulham to the east.

The area of the borough is flat and almost entirely built up. Hounslow Heath, now much diminished through the expansion of Heathrow Airport, was once the site of military encampments for both Oliver Cromwell and James II. It subsequently became the notorious haunt of highwaymen and footpads, preying on those using the roads to Bath and the West. The Great West Road was the site of some Art Deco factories in the 1930s but a number of these have been demolished. The traffic on both the M4 and the A4 roars through.

The major market town is Brentford, once the site of the notoriously riotous Middlesex county elections. It lies on the Thames where it is the first fordable spot. It has suffered from redevelopment but does retain The Butts, an attractive grouping of late 17th century and early 18th century houses. Brentford's chief landmark is its 19th century minaret-like water tower surmounted by a cupola. Both Chiswick and Isleworth on the River Thames have attractive 18th century buildings. The other towns of the borough are more nondescript.

What Hounslow does have is a substantial number of large country houses which have somehow escaped demolition. Boston Manor is 17th century. Chiswick House is a Palladian villa designed by Richard Boyle, 3rd Earl of Burlington in 1727–9 and inspired by the Villa Rotonda outside Vicenza. It came through descent to the Dukes of Devonshire and has eventually ended up in the possession of English Heritage. Gunnersbury Park was the summer residence of Princess Amelia, George III's aunt 1762–86. It was rebuilt in 1802 and acquired by Nathan Mayer Rothschild in 1835. It is now municipally owned. Osterley Park was built for the banking Child family in the 18th century and was decorated by Robert Adam. The Child-Villiers Earls of Jersey made over the house to the National Trust in 1949. Syon House remains in the possession of the Duke of Northumberland. From 1431 until the Reformation it was the site of a Bridgettine nunnery originally set up by Henry V at Twickenham in 1415. Robert Adam created an exciting set of interiors in the 1760s for Sir Hugh Smithson, 1st Duke of Northumberland, who married the Percy heiress. He was described by Adam as "a person of extensive knowledge and correct taste". The gardens were laid out by Capability Brown.

Two churches of interest, Holy Trinity, Hounslow and All Saints, Islington, were both burnt by the same set of boy arsonists in 1943.

St Mary, East Bedfont outside is most remarkable for its extraordinary topiary (1). This is said to represent two vain young women who irritated other worshippers by displaying their finery. Thomas Hood wrote a poem *The Two Peacocks of Bedfont*: "And where two haughty maidens used to be ... There, gentle stranger, thou mays't only see two sombre Peacocks – Age with sapient nod marking the spot still tarries to declare how they once lived". 12th century work survives in the north chancel and the south aisle as well; the south doorway is also Norman. The chancel was lengthened in the 15th century. The Norman chancel arch is carved in zigzags (2). The church has some 13th century wall paintings representing the Last Judgement (3) and the Crucifixion.

St Leonard, Heston (open the first Saturday of each month after 9.30 requiem until 12 noon) has a Perpendicular west tower and west door (4). The rest of the church was rebuilt 1863–5 by T. Bellamy. It was described at the time by *The Ecclesiologist* as "such an act of vandalism as our age has never seen". The church has a good font (5), 18th century monuments including one to Robert Child of Osterley Park (died 1782) by Robert Adam (6), and 19th century stained glass by Kempe and others.

St Nicholas, Church Street, Chiswick has an early 15th century ragstone tower (7). The rest of the church was rebuilt by Pearson in 1882–4, and the fittings (screens and reredos – 8) are to match. The cost was defrayed by Henry Smith of the adjacent brewers Fuller, Smith and Turner as to £6,850 and the Duke of Devonshire at Chiswick House as to £1,000. The church has much stained glass, some by Clayton & Bell (10, 11). Of the many monuments, the most interesting is an alabaster one to Sir Thomas Challoner (obit 1611) and his wife; he was Chamberlain to Henry, Prince of Wales. The font is of the 1860s (9). Sir Stephen Fox was married in the church and his grandson Charles James Fox was baptised here. Field Marshal Montgomery was married in the church by his father in 1927. Many interesting figures lie buried in the churchyard; these include Barbara Villiers (Duchess of Cleveland), Hogarth, Garrick, Thornhill, Richmond and Whistler.

Hounslow possesses two 19th century Anglican churches of interest.

The first is **St Stephen, St Stephen's Road, Hounslow**. It is a large red brick building of 1875–6

by Ewan Christian with a rather dramatic tower and doorway added by Cachemaille-Day in 1935 (13). It has a mosaic reredos (12).

More important is **St Michael and All Angels, Bedford Park** (open daily) of 1879–80 by Norman Shaw. It and the Tabard Inn form the centre of the Bedford Park estate. The exterior is extremely inventive, being Perpendicular at street level with 17th and 18th century upper features. The exterior has red brick gables, a belfry over the crossing and a white timber balcony (16). Street described the church as "very novel but not very ecclesiastical". Inside the green pews are by Shaw (17) and there is Arts and Crafts stained glass (14) although much was lost in the Blitz. When opened the church was denounced by Henry Smith, churchwarden of St Nicholas, Chiswick for its "popish and pagan mummeries" (15).

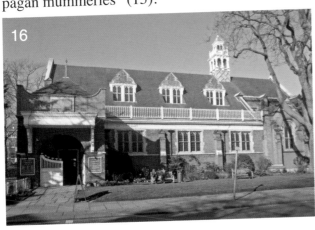

The 20th century has also provided Hounslow with a number of interesting Anglican churches.

St Faith, Windmill Road, Brentford is of 1906–7 by Bodley & Hare. It is of red brick and towerless. Betjeman said "It rises like a great ship above the housetops" (19). It was designed at the very end of Bodley's life and was built fairly cheaply for £8,000 for a congregation that was described as consisting of "clerks, artisans, ... labourers". The contemporary architect Maurice B. Adams wrote "What struck one looking at St Faith, Brentford was the juvenile enthusiasm with which the whole thing was inspired. That a man of Mr Bodley's years could design such a virile church as that seemed truly remarkable." The church has tall clerestory windows and no screen (18), with glass probably by Burlison & Grylls, and by Comper (20).

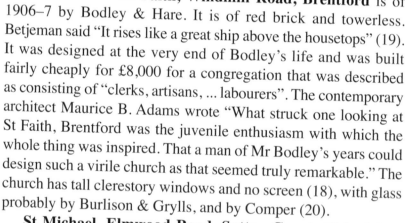

St Michael, Elmwood Road, Sutton Court, Chiswick is 1908–9 by Caroe. It is red brick and attractive (21). The chairs have been preserved inside (22).

St Francis of Assisi, Great West Road, Osterley is by Shearman with its apse facing the main road (23, 24, 25). It is a large brick church based on Albi Cathedral with a very tall interior (26).

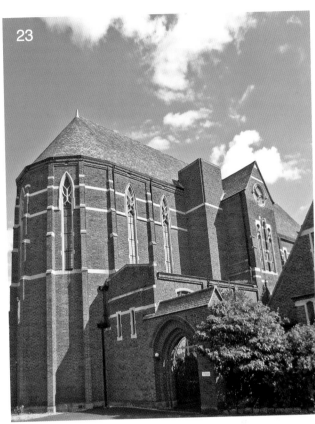

All Saints, Uxbridge Road, Hanworth is by Cachemaille Day of 1951–7. It has a stout exterior of pale brick surmounted by a circular lantern (27). Inside, it has various contemporary fittings (28).

Of Catholic churches, **St John the Evangelist, Boston Park Road, Brentford** is by an unknown architect, a Mr Jackman. It is a stock brick building with a squat tower (29). The inside has an interesting cast iron arcade (30). The church has some Victorian glass. In 1883 Bentley was brought in to make fittings but these have all been mostly destroyed with the exception of the screen at the west end of the nave (31, next page). Anthony Delarue is currently superintending the restoration of the church.

Ecclesiastical grants in Hounslow made by the Heritage of London Trust

1991 £2500 for monuments in the churchyard of St Nicholas, Chiswick

1992 £1786 for stonework at St Mary's Convent, Chiswick

1992 £3356 for the restoration of medieval glass at St George, Hanworth

1994 £200 for the tomb of Whistler at St Nicholas, Chiswick

2001 £2500 for the restoration of the Challoner tomb at St Nicholas, Chiswick

2001 £4000 for the medieval lych gate at St Leonard, Heston

2005 £4000 for the restoration of the reredos screen at St George, Hanworth

2009 £2000 for the restoration of the Hogarth monument at St Nicholas, Chiswick

2012 £2,000 for restoration of tombs at St Nicholas, Chiswick

2013 £2,500 for exterior clock faces at Christ Church, Turnham Green

2014 £1,600 for gable cross at St George, Hanworth

Barry stock brick at St John the Evangelist, Holloway Road

ISLINGTON

The London Borough of Islington was formed in 1965 out of the former boroughs of Finsbury and Islington.

Islington is due north of the City with Hackney to the east, Haringey to the north, Camden to the west and Westminster to the south west.

Finsbury lies on the northern fringe of the City. Until the Reformation it was dominated by religious houses. The Priory of St John in Clerkenwell, founded in 1141, was the headquarters of the Knights Hospitaller in England and the Grand Prior of England was based there. The Order was dissolved in England at the Reformation "for maliciously and traitorously upholding the Bishop of Rome to be Supreme Head of Christ's Church" and three Knights were executed. The gateway and the church survive. The Charterhouse was founded by Sir William de Manny in 1370. At the time of the Reformation the Prior John Houghton was hung, drawn and quartered at Tyburn. Ten Carthusian monks were taken to the Tower of London; nine starved to death and the tenth was executed three years later. After ownership by Lord North and the Duke of Norfolk the site was purchased in 1611 by Sir Thomas Sutton for use as a hospital; the school grew up around it.

In 1607 R. Johnson described Moorfields as "a garden to the City ... for citizens to walk and take the air". The neighbourhood became fashionable and Stow talks of the "many fair houses for gentlemen" in Clerkenwell. As in Shoreditch, various theatres were set up outside the walls of the City. In the 18th century the area became a centre of nonconformity with Wesley's Chapel in City Road. To counter this (perhaps) Whitbread's Brewery was set up in Chiswell Street. In the northern part of Finsbury chalybeate springs were discovered late in the 18th century; the name is preserved in Sadler's Wells. The population grew by the end of the 18th century and Finsbury became overcrowded and less fashionable. Small scale industries developed. At the start of the 20th century Finsbury became known for its slums and there was much subsequent clearing and redevelopment.

Islington remained a rural village until the 18th century. The Knights Hospitaller had been here too, in Highbury, until the Reformation. Development started in 1790s at the Marquess of Northampton's Canonbury estate and continued in Barnsbury. The North London Railway arrived in 1850 leading to the expansion of the population and industrial growth. Fifty years later the borough was seriously overcrowded. Pentonville Prison was built in 1840–2 and Holloway Prison in 1849–51.

In George and Weedon Grossmith's *The Diary of a Nobody* (1892), the Pooters moved into "The Laurels", Brickfield Terrace, Holloway – "a nice six roomed residence, not counting basement with a front breakfast-parlour".

The Knights Hospitallers' Priory of St John of Jerusalem, Clerkenwell (Museum open daily 10 am – 5 pm) was founded in 1144 and flourished on its six-acre site until the Reformation. The upper church is undistinguished architecturally (1) and has a simple Georgian sanctuary of 1721–3. It was gutted in the Second World war and restored (3). The 12th century crypt with its ribbed vaulting is however fascinating. It contains the exquisite late 16th century alabaster recumbent effigy of a Knight of St John, Juan Ruiz de Vergara, Proctor of the Langue of Castile, Maltese cross on his chest (4), with a sleeping page; it was brought from Valladolid Cathedral in 1914. John Wilkes, the radical 18th century politician, was married in the church. The gateway of the Priory survives (2).

St Luke, Old Street was built 1727–33 to designs by Nicholas Hawksmoor and John James under the Fifty New Churches Act. It was made redundant in 1960 and subsequently became derelict. The stone walls survive with a Venetian east window. The west tower has an obelisk of Portland stone as its spire (5). The church is now used by the London Symphony Orchestra as a concert hall.

St Mary, Upper Street (open Wednesday and Saturday, 9.30 am – 12 noon) was built by Launcelot Dowbiggin in 1751–4. Only the tower and spire of this church survived bombing in the War (6). The rest was rebuilt 1954–6 by Seely & Paget as a brick box. The interior has black Egyptian columns framing the sanctuary (7) and modern paintings by Brian Thomas (8). The church has a longstanding evangelical reputation. John Wesley preached here and both Donald Coggan and David Sheppard were curates at different times.

James Carr built **St James, Clerkenwell Close** in 1788–92 to replace a 12th century church used by a nunnery as a chapel until the Reformation. The rebuilt church is attractively sited on Clerkenwell Green, a brick square with a stone tower at the west end. The steeple is an obelisk in Portland stone (9). The west front is stone-fronted. The church has Georgian fittings (11), a moulded ceiling and a number of monuments (including one to Bishop Burnet) from the earlier church. The best is probably that of Thomas Crosse (died 1712) and his wife; this was formerly attributed to Roubiliac (12). The Venetian east window has bright glass of the Ascension, and other stained glass can be found elsewhere (10).

Islington itself has a large number of early 19th century churches. The borough has in the main tended to the more protestant side of Anglicanism.

St Mary Magdalene, Holloway Road (open Monday to Friday, 13.30 – 15.30) is by Wickins in 1812–14. Until 1894 it was a chapel of ease to St Mary, Upper Street. It is a six-bay Georgian brick box (13) set in a large graveyard. The choir stalls and pews were removed in 1983, the church being Evangelical. The east end is intact with an early 19th century "Noli me tangere" painted by a churchwarden (14).

Holy Trinity, Cloudesley Square (now the Celestial Church of Christ) (open Tuesday to Friday, 9 am – 5 pm) was built by Charles Barry in 1826 in a Perpendicular style. The turrets are in need of repair and currently swathed in blue plastic (15). The church was made redundant in 1978 and taken over by a Pentecostalist sect. The inside is dark (16). The church retains some Victorian glass.

St John the Evangelist, Holloway Road is also by Barry in the same year in yellow stock brick (17). The interior has its original fittings including the galleries (18).

St Clement, King Square (open Tuesday 10 am – 1 pm) (originally St Barnabas) is by Hardwicke in 1824 with Ionian front and a thin spire (19). It a 'Waterloo' church and is firmly Anglo-Catholic in liturgy (20, 21).

St Saviour, Aberdeen Park, High-bury (since 1990 the Florence Trust artists' studios and open to the public during exhibitions) with its poly-chromatic brickwork was built 1864–6 by William White for the Anglo-Catholic vicar, the Rev R.W. Morrice, and has beautiful proportions (22). Sir John Betjeman worshipped here as a child and wrote a poem about the building. ("Great red church of my parents, cruciform crossing they knew") (23). A statue of Christ still observes proceedings (24). Some of the glass is by Lavers & Bar-raud. Sir Henry Layard, the archaeologist who discovered the remains of Nimrud and Nineveh, was responsible for the reredos with its mosaic of the Crucifix-ion.

Holy Redeemer, Exmouth Market (open mornings) was built on the site of the former Spa Fields Chapel (Countess of Huntingdon's Connection) in 1887–88 by John Dando Sedding. It is an Italian Renaissance church rather oddly transplanted to north London, built of brick with a towering front with a round doorway, with the inscription "Christo Liberatori" on the frieze above (25). The campanile was added by H. Wilson later. The interior is dominated by the marble high altar with a large baldacchino with red columns and blue dome (26); according to Pevsner this was based on the Santo Spirito, Florence. The organ, originally from the Chapel Royal, Windsor, belonged to the Prince Consort. The church is full of Anglo-Catholic fittings (27).

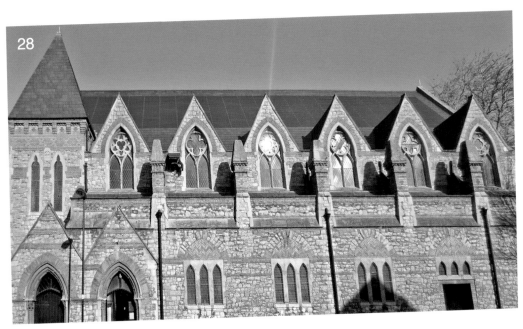

St Silas, Penton Street, Pentonville is a Gothic building in Kentish ragstone. It was designed by Teulon and opened in 1863 (28). Its current Anglo-Papalist tradition (29) has developed subsequently. The Travers altar of Our Lady of Walsingham was paid for by an American gin distiller (30). The organ came from St Thomas, Regent Street.

Islington has two Catholic churches of merit.

The first of these is **St John the Evangelist, Duncan Terrace** by J.J. Scoles of 1841–3. It has a classical façade dominated by twin towers (31). An external war memorial is placed outside (32). The interior is large and

variously believed to be based on San Clemente or the Gesu in Rome. Pugin hated it and called it "the most original combination of modern deformity that has been executed for some time past". The chancel is classical (33). The font is in front of a fresco of Jesus raising Lazarus from the dead (34). The convert Frederick Oakeley, baronet's son, former Balliol don, friend of Newman and translator of "Adeste Fideles", was parish priest here.

St Joseph, Highgate Hill was built for the Passionists by Albert Vicars, 1887–9. It is large and dominates the surrounding landscape (35) with its high octagon (36). The style is Italianate with a lavish west front; the barrel-vaulted nave is dominated by a baldacchino (37).

Ecclesiastical grants in Islington made by the Heritage of London Trust

1988 £3000 for stained glass at St Saviour, Aberdeen Park

1989 £6500 for the Priory of St John of Jerusalem, Clerkenwell

1991 £3000 for railings at St Saviour, Aberdeen Park

1994 £7500 for the Union Chapel, Highbury

1996 £5000 for tombs at St Luke, Old Street

1998 £2500 for the restoration of the porch at St Luke, West Holloway

1999 £1500 for stone crosses at St Thomas, Finsbury Park, Islington

2001 £3500 for the spire of St Stephen, Canonbury

2001 £3500 for restoration of statues at St Joseph, Highgate Hill

2002 £4000 for the rose window of Holy Redeemer, Exmouth Market

2003 £3000 for the Celestial Church of Christ, Cloudesley Square

2006 £4165 for the Union Chapel, Highbury

2006 £4000 for stone repairs at St John the Evangelist, Duncan Terrace

2008 £4000 for painting restoration at St John the Evangelist, Duncan Terrace

2009 £2000 for St Silas Church, Pentonville Road

2013 £2000 for chapel redecoration, St John the Evangelist, Duncan Terrace

2013 £1000 for Kempe window restoration, St Thomas the Apostle, Finsbury Park

The extraordinary baroque altar at St Augustine, Queen's Gate

KENSINGTON AND CHELSEA

The Royal Borough of Kensington and Chelsea was formed in 1965 by the union of the two former boroughs of Kensington and Chelsea. Kensington was made a royal borough in 1901 by Edward VII. The borough is the smallest and the most densely populated in the Greater London area.

The Royal Borough has the City of Westminster to the east, Brent to the north, Hammersmith & Fulham to the west and the River Thames to the south.

Kensington is mentioned in Domesday Book. It belonged at the time to Geoffrey de Mowbray, Bishop of Coutances. The manor was subsequently split between the Abbey of Abingdon and the de Vere Earls of Oxford (hence Earl's Court). It remained very rural until the late 17th century. There were a number of country houses such as Holland House (named after Sir Henry Rich, Earl of Holland and subsequently owned by the Earls of Ilchester; ruined in the Blitz) and Nottingham House, which was sold to William and Mary in 1689 and redeveloped by Christopher Wren as Kensington Palace. Thomas Young built Kensington Square in 1685. Proper development over what had been market gardens started with Lord Kensington selling building leases in 1811; seventy years later the borough was completely urban, either stuccoed or red brick. The Brompton and Kensal Green cemeteries were built in the 1830s. 'Albertopolis' came in the wake of the Great Exhibition of 1851 when 87 acres were purchased for museums, etc. In the 19th century Notting Hill was notorious for its Potteries and Piggeries. There was a short-lived attempt in 1837–1842 to build a hippodrome for racing. Industry came along the Grand Union Canal. The area became poor and overcrowded.

The name of Chelsea derives from "landing place for chalk". Until the late 18th century it remained a riverside village. Henry VIII bought the Manor in 1536 and Anne of Cleves resided there after her divorce. Thomas More lived in the now vanished Beaufort House. In 1682 Charles II founded the Royal Hospital designed by Christopher Wren. In the 18th century Chelsea was known for its pleasure gardens at Cremorne and Ranelagh. In 1777 Henry Holland started developing Hans Place and Sloane Street for what eventually became the Cadogan Estate. "Pont Street Dutch" (the term derived by Osbert Lancaster) followed, "her new built red as hard as the morning gaslight" (Betjeman). The west of Chelsea around World's End was historically poorer and Trollope's George Vavasour was Radical MP for Chelsea Districts. Chelsea enjoyed an artistic Bohemian Pre-Raphaelite and later reputation but alas no longer.

All Saints, Cheyne Row, Chelsea (Chelsea Old Church) (usually open Tuesday to Thursday, 2 pm – 4 pm) is the only church in the Royal Borough to retain anything of the Middle Ages. It lies on the bank of the Thames. Bombed in 1941, it was carefully restored in 1949–58. The appearance of the church is mainly that of a brick classical building of 1667–74 (1). The chancel and various chapels date from the 13th and 14th centuries, the southern (More) chapel being adorned by Renaissance carving in 1528 (2). The chief interest of the church lies in its monuments, including one to Sir Thomas More whose body was buried in two pieces elsewhere. The effigies of Lord and Lady Dacre date from the 1590s (3). Sara Colvile (obit 1632) rises in her shroud, her eyes and hands raised to heaven. In 1672 Pietro Bernini designed the monument to Charles and Jane Cheyne, Viscount and Viscountess Newhaven (4). Sir Hans Sloane lies outside the church.

St Mary Abbots Church, Kensington High Street (open daily) was built by Giles Gilbert Scott to replace the original parish church of Kensington. The name derives from ownership by Abingdon Abbey up to the Reformation. It is a dark building approached by a later, winding cloister and dominated by the tallest spire in London (254 feet), based on that of St Mary Redcliffe in Bristol (5). The church is Decorated in inspiration (6) and retains many Victorian fittings such as the reredos (8). The hexagonal font is dated 1697 and may have been the gift of William III, who worshipped here. The building is adorned with much Victorian glass. A number of monuments survive from the earlier church, the most ambitious being that to Edward, Earl of Warwick and Holland (obit 1721), Addison's stepson, who is depicted as a seated figure in Roman costume; it was completed in 1730 by Guelfi (7). Newton, Wilberforce, Canning, Beatrix Potter and David Cameron have all worshipped here.

Various churches were built in the Royal Borough before the full force of the Gothic Revival hit London.

St Luke, Sydney Street, Chelsea (open daily, 9 – 4pm) is a long narrow neo-Perpendicular edifice with stone vaulting and whispy flying buttresses. It is ashlar faced and has a tall west tower with a five bay porch (9). It was built in 1820 by James Savage for the Hon and Rev Gerald Valerian Wellesley, brother of the Duke of Wellington, an expensive church costing £40,000. It has a high 60-foot nave (10). The glass in the east window is by Hugh Easton (11) to replace earlier glass destroyed in the War. Charles Dickens was married in the building.

Holy Trinity, Brompton Road, Kensington, that current powerhouse of modern Evangelical Anglicanism, whence Justin Welby, Archbishop of Canterbury, sprang, is a Commissioners' church built 1826–9 by T.L. Donaldson. It is of light brick with a thin west tower (13). The chancel with its large gold mosaic reredos by Clayton & Bell was an improvement of the 1880s and survives to date (12).

St Barnabas, Addison Road, Kensington (now a HTB 'plant') was designed by Vulliamy and built in 1827–9; it is of the King's College Cambridge type, in light brick, popular at the time (15). It has glass designed by Burne-Jones and made by Morris, and retains the reredos (14).

The Assumption and All Saints (formerly All Saints), Ennismore Gardens, Kensington (open frequently) was also built, in 1848–9, by Vulliamy. It has an Italianate front with a campanile (16). Inside the church has high Corinthian columns not dissimilar to Wilton church in Wiltshire (18). It has sgraffito by Heywood Sumner and stained glass. It is now the Russian Orthodox cathedral (17).

St Peter, Kensington Park Road, Kensington (parish office open Monday, Wednesday and Friday, 10 am – 3 pm; Tuesday and Thursday, 10 am – 4 pm) is a classical building of 1852 by T. Allom with portico, tower and cupola (19). The inside has giant Corinthian columns painted in white and gold. The furnishings in the main date from the 1880s (20, 21). The church has much Victorian glass (22). The site was developed by the property developer Charles Henry Blake who made his initial fortune from indigo in India. The church was consecrated by Bishop Tait in London in 1857. Seating was available for 1400 parishioners. It is believed to be the last Anglican 19th century church in London for which a classical design was used.

The Oxford Movement endowed the Royal Borough with a considerable number of churches built in that tradition.

All Saints, Talbot Road, Kensington is by William White, 1852–61 (23). The first vicar went bankrupt and the building was uncompleted for a number of years during which period it was known as "All Sinners-in-the-Mud". The 100-foot tower resembles the medieval Belfry in Bruges; the spire was never built. The interior was whitewashed in the 1930s and the church suffered from bomb damage. The Flemish Gothic reredos is by Cecil Hare (25). Some glass (24) and another reredos (26) are by Comper and there are many other high church fittings (27). The Vicar 1931–61 was the flamboyant tricycle-riding Father John Twisaday who attracted Protestant demonstrations at the rededication after the War, and who eventually retired to Walsingham. All Saints seems to have been the model for St Luke's in Barbara Pym's *A Glass of Blessings*.

St Stephen, Gloucester Road, Kensington (open Monday to Tuesday, Thursday to Friday, 8.30 am – 2 pm) was built by Joseph Peacock in 1866–7 for a lowish vicar. The stone exterior (28) does not prepare the visitor for the early 20th century High Church fittings (29) built for Lord Victor Seymour, Vicar 1900–29, the huge reredos by Bodley (31) and the rood by Tapper (32). Goodhart Rendel remarked Peacock's building had been "tamed by other hands". T.S. Eliot worshipped here and is remembered by a memorial (30). The Victorian glass is by Mayer, and Lavers, Barraud and Westlake.

St Augustine, Queen's Gate, Kensington was built by Butterfield in 1871–6, his last major church in London. It has a tall brick façade surmounted by a belfry (33). Some attempt was made in the past to restore the internal polychromy, whitewashed in 1925 (36). Butterfield was responsible for the pulpit (34), lectern and font. The Baroque reredos (35) and the Lady Altar (36) are by Martin Travers (1928) as are the Stations of the Cross.

Betjeman described the Travers fittings as "a period piece of rare delight". The church was in its time the apotheosis of the Anglo-Catholic Congress movement. The church has recently been taken over by HTB and there are fears as to whether the distinctly High Church fittings will be preserved. The pews have already gone.

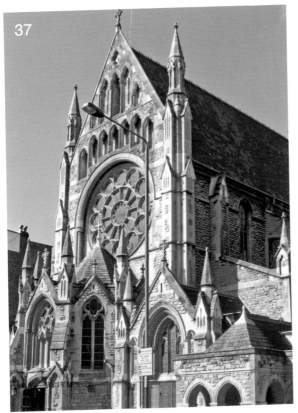

St John the Baptist, Holland Road, Kensington is 1872–89 by James Brooks on an early French Gothic model although the west front is later (1909–11), by J.S. Adkins (37). The interior is lofty and vaulted with screen and rood dividing the nave from the chancel (38) with high church fittings (39) and much Victorian glass (40), mainly by Clayton & Bell. Once known as 'St John the Papist' the church is less 'High' than it was historically. On Saturday and Sunday mornings the building is used by a thriving Eritrean community.

St Cuthbert, Philbeach Gardens, Kensington (open Sunday, 9 am – 1 pm) is 1884–8 by Roumieu Gough with an exterior of red brick surmounted by a fleche spire (41) and a tall interior (43). It was lavishly embellished 1887 to 1914 (43, 45). The enormous reredos was designed by the Rev Ernest Geldart (44). Betjeman described the church to Father Gerard Irvine, quondam vicar, as "Nouveau Viking" in style. The stalls in the chancel have a number of misericords, one showing the Protestant agitator, Kensit, with asses' ears (42). The metal screens, altar rails and lectern are by Bainbridge Reynolds. This was the first Anglican church to reserve the host. In

2013 Father Paul Bagott replaced the very long standing Father John Vine as Vicar and is actively setting up a group of Friends.

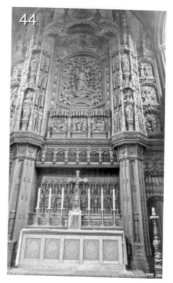

Holy Trinity, Sloane Street, Chelsea (open daily) is by John Dando Sedding of 1888–90 and is a red brick shrine of ecclesiastical Arts and Crafts, paid for by the then Earl of Cadogan. There was a subsequent disgraceful attempt by the Cadogan Estate and the Diocese of London to close and demolish the church in the 1970s but this was fought off by John Betjeman, Gavin Stamp and others. Bishop Michael Marshall was recently incumbent here and it was during his tenure that the church was restored to its current gleaming form. The west front is based on King's College, Cambridge (46, 47). Henry Wilson designed the screens. The baldacchino is by Sedding. The font and pulpit (51) are of coloured marble. The excellent stained glass in the east window of apostles, etc., is by Burne-Jones and Morris (49). The church is only marred by the bright blue modern chairs. The reredos is good (50).

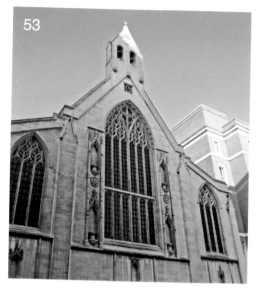

Holy Trinity, Prince Consort Road, Kensington (open Wednesday, 1 pm – 5 pm) is one of Bodley's last works, being built between 1901 and 1906. It is a Perpendicular church, built in stone with a plain front (53), disguising the lofty interior (52). Bodley, to whom there is a monument and bust, designed most of the fittings including the excellent reredos (54), installed in 1912 after his death; Our Lord is on the Cross with Our Lady and St John on either side above the Nativity and the Annunciation. The stained glass in the chancel window and elsewhere is by Burlison and Grylls.

St Simon Zelotes, Moore Street, Chelsea does not fall in the high church tradition. It is of 1858 by Peacock and is a fairly memorable building with its overfull Gothic west front surmounted by a tall bell gable (55) and riotous interior with polychrome white and black brick walls (56). *The Ecclesiologist* did not approve: "Altogether we fear this building will be no gain to art". Goodhart Rendel commented "Details of the Decorated period are piled up in a riotous conglomeration ... never can there have been more architecture in less space".

St Helen, St Helen's Gardens, Kensington is one post-war Anglican church of interest. It was designed in 1954–66 by J.B.S. Comper in red brick (57). It contains a large organ case and stained glass (58) by his father, Sir Ninian. The pews are by Norman Shaw and come from his now closed Harrow Mission church.

The Royal Borough is unsurprisingly fairly rich in Catholic churches.

St Francis, Pottery Lane, Kensington (usually 10 – 12 am, Mondays, Thursdays and Fridays) was built in 1859–60 for the Oblates of St Charles, founded by Manning, to serve the poor of Notting Dale. There is a pleasant courtyard outside (59). This fairly small church in French Gothic was designed by Henry Clutton and subsequently embellished both architecturally and decoratively by J.F. Bentley (the architect of Westminster Cathedral); thankfully the rich and colourful fittings (60) (altars, Stations of the Cross, font, screens, etc.) have in the main survived modern Catholic iconoclasm.

St Mary, Cadogan Street, Chelsea (open daily) was originally founded by Abbe Voxaux de Franous (whose memorial (63) remains) in 1811 for the Catholic pensioners of the Royal Hospital. This church was opened by the Duchesse d'Angouleme. Bentley built a new church in 1877–8 (61) although earlier work in the chapels in the south side built by A.W. Pugin and E.W. Pugin survive. The sanctuary itself is rather bleak following reordering. The elaborate altarpiece (moved to the north east chapel) and the pulpit are by Bentley. Other attractive fittings remain (62).

The Catholic tour-de-force is of course the **Oratory (The Church of the Immaculate Heart of Mary), Brompton Road, Kensington** (open daily, 7 am – 6 pm). It was founded by Father Faber and came to the present site in 1854. The church is by Herbert Gribble, 1878 to 1884. With its massive (later) dome dominating the area, it looks as if it was bodily plucked up from Rome and deposited in Kensington (64). The interior with its Corinthian pilasters is huge and can seat 2000 (65).The church is served by a college of secular Oratorian priests, currently numbering 10. The internal decoration is a slightly severe Italianate. The gigantic 17th century statues of the Apostles for instance come from Siena Cathedral. The triptych in the chapel of the English Martyrs is by Rex Whistler. Very recently a Calvary has been installed with newly carved, and rather moving Spanish statues, against a backdrop of Jerusalem by Alan Dodd (67). The Brompton Oratory was thankfully spared much destruction emanating from any misinterpretation of the decrees of the Second Vatican Council, and the numerous individual altars survive (66). A new altar has recently been set up for the Blessed John Henry Newman (68).

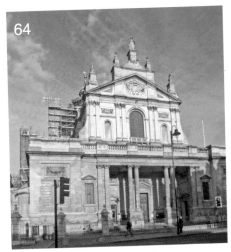

Our Lady of the Holy Souls, Bosworth Road, Kensal Town is a fairly simple red brick Gothic building by Bentley of 1882 for the Oblates of St Charles; the foundation stone of the church was laid by Cardinal Manning (69). It has been re-ordered several times and not much of Bentley's decoration survives. His pulpit has been recently uncovered. The reredos was designed by Father Arnold Baker (70). Attempts at restoration of the church are now under way.

The Most Holy Redeemer and St Thomas More, Cheyne Row is by Goldie of 1895 in red brick Italianate style (71). It was consecrated by Archbishop (later Cardinal) Bourne in 1906. The church was reordered after Vatican II by Canon Alfonso de Zulueta, Count of Torre Diaz, parish priest between 1945 and his death in 1980 (72). Alan Hopes, currently Bishop of East Anglia, was parish priest between 1997 and 2001. There are modern (2000) Stations of the Cross by Ken Thompson (73).

The Transfiguration, Kensal Rise was built as a Methodist church in 1899 and acquired as a Catholic Church in 1977. It was extensively refurbished by Anthony Delarue in 2010 . The exterior is red brick Decorated Gothic with stone facings (74). The interior is white with a blue roof and decent modern furnishings (75).

St Pius X, St Charles Square started life as in 1908 as the chapel of the St Charles Teacher Training College run by the nuns of the Sacred Heart. The building was designed by Percy Lamb and Robert O'Brien North as a classical building (77). Lamb was Bentley's Clerk of Works at Westminster Cathedral. The interior is baroque with a colourful reredos, blue at the time of writing being the dominant colour (76, 78). Following restoration in 1955 the building became a parish church.

Our Lady of Mount Carmel and St Simon Stock, Kensington Church Street (open daily) was built in 1954–9 by Sir Giles Scott in brick Gothic (79) to replace an earlier church by E.W. Pugin lost in the Blitz. The Carmelites started as a community of hermits on Mount Carmel in the 12th century. They arrived in England as mendicant friars in 1242. Three years later St Simon Stock was elected Prior General. He had a vision of the Blessed Virgin Mary who handed him the Carmelite habit, the Brown Scapular. The Discalced Carmelites (a Spanish refoundation by St Teresa of Avila) originally arrived on the site in 1864. The Stations of the Cross set in the tympana of the side aisles are by A. Stafford (80). Scott designed the reredos (81).

Ecclesiastical grants in Kensington and Chelsea made by the Heritage of London Trust

1988 £5000 for tower stonework at All Saints, Talbot Road, Kensington

1989 £7164 for stained glass at St Cuthbert, Philbeach Gardens, Kensington

1993 £7500 for restoration of painting at St Peter, Kensington Park Road

1994 £5000 for the statue of Cardinal Newman at the Brompton Oratory

1994 £2000 for railings at Holy Trinity, Brompton, Kensington

2001 £3000 for St Cuthbert, Philbeach Gardens, Kensington

2007 £2500 for St Cuthbert, Philbeach Gardens, Kensington

2007 £3000 for the façade of St Peter, Kensington

2009 £4000 to restore stone and brickwork at St Augustine, Queen's Gate

2013 £2000 for repair of clock faces at St Clement, Notting Dale

2013 £2000 for final repairs at St John the Baptist, Holland Road

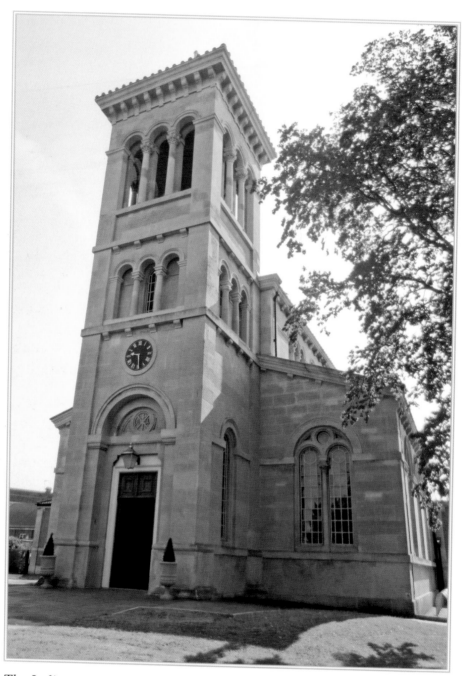

The Italianate campanile of St Raphael, Kingston

KINGSTON UPON THAMES

The Royal Borough of Kingston upon Thames was formed in 1965 out of the former boroughs of Kingston, Surbiton and the Maldens and Combe.

Kingston has Surrey, the River Thames and Richmond upon Thames to the west and north, and Wandsworth, Merton and Sutton to the east.

It stretches from the riverside to sandy and hilly heath land in the east and clay in the south.

Eight West Saxon kings either were or may have been crowned at Kingston – hence the name. These were Edward the Elder (902), Athelstan (925), Edmund (939), Eadred (946), Eadwig (956), Edgar (960), Edward the Martyr (975), and Aethelred (979). The Coronation Stone is now preserved in the market place.

In 1193 a bridge was built, the first upstream from London Bridge. Kingston received its first charter in 1200. Both King John and the Bishop of Winchester had residences in the town. In 1513 a Lollard was burnt. Cardinal Wolsey's construction of Hampton Court was important for Kingston where many associated with the palace built lodgings. There were skirmishes in the Civil War. Various minor industries grew up in Kingston – malting, brewing, tanning, fishing, brick-making.

In 1836 the London and South Western Railway went to Surbiton rather than Kingston, which preserved the latter from the development of housing for commuters. The west side of Surbiton was the one initially developed.

Galsworthy was brought up at Coombe Court in the hills north east of Kingston and this formed the model for Robin Hill, the house built for *The Man of Property*, Soames Forsyte, designed by Bossiney the architect and lover of his wife Irene. In *Three Men in a Boat* by Jerome K. Jerome the three rowers accompanied by Montmorency the Dog commenced their excursion from Kingston: "The quaint back streets of Kingston where they came down to the water's edge, looked quite picturesque in the flashing sunlight, the glinting river with its drifting barges, the wooded towpath, the trim-kept villas. I mused on Kingston or 'Kingeston' as it was called in the days Saxon 'kinges' were crowned there. Great Caesar crossed the river there and the Roman legions camped on its sloping upland."

Various artistic and literary luminaries spent time in Surbiton; these included John Millais, William Holman Hunt, Thomas Hardy and Enid Blyton.

In the 20th century Kingston was a major centre for the manufacture of military aircraft at Canbury Park – Sopwith Camels in the First World War and Hawker Hurricanes in the Second.

Chessington, Malden and Tolworth all lack excitement as destinations.

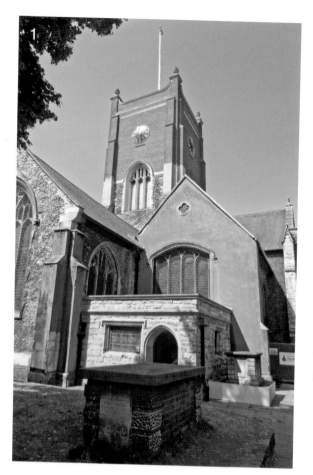

All Saints, Church Street, Kingston (open daily) is mostly 15th century with an 18th century brick tower (1). It was restored by both Brandon and Pearson in the 19th century. The high altar by Comper has been made obsolete by later re-ordering. A 14th century wall painting of St Blaise, a monument of Sir Anthony Benn, Recorder of London, who died in 1618, depicted in his lawyer's robes with ruff and cuffs (2), and much Victorian glass by Lavers & Barraud (3) all survive. A statue by Chantry commemorates Theodosia, Countess of Liverpool, wife of the Prime Minister, who died in 1825.

Christ Church, King Charles Road, Surbiton was built in 1862–3 by the local architect C.L. Luck (4), who worshipped in the church. The proposed tower was never built. Goodhart-Rendel described the west front as "chapelly". The church is brick with a polychromatic interior and ornate painted roofs (5, 6). It was re-ordered (in fact effectively wrecked) in 1979 with a pop music stage masquerading as the new sanctuary on the north side of the nave (7). There is apparently now some desire to make things better. Much good Victorian glass by Clayton & Bell (east window), Heaton, Butler & Bayne and Lavers & Barraud remains (8).

St Andrew, Maple Road, Surbiton was built by Blomfield in 1871 in yellow and red brick in a robust style (9). The tower was completed as a thanksgiving for the recovery of the Prince of Wales from illness. The church has a polychromatic brick interior (10) and stained glass by Lavers, Westlake & Co. (11).

The best church in the borough is probably the Catholic **St Raphael, Portsmouth Road, Kingston** (open Monday to Friday, 9 am to 11 am) built by Charles Parker of 1846–7 for Alexander Raphael, an Armenian immigrant who became an MP. The square campanile dominates this stretch of the Thames (12). The church is eclectic Italian Renaissance and has recently been well restored (14) It has gilded Ionian columns and marble fittings in the sanctuary. Louis-Philippe attended Mass here in his exile after 1848. An interesting memorial remembers Princess Ann of Loewenstein Wertheim, daughter of an Earl of Mexborough (13).

Ecclesiastical grants in Kingston upon Thames made by the Heritage of London Trust

2012   £2000 for restoration of Benn monument at All Saints, Kingston

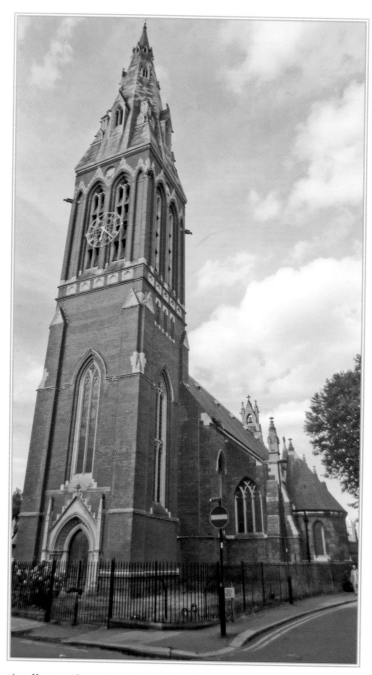

A tall stone broach spire and red brick tower by Street at St John the Divine, Vassall Road

LAMBETH

The London Borough of Lambeth was formed in 1965 out of the medieval parish together with parts of Streatham and Clapham.

Wandsworth lies to the west, Merton to the south west, Croydon to the south, Southwark to the east and the River Thames to the north.

Lambeth itself historically was divided between the Archbishops of Canterbury who purchased the site of Lambeth Palace in the late 12th century and the Princes of Wales / Dukes of Cornwall; the Kennington Estate was granted to the Black Prince in 1337 and is owned still by the Duchy of Cornwall. Lambeth Palace is an architectural mixture. The Lollards' Tower dates from 1435–40 and the Gatehouse was built by Cardinal Morton. Archbishop Juxon rebuilt the Great Hall after it was damaged in the Civil War. Blore did much work in the early 19th century.

The famous Vauxhall Pleasure Gardens started life in the late 17th century as the New Spring Gardens. Evelyn described them as "a very pretty contrived plantation". In the 18th century various buildings such as a Turkish tent were added. The gardens finally closed in 1859 and were built over.

The area along the river became industrialised over the years with factories making glass, pottery and Coade stone (otherwise known as lithodypyra); there was also the Lion Brewery. The rest of the area was increasingly covered with working class houses. The LCC built many council estates in the 20th century.

Lambeth has a number of buildings of national significance in addition to Lambeth Palace. There include Westminster Bridge (originally 1750), Vauxhall Bridge (originally 1816), Brixton Prison (1819), St Thomas's Hospital (1868–71 and later), Waterloo Station (1901–22), County Hall (1912–22), The Royal Festival Hall (1948–51) and The National Theatre (1961–76). Brixton was developed in the 19th century as was Herne Hill; in 1841 R. Brown talked of the latter as "a spot bespangled with suburban villas, most of which (are) in the Italianate style". Norwood with its woods and hill remained agricultural until the sale of the estate of Lord Thurlow in 1810. The Crystal Palace Railway opened in 1856.

Clapham was a separate village from London until c.1840. Thackeray wrote of it "Of all the pretty suburbs that still adorn our Metropolis there are few that exceed in charm Clapham Common". Clapham Park to the east of the Common was developed from 1825 by Thomas Cubitt with villas for wealthy City men; most of these have been demolished in favour of council housing. Streatham historically clustered around its parish church. The Russell Dukes of Bedford inherited land through marriage and built substantial if now vanished manor houses such as Bedford House and Russell House. Development came with the railway.

St Mary, Lambeth Road (museum open daily 10.30 am – 5 pm; 4 pm on Saturday), situated outside the gate of Lambeth Palace, is the only medieval church surviving in the borough. It is substantially of the 1370s (1). The church became redundant in 1972, having suffered bomb damage, and in 1979 was taken over by the Tradescant Trust as a Museum of Garden History. It has good proportions and a five bay nave. The church has many monuments including several to Archbishops of Canterbury (2). Archbishop Benson curiously installed a total immersion font. Captain Bligh of HMS Bounty lies in the churchyard (3).

Holy Trinity, Clapham Common (open Monday – Wednesday and Friday 9 am – 12 noon / Saturday 10 am – 1 pm) has been the parish church of Clapham since its construction in 1774–6 by Kenton Couse. It is a simple brick rectangle with a slightly later portico. A stone turret is surmounted by an octagonal cupola (4). The chancel is of 1903 by Beresford Pite. The church has some contemporary 18th century fittings (5). It suffered bomb damage in the Second World War. It was thereafter restored and some new glass installed (6). The Evangelical movement known as the Clapham Sect (of which William Wilberforce was a member) operated from the church.

St Paul, Rectory Grove, Clapham had been the earlier parish church which was demolished at the time of the construction of Holy Trinity. The present church was built in 1815 by C. Edmondes as a chapel of ease. It is of brick with a western pediment (7). It has a number of monuments now in the north transept, the most interesting of which is that to Sir Richard Atkyns, obit 1689, together with his wife and daughter, the latter dying at the age of eight. "Reader, survey with piteous eye the merciless hand of destinye which from a tender parent's breast with fury tore the welcome guest" (8). In 1691 effigies of his parents were added (9). The Atkyns became Lords of the Manor of Clapham in 1616.

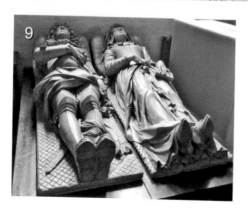

Lambeth is endowed with four Commissioners' churches, all begun in 1822, and named after the four Evangelists.

St John, Waterloo Road, Lambeth (open daily) is by Bedford. It has a Greek Doric portico with a thin spire ending in an obelisk (10). Summerson remarked "It was the kind of tower that Ictinus might have put on the Parthenon, if the Athenians had had the advantage

10

of belonging to the Church of England". The interior was mostly destroyed in the war. The font survived (11). There are curious mobile pulpits (12) and a Feibusch altar mural (13).

11

12

13

St Luke, West Norwood, Lambeth is by the same architect. It is well sited. There is a portico with Corinthian columns (15). Street was responsible subsequently for the chancel, now much altered (14).

St Mark, Clapham Road, Kennington is by Roper. It has a Doric four-column portico. The tower is surmounted by a cupola (16). The interior is dominated by Greek columns. There was much bomb damage in the war. The reredos survived and dates from Teulon's restoration of 1873–4 (17). The 17th century font came from St Michael, Wood Street. The Rev William Otter, subsequently Bishop of Chichester, was the first Vicar. Charlie Chaplin was a resident of the parish in early life, as was Field Marshal Montgomery whose father was Vicar.

St Matthew, St Matthew's Road, Brixton is by Pordern, again with a Doric four column portico. The tower is unusually at the east end (18, 19). The church was gutted for conversion in 1976. It is now shared with Babalou, a live music venue and the Brix, a community centre.

St Leonard, Streatham (open daily, 11 am – 2 pm; Friday until 1.30 pm) is the parish church of Streatham. The main body of the church is of 1830–31 by Parkinson (20). It is brick with Decorated windows. The tower base is medieval and the chancel Early English of the 1860s by Ferrey. The interior still has wooden galleries on cast iron columns. There was a bad fire in 1975. The church has a number of monuments of interest including a battered effigy of a knight (21) and a 17th century monument to John Howland, possibly by Van Nost (22); the former's descendants married into the family of the Dukes of Bedford, hence their adoption of the courtesy title of Viscount Howland. Dr Johnson's friend, Henry Thrale, the brewer, is also commemorated here.

23

24

Christ Church, Christchurch Road, Streatham Hill is rather remarkable. It was built 1840–2 by J. Wild in polychromatic brick as an Italianate church with porch and a tall campanile (23). The interior decoration was by Owen Jones; a certain amount survives in the sanctuary and elsewhere (24). The church has some reasonable modern stained glass (25). The nave columns are painted red (26).

25

26

Lambeth has four interesting surviving works of the Anglican Gothic Revival.

St Peter, Kennington Lane, Vauxhall (Open Tuesdays and Thursdays, 12 noon – 2 pm) of 1863– 4 is Pearson's first important urban church. It is located on what was the site of the Neptune Fountain in the Vauxhall Pleasure Gardens for the Reverend Robert Gregory. The foundation stone was laid by the Prince of Wales. The church is of brick with some polychromy (27). The interior is vaulted (28). Clayton & Bell designed the murals and stained glass. Many contemporary fittings survive (29). The capitals are elaborately carved.

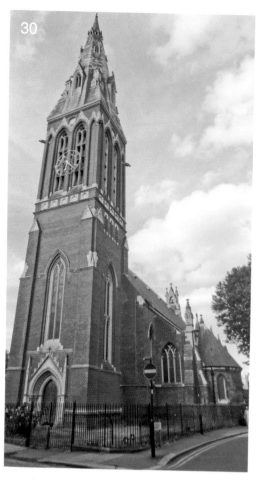

St John the Divine, Vassall Road, Lambeth is by Street 1870–4 . It has a west tower and broached stone spire, the tallest in south London; the church is of red brick (30, 32). The church has a broad nave and arcades. The chancel is apsidical. Betjeman said St John the Divine was the most magnificent church in south London. The church had originally been decorated in the 1890s by Bodley. After bombing in 1940 it was restored by Goodhart-Rendel. The 'Kelham' Rood is by Jagger and is on loan from the Society of the Sacred Mission (31). Some glass by Kempe survives.

St Peter, Leigham Park Road, Streatham is an excellent building (33). It is a tall church of polychromatic brick by R.C. Drew, a nephew of Butterfield. Fellowes Prynne was responsible for the baptistery in 1886–7. It was curiously reordered on a back-to-front basis by John Hall, now Dean of Westminster Abbey, during his incumbency. Numerous good fittings survive (34–37).

All Saints, West Dulwich is of 1887–91 by Fellowes Prynne. It is of red brick and has stone tracery with lancet windows (38, 40). It was badly damaged by fire in 2000 but was restored with a modern west entrance (41). Remembrances of the past survive (39, 42).

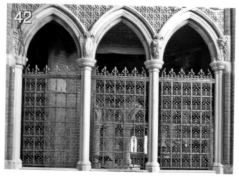

Christ Church, Brixton Road by Beresford Pite of 1899–1902 is quite different, being cruciform and Byzantine Romanesque. It is built of brown layered brick and Portland stone stripes (43). There is an outside pulpit (44). The church has a shallow sanctuary (45). The interior is domed. It has been subdivided and almost all the pews have gone (46).

47

48

St Margaret, Barcombe Avenue, Streatham is a grand red brick cruciform church built 1889–1907 by Rowlande Plumbe & Harvey (47). The reredos and various other fittings are by Caroe (50), and the church has much stained glass in the building (48, 49).

49

50

Holy Spirit, Narbonne Avenue, Clapham was built in 1912–13 by Burke-Downing as a tall Gothic church (51, 52), with a whitewashed interior.

St Anselm, Kennington Road was designed in 1911 by Adshead & Ramsey but not built until 1931. It is in a tall neo-Byzantine style of yellow brick (54) with a simple white interior. A baldacchino stands over the high altar (55). The font is interesting (53).

56

Holy Redeemer, Streatham Vale is by Martin Travers and T.F.W. Grant of 1931–2 and apparently has Baroque fittings. The church is currently locked and inaccessible (56).

St Agnes, St Agnes Place, Kennington was built after the war to replace the damaged, great church of the same name by George Gilbert Scott Junior. The new building is serviceable and red brick (59), but inside are to be found some surviving fittings by Temple Moore and others, some of which have recently returned from the Holy Spirit, Southsea (57, 58, 60).

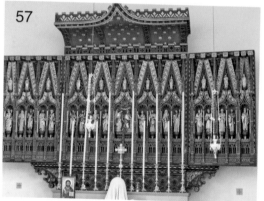

57

58

59

60

St James, Park Hill, Clapham Park (open Friday, 11 am – 5 pm) is a yellow brick, somewhat traditionalist building of 1957–8 by Cachemaille Day (61).

There are various Catholic churches of interest in Lambeth.

Our Lady of Victories, Clapham Park Road is a building of 1849–51 for the Redemptorists by William Wardell with later work by Bentley. The church was opened by Cardinal Wiseman in 1851 and consecrated the next year (64), the debt having been paid off by Father Edmund Douglas, a wealthy convert who had joined the Redemptorists. It has a spire and a six-bay (unwrecked) interior (65). It has excellent fittings, some by Bentley (62, 63). The church has a Pugin window, and also later glass including a rather fetching representation of Eve (66).

Corpus Christi, Brixton Hill was begun in 1886 by Bentley for the Flemish Father Hendrick Van Doorne in a very tall gothic style modelled on the Sainte Chapelle in Paris (67). The material is striped brick and stone. Only the chancel and transepts were built (69). The church has some excellent fittings (68, 70). From 1980 to 2005 the parish was looked after by the Society of Jesus.

71

72

The Church of the English Martyrs, Mitcham Lane, Streatham is by Purdie in 1892. It is large, spired and built in Decorated style in Kentish ragstone (71, 72). It has much statuary (73) inside, and Victorian glass mainly by Hardman (74). It was opened by Cardinal Vaughan in 1893. In 1965 a new transeptal chapel was opened to cater for increasing Mass attendance.

74

73

St Anne, Kennington Lane, Vauxhall (1903–7 by Walters) is a red brick church with a distinctive saddleback tower for Father (later Bishop) William Brown (75). The church was opened by Bishop Bourne (then of Southwark but later of Westminster) in 1903 and cost £13,000. It has a stencilled Arts and Crafts chancel (76) and richly decorated side chapels (77).

St Bede, Clapham Park is one of the many churches built with the help of Miss Frances Ellis who was a major benefactor to the Diocese of Southwark in the early years of the 20th century. The church is attached to the stucco villa where she lived, and which is now the Presbytery (78). The architect is unknown but it was built 1905–7 in an economic classical style. Inside Mayer of Munich designed a statue of the Queen of Heaven. The church nowadays has close links with the Latin Mass Society.

Ecclesiastical grants in Lambeth made by the Heritage of London Trust

1984 £5000 for the installation of window at All Saints, Clapham Park
1988 £4120 for stained glass repair at St John the Divine, Vassall Road
1989 £5000 for railings at St Michael, Stockwell Park Road
1990 £3000 for the external pulpit of Christ Church, Brixton Road
1991 £10,000 for stained glass window at Corpus Christi RC Church, Brixton Hill
1994 £10000 for wall painting restoration at St Peter, Vauxhall
1996 £5000 for external bronze wreaths at St John, Waterloo Road
1997 £5000 for restoration of Owen Jones murals at Christchurch, Streatham
1997 £1000 for restoration of interior frieze at St John, Waterloo Road
1999 £3000 for restoration of chest tombs at St Leonard, Streatham
2000 £5000 for classical porch of St John the Evangelist, Clapham Road
2000 £2500 for the clock at St Matthew, Brixton
2002 £3500 for stonework at St Paul, Clapham
2002 £3000 for work on the font at St John, Angell Town, Brixton
2004 £4000 for the external pulpit of Christ Church, Brixton Road
2006 £6000 for the spire of Holy Trinity, Tulse Hill
2007 £2500 for hard landscaping at All Saints, Rosendale Road, Brixton

The fine entrance of St Paul, High Street, Deptford

LEWISHAM

The London Borough of Lewisham was formed in 1965 out of the former boroughs of Lewisham and Deptford.

Lewisham has Southwark to the west, Bromley to the south, Greenwich to the east and a small stretch of the River Thames to the north.

Lewisham historically was a village on the road running south. The name means "a house close to the meadows". In the Middle Ages the manor belonged to the Abbey of St Peter in Ghent. In the late 17th century it was purchased by George Legge, Baron Dartmouth; in 1711 his son was created Earl of Dartmouth and Viscount Lewisham. The arrival of the railway in 1849 turned it into a working class suburb, residential in the main rather than industrial.

South of Lewisham itself there are a number of other suburbs. Lee was the most ancient village. Blackheath started life as a small cluster of houses called Dowager's Bottom. Known at one stage as a notorious haunt of highwaymen, the area became developed with detached houses in the late 18th and early 19th centuries. The most interesting house is The Pagoda which was built by Sir William Chambers c 1760 for the 4th Earl of Cardigan who lived at Montague House nearby. In the 1780s it was owned by the Duke of Buccleuch. There are hills in the south west of the borough. Sydenham was a minor spa from the 17th to the 19th centuries. It became a smart suburb because of its proximity to Crystal Palace in the middle of the 19th century. Forest Hill has the Horniman Museum of 1902 designed by Harrison Townsend in a mixture of Arts and Crafts and Art Nouveau style.

Deptford in the north of the borough is very different. It was originally the "deep ford" over the Ravensbourne. After the Conquest it was granted to Maminot, Bishop of Lisieux. It was a modest fishing village in the Middle Ages. In 1513 Henry VIII set up the Royal Dockyard at Deptford. It had a glamorous existence for a couple of centuries. In 1581 Elizabeth I knighted Francis Drake there aboard the Golden Hind. Christopher Marlowe was stabbed to death in 1597 at the youthful age of 29. Samuel Pepys was a frequent visitor as Clerk to the Navy Board. John Evelyn owned Sayes Court (described by Pepys as "a most beautiful place") from 1652. Peter the Great stayed there for three months in 1698 and spent most of the time getting drunk. The house was demolished in 1728–9. The dockyard declined from the late 18th century with increasing competition from Chatham, Plymouth and Portsmouth. It was closed in 1869. From 1871 until the First World War the site was used as the Foreign Cattle Market. Deptford was a station on the London to Greenwich Railway, London's first, opened in 1836. In the Second World War a V-2 rocket exploded at Woolworths next to Deptford Town Hall, killing 160.

St Mary, Lewisham High Street is the parish church of Lewisham. There is late Perpendicular work at the base of the tower; the top is 18th century (1). The 18th century interior was restored rather inadequately by Blomfield (2). The church has a number of 18th and 19th century monuments, one by Flaxman of Mary Lushington who died in 1797 and some modern stained glass (3).

St Nicholas, Deptford Green also has a late medieval tower but the church is of 1697 by C. Stanton (4). It was bombed in the war although some contemporary woodwork survives (6, 7) as do various monuments including one to Roger Boyle, Earl of Cork, who died in 1615 (5). Christopher Marlowe is commemorated by a modern memorial (8).

TO THE IMMORTAL MEMORY OF
CHRISTOPHER MARLOWE
WHO MET A TRAGIC DEATH
NEAR THIS SPOT ON THE 30th
MAY 1593. THIS TABLET IS ERECTED
IN 1957 BY THE ASSOCIATION
OF MEN OF KENT AND KENTISH
MEN TO REPLACE AN EARLIER
MEMORIAL UNVEILED BY
SIR FRANK BENSON ON THE
3rd JUNE 1919 AND DESTROYED
BY ENEMY ACTION IN 1940

Cut is the branch that might have grown full straight

The Ascension, Dartmouth Row, Blackheath started life as a chapel of ease for the Earls of Dartmouth in 1697. It is an unassuming brick building with a cupola (10). The apse with its rich decoration dates from 1750 (9). The nave was rebuilt in the 19th century and subsequently suffered war damage.

The greatest church in Lewisham is undoubtedly **St Paul, High Street, Deptford** (open Saturday morning). It stands in a wide open space and was built by Thomas Archer in 1712–30 under the Fifty New Churches Act of 1711 in a splendid Baroque style. Archer combined a semi-circular portico of tall columns (based on S. Maria della Pace in Rome) with a circular tower above it (12). The interior (based on S. Agnese in Rome)

is cruciform with giant Corinthian columns, an apsidical sanctuary and good plasterwork (13). The fittings do not match the architecture. The church has a number of monuments (11) and statues. From 1969 to 1992 the famous Father David Diamond was parish priest.

St Margaret, Lee was built in 1839–41 by John Brown of Norwich (14) to replace an earlier church on the other side of the road (15). It has lavish furnishings and glass (16, 17). It was remodelled in 1875 by Brooks who lengthened the chancel. The reredos was carved by Earp.

All Saints, Blackheath is by Ferrey of 1857–67 in Decorated style. It is built in Kentish ragstone. With its spire on the southern side it is a major landmark on Blackheath Common, surrounded as it is entirely by grass (18). The vestries and porch were added by Blomfield in 1890 and 1899 respectively. It has good high church fittings (19–22). The Patron is the Vicar of St Mary's, Lewisham, from which parish the new parish was originally carved out.

St Stephen, Lewisham High Street is by Sir George Gilbert Scott in 1865 in an Early English style, in Kentish ragstone (23). The high altar is by

Westlake and Buckeridge provided the alabaster reredos (24). Brooks was responsible for the chancel rood and a small amount of Clayton & Bell glass survived a bomb in World War II.

St Andrew, Sandhurst Road, Catford is 1904 by P.A. Robson. It is in red brick without a tower and on a hill (25). It has a wide interior with brick piers. The aisles are narrow with buttresses inside. Martin Travers designed some excellent glass between the Wars (26–28). The nave aisle is now divided off.

St Hilda, Stondon Park, Forest Hill is Arts and Crafts Gothic of 1907 by Greenaway & Newberry (30). It suffered a degree of damage in the Second World War. It has a high church tradition (29).

St John, South End, Bromley Road, Lewisham is a large Perpendicular brick church of 1928 by Sir Charles Nicholson, here photographed on a misty morning (33). The church (32) has a 20th century monument (31) and stained glass by Karl Parsons and furnishings by John Hayward. The attractive old chapel of 1824 with cupola and Tuscan porch is now used as the parish hall.

The Catholic church of **St Saviour and SS John the Baptist and Evangelist, Lewisham High Street** is a red brick Italian building of 1909 by Kelly and Dickie (34). A large open red brick Tuscan pediment with statues of St Peter and St Patrick dominates the exterior. The 126-foot campanile of 1929 is crowned by a figure of Christ (36). The church has much marble decoration inside, here seen in the southern Sacred Heart Chapel (35). The church was hit by a bomb in 1940.

Ecclesiastical grants in Lewisham made by the Heritage of London Trust

1983-5	£17,000 for the restoration of the outside steps at St Paul, Deptford
1984	£1000 for the restoration of the font at St Stephen, Lewisham
1999	£3000 for the restoration of the clock on spire at All Saints, Blackheath
2003	£1500 for restoration of tomb at St Bartholomew, Sydenham
2004	£5000 for restoration of pulpit at St Paul, Deptford
2007	£1000 for restoration of west window at St John, Deptford
2008	£3000 for organ case at St Andrew, Catford
2009	£2000 for restoration of clock at St Bartholomew, Sydenham

East Anglian Decorated by F.A. Walter for the Jesuits at the Sacred Heart, Wimbledon

MERTON

The London borough of Merton was formed in 1965 out of the borough of Wimbledon and the urban district councils of Merton and Mitcham.

The borough has Wandsworth and Lambeth to the north, Croydon to the east, Sutton to the south and Richmond upon Thames to the west.

In Domesday Book Wimbledon is mentioned as part of the manor of Mortlake. The Manor of Wimbledon belonged to the Church until 1398 when Thomas Arundel, Archbishop of Canterbury, fell out with Richard II. In 1588 Thomas Cecil, Earl of Exeter, built a now vanished house. Wimbledon Park House was built for Earl Spencer by Henry Holland in 1799–1802. This survived until 1949. Wimbledon has some 17th century houses of interest but is essentially a wealthy 19th century suburb with housing to match. One surviving 18th century house of interest is Cannizaro House, which was leased from 1785 to 1806 by Henry Dundas, Viscount Melville; from 1801 to 1804 it was used by Henry Addington as Prime Minister. It is now a hotel. The arrival of the London and South Western Railway in 1838 led to a rapid expansion in population. The Apostolic Nunciature of the Roman Catholic Church overlooks Wimbledon Common.

Merton is mentioned as 'Meretown' in Domesday Book when it belonged to William the Conqueror. Merton was the site of an Augustinian priory founded in 1114. Thomas a Becket and Nicholas Breakspear (Pope Adrian IV) were both educated there. The Statute of Merton in 1235 *inter alia* set out the rights of landlords to enclose common land. Walter de Merton, sometime Bishop of Rochester, founded Merton College in Oxford in 1274. The Priory was dissolved in 1538. For a number of centuries there had been water mills along the River Wandle and in 1660 a silk mill and bleaching works were in operation. Calico printing began in the 1720s. William Morris opened a works at Merton Abbey Mills in 1881 and Liberty & Co in Regent Street had an adjacent works. Merton was however mainly rural at the start of the 19th century. In 1802 Admiral Nelson bought Merton Place and lived there intermittently with Emma Hamilton. After his death at Trafalgar in 1805 his clerical elder brother was created Earl Nelson and Viscount Merton. The house was demolished in 1821. The fields of Merton predominantly survived until the first two decades of the 20th century when large-scale residential development arrived.

Mitcham ('Michelham') and Morden are both mentioned in Domesday Book, the former belonging to the Canons of Bayeux and the latter to Westminster Abbey. Both remained rural until well into the 20th century when the Northern Line arrived. Mitcham was once known for both lavender fields and calico printing.

The earliest church by date in the borough is **St Mary, Church Lane, Merton** (open Monday to Friday 8 am – 12 noon / Saturday 10 am –12 noon / all day Sunday) (2). The nave was built between 1114 and 1125 although it is now much Victorianised (4). The chancel is 13th century. It has a 15th century porch. Morris (5) and other (6) glass is to be found as is a monument of 1597 to Gregory Lovell, Cofferer of the Household to Queen Elizabeth I, and his wives (3). In the large churchyard an elaborate doorway of c 1175 survives from the vanished Merton Priory (1).

St Mary, Church Road, Wimbledon ("open when parish office is") is the ancient parish church of Wimbledon. Certain medieval stone work survives. The rest was rebuilt in the 18th and 19th centuries, in the latter case by Sir George Gilbert Scott. The roof is decorated (7). Sir Edward Cecil, Viscount Wimbledon, who died in 1638, has a monument (11). The church has some 14th century glass of St George (8) and some Morris glass (10). A monument to James Perry obit 1821 erected by the Fox Club is of a seated figure below a bust of Charles James Fox. The large mausoleum of Sir Joseph Bazalgette, the engineer of London's sewage system, lies at the east end of the churchyard; a grateful populace should cover it in flowers.

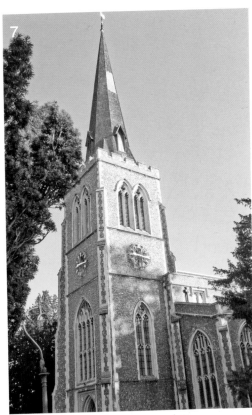

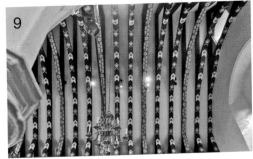

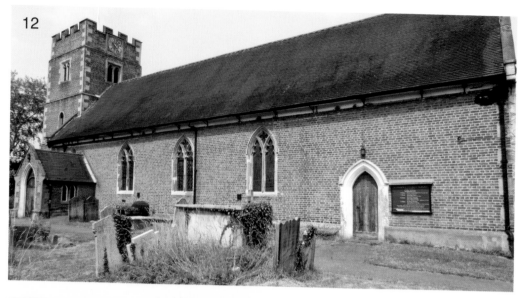

St Lawrence, London Road, Morden was built in 1636 and is red brick with a tower (12). The nave and chancel are one. The 17th century painted glass in the east window shows Moses and Aaron with the Ten Commandments between them (14). The church has 18th century fittings such as the wooden pulpit and a number of monuments (13). The one on the left with a bust is that of Sir Peter Leheup, a Whig place-man (1699–1777). Of Huguenot descent he was Underclerk of the Treasury 1721–52 and Clerk 1752–5 but had to resign in 1755 when he was caught running an 'irregular' lottery (he abducted £1000 for his own use) to raise funds for the purchase by the British Museum of the Harleian and Sloane collections.

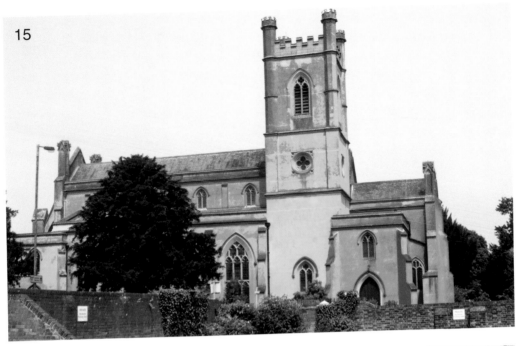

15

St Peter and St Paul, Church Road, Mitcham was rebuilt in 1819–21 by George Smith (15) in vaguely Perpendicular style with attractive vaults (16). It has an early 18th century monument to Sir Ambrose and Lady Cowley probably by Rysbrack (18). The church has a fair amount of Victorian glass (17).

16

17

18

Christ Church, Copse Hill, Wimbledon is by Teulon of 1859–60. It has a muscular tower above the chancel (19). The nave is long without a clerestorey (20). The reredos is by Shearman. The tracery is elaborate (21).

T.G. Jackson built one church in the borough. **St John, Spencer Hill, Wimbledon** (1875) is towerless red brick (22). The inside is now whitened. The church has one window by Morris. Travers was responsible for the reredos of the Lady Chapel (23).

There are two Catholic churches of interest in the borough.

One is the **Sacred Heart, Edge Hill, Wimbledon** (open daily; entrance via the shop), built for the Jesuits by F.A. Walter in 1886–1901 (24 and p.246). This large church is in flint and stone, and long, ending in an ambulatory leading to three chapels (25). The style is Decorated. The interior has much stone decoration (26), a good rood (27) and an interesting monument to Caroline Currie of 1904 (28).

The other is **St Winefride, Latimer Road, Wimbledon**, by the same architect (1905), which is red brick and white outside (29). It has a fine polychromatic brick interior (31, 32) and good fittings including a blueish font (30).

Ecclesiastical grants in Merton made by the Heritage of London Trust

1987   £250 for hatchments at St Mary, Merton
1988   £3250 for heraldic shields at St Mary, Merton
1989   £6100 for north west porch of St Peter and St Paul, Mitcham
1998   £3350 for St Peter and St Paul, Mitcham
1993   £2510 for stonework at Raynes Park Methodist Church
1996   £2500 for Kempe stained glass at All Saints, South Wimbledon

Eve offers Adam the forbidden fruit in Victorian window at St Chad and St Andrew, St Andrew's Road, Plaistow

NEWHAM

The London Borough of Newham was formed in 1965 out of East Ham and West Ham, both previously in Essex. The name had to be invented as neither constituent part was prepared to cede to the other in naming terms.

It is bounded by Barking in the east, Redbridge and Waltham Forest to the north, Hackney and Tower Hamlets to the west and the River Thames to the south.

West Ham is separated from Tower Hamlets by the River Lea. The ancient village fairly early on yielded commercial supremacy to Stratford where the main road to Romford crossed the Lea. The area was dominated in the Middle Ages by the Cistercian Abbey of Stratford Langthorne. The mills originally established by the Abbey along the Lea attracted heavy chemical industries in the 19th century. A massive railway engineering works was established at Stratford in 1847. The Abbey Mills Pumping Station (for sewage) was built in 1865-8 by Charles Driver for Sir Joseph Bazalgette. West Ham, Forest Gate and Plaistow were all more residential. Canning Town was known for the Thames Iron Works at Bow Creek and for the huge Brunner Mond armaments works. An explosion at the latter in the First World War killed 73. All this industry attracted extremely heavy bombing in the Blitz in the Second World War with the result that some 14,000 homes in West Ham were destroyed by enemy action. Canning Town is the most deprived ward in the most deprived borough in the country.

East Ham was originally owned by Westminster Abbey. It remained rural for longer than West Ham. Between 1850 and 1981(when the final dock closed) it was dominated by the Royal Docks. These were vast, and stretched three miles along the River Thames. The freight railway in the middle of the 19th century brought industry – rubber to Silver Town, ferry, railway and telegraph cable works to North Woolwich and the Gas Light and Coke Co large gasworks to Beckton. The Royal Victoria Dock was built in 1864 and the Royal Albert Dock to the east in 1875–80. The Port of London Authority finally added the King George V dock in 1912. A cold stores, a tobacco complex, flour mills and shipbuilding repair facilities followed the building of the docks. The setting up of the container port further downstream in Tilbury together with the strike-prone working practices of the unions brought the Royal Docks to an end. The London City Airport has been built on part of the George V Dock.

West Ham United (founded 1895) Football Stadium is rather confusingly situated in East Ham.

Little Ilford and Manor Park to the north of the Docks are more residential. The vast City of London Cemetery was built in Little Ilford in the 1860s.

Away from the centre of London, more of the medieval has survived than might have been anticipated. **St Mary Magdalen, High Street South, East Ham** is essentially of 1130. It is situated in a large (9.5 acres) slightly ragged churchyard near the docks. It is mainly but not exclusively built in Kentish ragstone; the squat tower is probably 13th century (1). The apse, chancel, blind arcading on the north wall and unaisled nave are all Norman (3). An early 17th century painted alabaster monument to Edward Nevill, Earl of Westmoreland and his family dominates the chancel in a very protestant way (2). The font is of 1639. The wooden figure of St Mary Magdalen, given in the 1930s, is Flemish.

All Saints, Church Street, West Ham (normally open Mondays to Fridays, 10 am – 12 noon during summer months) has Norman walls but a 13th century aisle. The tower is 15th century (4). The roof is of 1500. The church was restored in 1866 by George Gilbert Scott, who was responsible for the elaborate reredos. Various monuments can be seen in the church. The grandest of these is that by Stanton to Sir Thomas Foote who died in 1688, the first Lord Mayor of London under the Commonwealth; he was knighted unavailingly by Cromwell but received a baronetcy at the Restoration (5). Another monument is that of 1743 to James Cooper and his wife; it is not signed (6). The east window is by Clayton & Bell. Sir William Reynolds-Stephens designed the War Memorial window in the north aisle (7). *Lavers & Barraud*

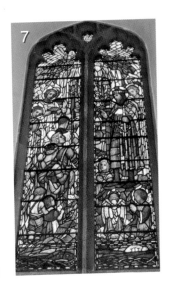

St Mary, Church Road, Little Ilford is a small 12th century survival. The nave is 12th century and the chancel 17th century (8). Georgian fittings survive (9). The 18th Lethieullier chapel lies to the north of the nave with contemporary monuments to the family (10). The most famous rector was the Elizabethan poet Thomas Newton, described in 1585 by the Puritans as "a great drunkard".

There are three interesting Anglican churches of the Gothic Revival in the borough.

The first is **St Mark, North Woolwich Road and Connaught Road, Silvertown** (open during performances) by Teulon in 1860–2 (11). It is now the Brick Lane Music Hall. It is distinguished by its polychromatic (red, black and yellow) brick work, its muscular tower over the chancel and its apse.

The second is **St Chad and St Andrew, St Andrew's Road, Plaistow**. This was built by James Brooks in 1868–79 in 13th century Gothic in ragstone (12). There is an apsidical east end. The proportions are no longer obvious since the church was sub-divided in 1982–5. The large reredos has vanished. A statue of St Andrew stands outside (13) and there is Victorian glass inside; here Eve offers Adam the forbidden fruit (14).

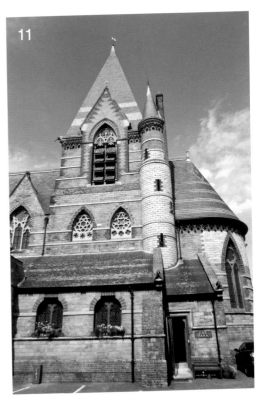

St Barnabas, Browning Road, Little Ilford is by Bucknall & Comper, 1900–9. The front away from the road is brick with stone Perpendicular windows (15). Part of Comper's high altar remains and the glass of the east window (1954) is by him (16, 17).

St Philip and St James, Plaistow is a stock brick building of 1954–5 with a north west tower by Gibbons (18). The interior is plain with white walls (19).

Of Roman Catholic churches, **St Francis of Assisi, Grove Crescent Road** has a brick front (21). It was built in 1868. Pevsner attributes the building to E.W. Pugin but this is probably a misattribution. The sanctuary of 1931–2 is certainly by W.C. Mangan (20). The figure of Christ crucified (22) comes from here. The Franciscans took over the running of the church in 1873.

St Margaret and All Saints, Canning Town (open mornings) is by Tasker of 1878 with a yellow stock brick exterior (23). The donors included Cardinal Manning and the Duke of Norfolk. It has a vaulted interior (24) and a marbled chancel (25).

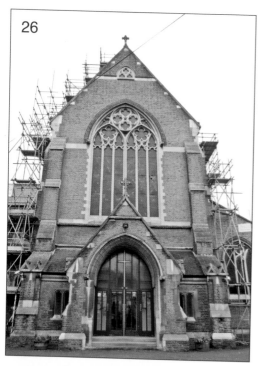

St Antony of Padua, Forest Gate (open mornings and Tuesday afternoons) is a vast brick church of 1884–91 built by Pugin & Pugin for the Franciscans, who finally left in 2001 (26). The church is large and Early English and was bleakly reordered in the 1960s (27). The Lady Altar was designed by P.P. Pugin. Good glass by Hardman and others survives, including a window of Eve being evicted from the Garden of Eden by the angel with the flaming sword NB the red serpent (28). There was some minor bomb damage in 1942. The French Community of St John (founded 1975) now runs the parish and intends over time to restore the church to some of its former glory.

In 1929–31 W.C. Mangan built **The Chapel of the Sacred Heart of Jesus at St Mary's Convent, Bethell Avenue, Canning Town**, for the Franciscan Sisters of Mary; it is now used by the parish of Canning Town. The slightly dull exterior is Lombard Romanesque (29). The interior is Renaissance and marbled. The large nave has a barrel vault above five arcades on Corinthian columns. The marble high altar is sumptuous (30).

Ecclesiastical grants in Newham made by the Heritage of London Trust

1990	£3000 for railings at St John's Stratford
1991	£7500 for church tower of St Mary Magdalene, East Ham
2003	£3500 for 13th century murals at St Mary Magdalene, East Ham
2007	£3000 for restoration of north turret at All Saints, West Ham
2007	£3000 for brickwork of the Memorial Baptist Church in Plaistow
2010	£500 for the restoration of bells at the Memorial Baptist Church in Plaistow

The spectacular monument to Sir Josiah Child in St Mary, Overton Drive, Wanstead

REDBRIDGE

The Borough of Redbridge consists of the former boroughs of Ilford, Wanstead and Woodford with parts of Chigwell and Dagenham, all formerly in Essex. The borough takes its name from the Red Bridge over the River Roding. The land is flat. Epping and Hainault Forests lay to the east of the borough

It is bounded by Barking and Dagenham to the east and south, by Havering to the east, by Essex to the north and by Newham to the west.

Ilford is mentioned in Domesday Book as 'Ilefort'. It belonged in the Middle Ages to the powerful Abbey of Barking. Ilford was on the main road to Colchester. It remained mainly rural until the 19th century. The 18th century Valentines house is now owned by the council. The railway came in 1839, and brick works, cement works, coal yards and steam laundries followed. In 1879 the Ilford Photographic Company was set up and only ceased trading early in the 21st century. Plessey moved to Ilford in 1919; in 1955 it was still employing 15,000 workers.

Wanstead is now mainly a residential suburb but in an earlier age was famous for the vanished Wanstead House, one of the major architectural losses of London. It had originally been a royal manor under the Tudors with for instance Robert Dudley, Earl of Leicester, being appointed Keeper. It was bought in 1673–4 by Sir Josiah Child. His son Sir Richard (Earl Tylney) in 1715 commissioned the building of a new Palladian house designed by Colen Campbell. This was completed in 1722. In 1784 the house was inherited by the Tylney-Long baronets. In 1812 Catherine, the daughter of the last baronet, was ill-advised enough to marry William Wellesley-Pole (subsequently 4th Earl of Mornington). He was a spendthrift who fled his creditors in 1822; his trustees had Wanstead House demolished three years later. The Park was sold to the City of London Corporation in 1881. A chain of ponds, a temple, a grotto and gateposts survive.

Woodford is an ancient settlement on the edge of Epping Forest. It is mentioned in Domesday Book as 'wdefort' and the name unsurprisingly means the ford (over the River Roding) in or by the wood. In the Middle Ages the manor was owned by the Canons of the Holy Cross at Waltham Abbey. After the Reformation it was owned by a variety of wealthy individuals including Lord Saye and Sele. In 1710 the manor was purchased by Sir Richard Child of Wanstead House (qv). An attempt was made in the early18th century to set up a minor spa. Rich city merchants built houses in Woodford as rural retreats; one survival is Hurst House, built for a brewer in 1714. Sydney Smith was born in Woodford, and William Morris spent his child-hood there. The railway arrived in 1856 but true suburbia only arrived in the 1930s. Sir Winston Churchill was MP for Woodford 1945–1964, and there is a statue to him on the green.

The earliest major ecclesiastical building to survive is that of **St Mary, Overton Drive, Wanstead** by Thomas Hardwick dating from 1790. The church stood next to the vanished Palladian house of the Earls Tylney. It is a rectangular classical building with a lofty porch held up on a pair of Doric pillars. The church has a high bell turret (1). The interior is painted white and is unspoilt with its box pews, high galleries and three-decker pulpit decorated with palm trees (2). The high point of the church is the grandiloquent monument to Sir Josiah Child of 1699 by Van Nost. Child is wearing a curious combination of Roman apparel and a wig, his son Bernard lying at his feet (3). Mourning women sit on either side (4) and two cherubs blowing golden trumpets. He was Governor of the East India Company, and described by John Evelyn as "a sudden monied man".

St Mary, High Road, Woodford
(open 10 am – 12 noon, Monday to
Friday) is essentially of 1817 by
Charles Bacon, albeit with a brick west
tower of 1708 with thickset pinnacles
(5). It was burnt down by an arsonist in
1969, but was restored by John Phillips
in 1971–2 (7). It has a good selection of
Tudor and later monuments including
one to Rowland Elrington and his wife
of 1595 (6). There are later ones to Elizabeth Elwes (obit 1625) and David
Bosanquet (obit 1741). The Blessed
John Larke, Rector in the 1520s, was
martyred at Tyburn in 1544 for defying
the supremacy of Henry VIII in matters
of religion.

Redbridge has two interesting Anglican Gothic revival churches.

The first is **Christ Church, Wanstead Place**. It was built in the 1860s as a chapel of ease by the rector of Wanstead and has later additions by George Gilbert Scott (nave and north aisle) and others (8). The interior is large with much late 19th century woodwork. The English Altar came from Nuremburg via Ely Theological College in 1974. There is stained glass in the east window by Kempe & Tower of Christ and some angels (9, 10).

The second is **St Alban, Albert Road, Ilford** by J.E.K & J.P. Cutts. Built in 1899 it is a big, decent red brick Gothic church (11). High Church fittings including the altar of 1900 (12) can be found. The late 17th/early 18th century pulpit came in 1949 from All Souls College, Oxford.

St Andrew, Ilford is a startling work. It was built 1923–4 by Sir Herbert Baker as a memorial to Bishop Edgar Jacobs of St Alban's. It is a red brick classical building with a western fleche (13). The small apsed western baptistery has a bronze figure of Peace by Sir Charles Wheeler surmounted on it (15). Karl Parsons was responsible for some of the beautiful glowing stained glass windows (17, 18). The quality of the brick work can be seen in the baptistery (14, 16).

There are two Catholic churches in Redbridge church worthy of mention.

The first is **St Thomas of Canterbury, High Road, Woodford**. It is Early English, a large Franciscan church of 1895 in red brick by Canon Scoles (19). Its elaborate furnishings were, alas, removed during a reordering in 1976 with only the high stained glass in the aisle walls a memory of past glories; many of these are of Franciscan saints: St Margaret of Cortona, St Rose of Viterbo, Blessed Agnellus of Pisa, St John Forrest, St Leonard of Port Maurice, St Didacus, St John Capistrano, St Bonaventure, St Pascal Baylon, etc. In the south east there is a slab to Henrietta Pelham-Clinton, convert Duchess of Newcastle, who died in 1913 and who paid for much of the church at the request of Cardinal Vaughan. She is represented as St Mary Magdalen in the life-size Calvary (20). She was the granddaughter and heiress of Thomas Hope of Deepdene (1769–1831) and niece of the ecclesiologist Alexander Beresford Hope. Her husband as Earl of Lincoln had had to flee the country in 1860 to escape his gambling debts. He fortuitously married her in Paris in 1861 and had his debts settled with an income of £50,000 per annum being given to the couple. He died in 1879. After her conversion she became a Franciscan tertiary.

The second is **St Peter and St Paul, Ilford**. The church is of 1898–9 by R.L. Curtis (21). Basil Clarke described the odd capitals of the arcades as "very horrid" (22).

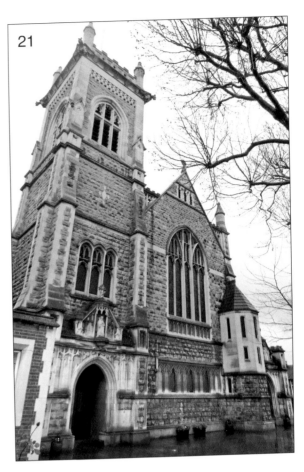

Ecclesiastical grants in Redbridge made by the Heritage of London Trust

1991 £2200 for repairs at St Mary, Wanstead
1995 £2000 for the Wood family sarcophagus at St Mary, Woodford
2007 £5000 for the Hospital Chapel of St Mary and St Thomas of Canterbury, Ilford
2008 £5000 for St Mary the Virgin, Great Ilford
2013 £2000 for tiled parapets at St Gabriel, Aldersbrook

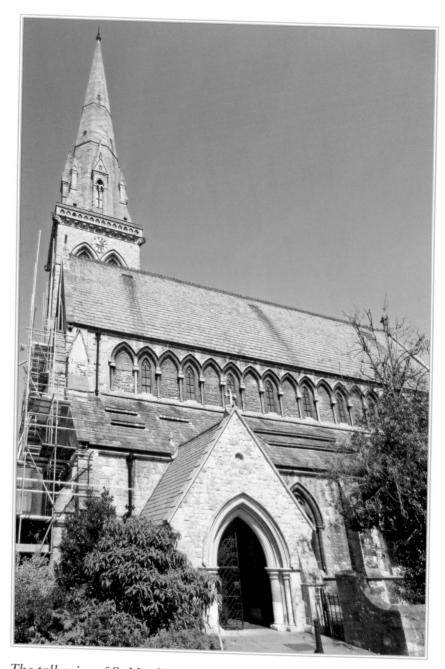

The tall spire of St Matthias near the top of Richmond Hill dominates the skyline for miles around.

RICHMOND UPON THAMES

The London Borough of Richmond upon Thames was formed in 1965 out of the Surrey boroughs of Barnes and Richmond and the Middlesex borough of Twickenham. It is the only London borough to straddle both sides of the River Thames with Hampton, Teddington and Twickenham one side and Ham, Petersham, Richmond, Kew, East Sheen and Barnes on the other.

The borough is bounded to the south by Kingston upon Thames and Surrey, to the west by Surrey, to the north by Hounslow, to the east by Hammersmith & Fulham and Wandsworth.

Richmond (or Sheen as it was originally known) attracted royal interest from early on. Edward III died at his favourite palace there. Henry V rebuilt it and set up a Carthusian monastery. The palace was again rebuilt by Henry VII and renamed after his earldom. Elizabeth I died at Richmond. The palace decayed towards the end of the 17th century. Hampton Court was leased by Cardinal Wolsey from the Hospitaller Knights of St John. He built the palace there from 1514 onwards. Henry VIII seized it on the fall of Wolsey in 1528 and continued to build. William and Mary employed Wren further to expand the palace. George II was the last monarch to use Hampton Court. Kew Palace was taken on a long lease by Frederick, Prince of Wales ("Here lies poor Fred..."). In 1738 Alexander Pope, who had a vanished villa at Twickenham, gave him a dog with the following couplet on its collar "I am His Highness's dog at Kew. Pray tell me, sir, whose dog are you?" Queen Charlotte died at Kew in 1818; Queen Victoria gave the palace and garden (subsequently known for its botanical splendours) to the nation on her accession. White Lodge in the 2000-acre Richmond Park was built for George II by Roger Morris as a hunting lodge. Lord Bute lived here from 1761 to 1782 and Henry Addington, Viscount Sidmouth from 1805 to 1844. Edward VIII was born in the building. From 1955 it has been the Royal Ballet School.

The royal presence attracted other mansions. Ham House was built for the Earls of Dysart in the 17th century. Orleans House was originally built in 1710–20 by John James and James Gibbs and lived in by Philippe Egalite, Duke of Orleans in the early 19th century. Marble Hill House was built for the mistress of George I, Henrietta Howard, subsequently Countess of Suffolk, by Roger Morris in 1724–9. Horace Walpole built his Gothick fantasy at Strawberry Hill between 1749 and 1766. Garrick bought his Villa in Hampton in 1754 and this was improved by Adam.

These buildings encouraged lesser Georgian houses to be built round them. These can be seen on Richmond Green and elsewhere. The view from Richmond Hill over Petersham and Ham, which remains surprisingly rural, has been preserved.

St Peter, Petersham (usually open 3 – 5pm, Sundays), an attractive church which lies down a footpath from the Dysart Arms, has a 13th century chancel; the rest was reconstructed in the early 16th century. The red brick tower was added in the early 17th century and the charming eight-sided lantern was added in 1790 (1). The transept is of 1840. The fittings are 18th century: double-decker pulpit, font, box pews, reading desk. There are effigies to George Cole obit 1624 and his wife; their grandson, another George Cole, lies beneath (2). In the churchyard stands an interesting monument to a Captain Stuart, the grandson of Lucien Bonaparte (3). The explorer George Vancouver also lies buried in the churchyard.

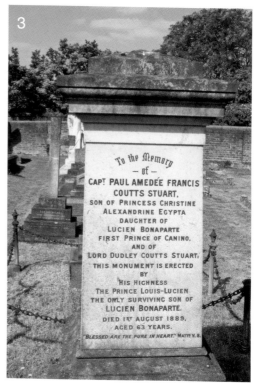

St Mary, Church Street, Twicken-ham with its riverside setting has a late 14th century tower of Kentish rag. The brick body of the church with its large pediments is however by John James in 1714–15 (4). The interior with its galleries is dignified (5). A number of monuments are in the church, including one to Francis Poulton and his wife of 1642 (6). Alexander Pope, a Catholic, lived in a villa in Twickenham. He died in 1744 and has various memorials in the church. He and his parents are com-memorated in the north gallery. His Anglican admirer Bishop Warburton of Gloucester erected a large obelisk mon-ument with a portrait, also in the north aisle. Sir Godfrey Kneller is buried here.

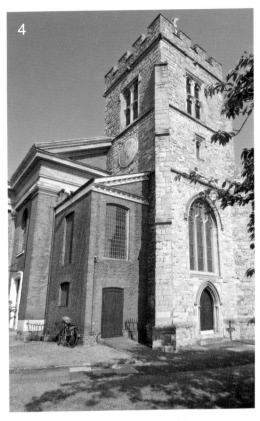

St Mary Magdalene, Paradise Road, Richmond (open 8 am – 3 pm, "most days") has a flint and stone tower of 1507. The rest of the red brick church is of 1750 (7). Blomfield made a number of alterations in 1864–5 (8). The chancel with its furnishings and decoration however is by Bodley of 1903–4. Monuments abound including one to Sophia Chaworth of 1689 (9).

St Anne, Kew Green (open 9 am to noon, except Thursday 1 pm – 3 pm) was originally built in 1710–14 as a chapel in yellow brick with red arched windows. It was enlarged in 1768, and again by Wyattville (who was responsible for the portico, tower and cupola) in the 19th century (10). The mausoleum of the Duke – much given to absent-mindedly interrupting services – and the Duchess of Cambridge was added in 1850–1. The interior has arcades of five bays with wooden Tuscan columns. The intersection has brown and imitation marble columns, the apse gold and white columns (11). The dome, redecorated by Comper, has gold stars on a blue sky (12). There is some Victorian stained glass and many monuments. Both Gainsborough and Zoffany are buried in the churchyard.

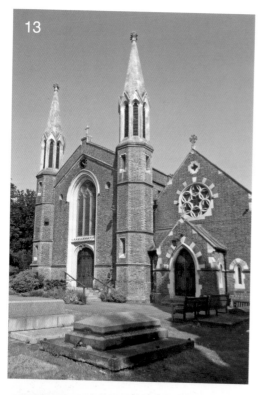

There are two churches in the borough by Lapidge, both begun in 1831.

St Andrew, Church Road, Ham is a red and grey brick building with octagonal turrets surmounted by stone pinnacles (13). Brandon built the south aisle (plus rose window) in 1860. It has an excellent chancel of 1900–1 by Bodley & Garner (14). A number of military monuments are placed on the walls of the church (15, 16).

St Mary, Hampton is a simple brick edifice also by Lapidge with lean lancet windows and a west tower (18). Blomfield added the lavish sanctuary in 1888. There are a number of monuments including one designed by Archer to a Mrs Thomas obit 1731 with

reclining figures of mother and daughter (17).

Vulliamy started **St John the Divine, Kew Road, Richmond** in 1831, finishing it five years later (19). A later carved crucifixion can be found outside the east end, high up on the wall. The chancel is early 20th century by Arthur Grove and has a contemporary collection of Anglo-Catholic fittings, including painted decoration by Westlake and ironwork by Bainbridge Reynolds (20).

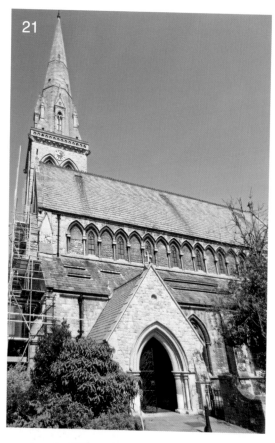

St Matthias, Friars Stile Road, Richmond (The St Matthias Centre has a coffee bar open weekday mornings during school term) is a large church by Sir Giles Gilbert Scott of 1857–8. There is a north west tower and a 195-feet high spire and rose window (21). *The Ecclesiologist* described it as "bold and artistic in its treatment but withal rather cold". The church was completed by John Oldrid Scott in 1884 with additional early 20th century work by Cecil Hare. Sir Arthur Blomfield was responsible for the screen and organ case. The chancel roof has a pretty painted ceiling (22). Furnishings in the decades both before and after 1900 survive. The west end has been subdivided. Hardman and others designed some decent stained glass (23, 24).

St Mary, Mortlake High Street (open 9 am – 4 pm, Monday to Friday) is mainly by Blomfield of 1885, although the Perpendicular tower dates from the 16th century (25). Viscount Sidmouth, Prime Minister as Henry Addington, who died in 1844, has a monument (27) as does his his daughter, Mary Anne Ursula (28). The reredos is attractive (26).

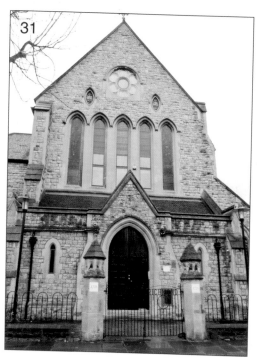

St Alban, Ferry Road, Teddington of 1887–9 for the Reverend Francis Leith Boyd (open during exhibitions) is by W. Niven, a huge incomplete French Gothic building (30). Once an Anglo-Catholic shrine and then abandoned by the Diocese of Southwark, it is now the Landmark Art Centre. The interior with its vaulted chancel soars (29). The sumptuous pulpit by A.H. Skipworth survives. Kempe designed the window on the eastern side of the north transept, depicting Jonah and the whale. Father Hope-Patten of Walsingham fame was curate here to Father Cazalet 1915–18.

Blomfield also built **Christ Church, Kew Road, Richmond** in 1893 in the style of the 13th century. The west front is dominated by five lancet windows (31). This church has been turned into flats.

All Saints, Bute Avenue, Petersham was commissioned by Rachel Laetitia Ward and begun in 1901 by John Kelly. It is a large red brick and terracotta Italian Romanesque church with a tall 118-foot campanile (32). It was requisitioned in World War II as a radar and anti-aircraft command post. Regular services ceased in 1962. It is now a private house so the "lavish interior" (Pevsner), if it survives, is no longer visible.

All Hallows, Chertsey Road, Twickenham is on the A316. It was erected in 1939–40 by Robert Atkinson, the 100-foot tower being Wren's from All Hallows, Lombard Street, that church having been demolished the year before by Arthur Winnington-Ingram, the Bishop of London (33). The church itself is a brick rectangle with stone dressings. The furnishings came from various City churches including All Hallows. Wesley is known to have preached from the pulpit (35). The font is from St Benet Gracechurch (34). The many memorials in the cloister and tower come from All Hallows, Lombard Street and St Dionis, Backchurch, including that of Edward Tyson, remembered as the father of modern comparative anatomy (died 1708), by Edward Stanton (36).

The Catholics possess two churches of interest in the borough, very different from each other.

St Mary Mortlake, North Worple Way is by Blount of 1852 (38). It is not unattractive (39). In the nearby cemetery is to be found the mausoleum designed by his wife (an Arundell) to Sir Robert Burton in the form of a tent (40, 37).

St Margaret, East Twicken-ham is by Williams & Winkley of 1968 (41) and is admired by some (including Pevsner who described it as "one of the best recent churches in London"). The exterior is functional. Inside it has seating centred on the sanctuary. The 19th century statue of St Margaret of Scotland comes from the earlier church (42). Patrick Reyntiens has provided some stained glass.

Ecclesiastical grants in Richmond upon Thames made by the Heritage of London Trust

1988   £6000 for the restoration of gargoyles on the tower of St Matthias, Richmond

1989   £5000 for the cupola of St Mary, Mortlake

1997   £2500 for the windows of St Mary, Twickenham

1999   £5000 for rose window of Grove Gardens Chapel, Richmond Cemetery

2006   £2500 for Churchyard wall of St Mary, Barnes

2006   £2500 for monument restoration at St Mary Magdalen, Richmond

2005   £3000 for railings at Christ Church, Richmond

2008   £5000 for tower etc at St Mary, Mortlake

2008   £3000 for Burton mausoleum at St Mary Magdalen, Mortlake (RC)

2009   £3000 for restoration of marble floor at St Alban,Teddington

2011   £2000 for De Vezlo mausoleum at St Mary Magdalen, Mortlake (RC)

2015   £3000 for the restoration of the gates to the Ladychapel, St John the Divine, Kew Road, Richmond.

The spectacular roof of St Stephen, College Road, Dulwich

SOUTHWARK

The London Borough of Southwark was formed in 1965 out of the boroughs of Southwark, Bermondsey and Camberwell.

The borough is bounded by Lewisham to the east, Bromley and Croydon to the south, Lambeth to the west and the River Thames to the north.

Southwark itself was an early suburb of London at the southern end of London Bridge, which, until 1729 when Putney Bridge opened, was the only bridge in London downstream of Kingston. The bridge was the subject of the nursery rhyme "London Bridge is falling down". Southwark had parliamentary representation from 1295. Inns such as Chaucer's Tabard and the still surviving George flourished. In the Middle Ages southern ecclesiastical dignitaries (such as the Bishops of Winchester and Rochester) had their palaces in the borough; a ruined part of the palace of the Bishop of Winchester remains. The Augustinian Priory of St Mary and St Saviour Overie survives intact, becoming Southwark Anglican Cathedral in 1905. There were theatres (outside the City) in the 16th century, such as the Globe for the Lord Chamberlain's Men. Southwark also became notorious for its numerous prisons such as the Clink and the Marshalsea. In 1815 Albion Mill with an early steam engine was set up near Blackfriars Bridge. The southern section of Southwark (Walworth) is now dominated by council housing. Southwark has a considerable number of interesting buildings: Guy's Hospital (1721–5), The Imperial War Museum (formerly the Bethlehem Hospital) (1811–14), St George Roman Catholic Cathedral (1841–1848; Pugin); Blackfriars Bridge (1869) and Bankside Power Station (now Tate Modern) (1954–60; Sir Giles Gilbert Scott).

Bermondsey was famous in the Middle Ages for its monastic foundation which possessed the Rood of Grace, a noted subject of devotion. It was originally founded in 1089 as a Cluniac priory from La Charite-sur-Loire. In 1390 it became an independent Benedictine Abbey. Elizabeth Woodville, the widow of Edward IV spent the last few years of her life there from 1487 to 1492. After the Reformation, Sir Thomas Pope, founder of Trinity College, Oxford built a house on the site. In 1823–43 the elder Brunel constructed Rotherhithe Tunnel. There were two miles of wharves along the river at Rotherhithe, which became docks. In 1864 the Surrey Commercial Docks were formally opened on a 460-acre site. This activity and other industry, e.g. leather making, caused a huge population increase and large scale slums. In their place the LCC eventually covered the borough with council estates. Bermondsey suffered considerable bomb damage in World War 2.

The only church with any medieval fabric surviving is **St Mary Magdalene, Bermondsey Street** (normally open Friday, 9.30 am – 12.30 pm) where the lower stages of the tower and possibly the north aisle have some 15th century work. The rest of the church was reconstructed by Charles Stanton in 1675–9 in classical style. The outside was stuccoed in 1830 and the erratic Gothic west front put on at the same time (1). The interior is 17th century (2). The arcades have Tuscan columns. The fittings including the pulpit, pews, organ case and font (3) are mainly 18th and 19th century.

St Mary, Rotherhithe was built between 1714 and 1737 by John James and others and is essentially a village church set in trees, but now enclosed by wharfs. The church is built in red brick with stone facings. It has a spire (4). Inside there are Ionic columns and a vaulted ceiling. The church was restored by Butterfield in 1876. The fittings are mainly 18th century. It has an attractive altar (6), candelabra (5), a 19th century painting of the Annunciation (8) and a moving memorial to Prince Lee Boo (1764-84), who was brought from Palau by Captain Henry Wilson aboard HMS Antelope; he unfortunately died from an attack of smallpox (7).

St George, Borough High Street (open Saturday morning) was built between 1734 and 1736 by John Price. It has a short stone tower and steeple at the west and the church is built in red brick (9). The east window is Venetian. Basil Champneys designed the plaster ceiling with cherubs (10, 11). The fittings are contemporary with the building. Bishop Bonner ("Bloody Bonner" of Protestant legend), who died in the Marshalsea prison, is buried in the churchyard.

St George, Wells Way, Camberwell was built by Bedford in 1822–4 as a Commissioners' church with a giant Greek Doric portico and myrtle wreathes on the frieze. It was consecrated by the Bishop of Winchester. Abandoned in 1970 it was wrecked by fire and vandalism. It has now been restored as flats (12).

St Peter, Liverpool Grove, Walworth (possible to enter through "Inspire" Monday to Thursday, 10 am – 1 pm) is another Commissioners' church of 1823–5 by Soane, his first church. The building is of yellow brick. The west front has four colossal Ionic columns and stone steeple (13). The interior has Doric columns supporting graceful galleries. The church was restored after war damage (84 people died in the Blitz here). The original altar survives at the east end (14).

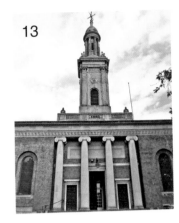

St James, St James's Road, Bermondsey (open Monday, 10 am – 12 noon and Thursday, 12 noon – 2 pm) is yet another Commissioners' church, this time by Savage in 1827–8 and rather more expensive (the cost was £21,000) and probably the best of its genre in London. The front is a colonnade with large uncarved Ionic columns (16). The church interior has been divided off at the west end and the aisles. The chancel is dominated by a very large painting of Christ's Ascension by John Wood (1844) (15).

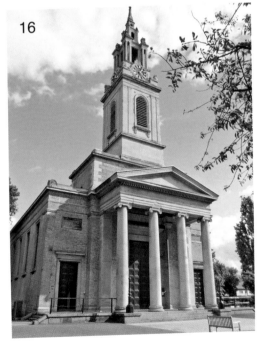

Southwark has not been fortunate in retaining its Victorian churches but the following remain.

St Giles, Camberwell Church Street (open Wednesday, 10 am – 10.45 am and Saturday, 1 pm – 2 pm) is a large Middle Pointed church completed in 1844 by G.G. Scott. It is stone and Early English, cruciform and with a 210-foot spire (17). *The Ecclesiologist* said "On the whole a magnificent work" while Eastlake wrote "In the neighbourhood of London no church was considered in purer style" (18). The 14th century sedilia and piscina of the earlier church remain. Some stained glass has also survived the bombing. It has fittings by Comper (19).

St Paul, Herne Hill was originally built by G. Alexander as a Commissioners' Church in 1844. It was destroyed by fire in 1858. Only the tower and spire survived from the earlier church (20). Street then enlarged the church; it was his first major commission after he moved to London. He beautified the interior with carving by Earp (22) and stained glass by Hardman (21) (mostly lost through bombing). The reredos and (later) rood screen survive, the latter at the west end. Ruskin described the church as "one of the loveliest churches of its time in the country and one that makes the fire a matter of rejoicing". Pevsner however described the church in his first edition as "disappointing".

St Stephen, College Road, Dulwich is by Banks & Barry of 1865–7, built in ragstone with a tall spire (23). Camille Pissaro painted the church in 1870, two years after its completion. It has rather a wonderful interior-font (25), chancel (24), roof (26) and fresco by Sir Edward Poynter of the stoning of St Stephen (27); the latter took 11 weeks to execute and cost £565. The east window was commissioned in 1924 from Kempe by Lord Vestey to commemorate his wife. The church was badly damaged by flying bombs in 1944.

St Augustine, Lynton Road, Bermondsey (1875–1883) is a large red brick church in Early English style built in an impoverished area by H. Jarvis. It has been turned into flats (28) .

St Paul, Lorrimore Square, Southwark was built 1955–60 by Woodroffe, Buchanan & Coulter to replace another church by Jarvis, destroyed in 1941. It is a modernistic construction looking rather like a series of beehives surmounted by green copper roof and spiky spire (29).

There are various Catholic Churches of interest.

Our Lady of Sorrows, Bird in the Bush Road, Peckham (open daily) was built 1859–66 for the Capuchin Friars (who remained until 2000) by E.W. Pugin. It is a huge building with a large rose window (30). Pugin altars remain in the sanctuary (31) and the south Lady Chapel.

Our Lady of La Salette, Bermondsey was built in 1861 to the designs of Edward Kelly. It is a modest brick building (32). It has fittings supplied by F.A. Walters and Sons in the 1920s (33, 34).

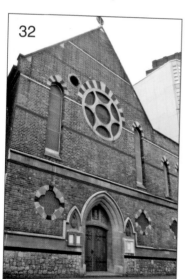

The **Most Precious Blood, O'Meara Street, Southwark** is by F.A. Walters in 1891–2 (36). It is neo-Norman with an apse and a large baldacchino based on that of S. Giorgio-in-Velabro in Rome (35). From 1981 until recently it was

looked after by the Society of Divine Compassion (Salvatorians). The church has not been well treated over the years (paint slapped on brickwork). However the Ordinariate of Our Lady of Walsingham has taken over the church, and matters are improving liturgically and aesthetically. In the north transept there are life-sized Calvary statues of 1893.

The English Martyrs, Rodney Road, Southwark is 1902 by Tasker, in yellow brick for the rector Father (later Bishop and Archbishop) Amigo (38). The interior with its red brick tall nave of five bays is more interesting than the exterior (39). It has decent fittings (37) including painted statues of Catholic martyrs executed at the North Surrey gallows.

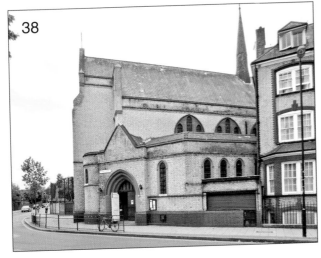

40

41

St Wilfrid, Lorrimore Road, Southwark was built in 1915 by Walters in red brick Perpendicular. In November 1940 the church was hit by a bomb. The exterior is fairly mean (40, 43) but good furnishings can be found inside, particularly the lady altar and the high altar with much gilding (41, 42).

42

43

St Thomas More, Dulwich
was built in 1927 by Joseph Goldie,
son of his more famous father Edward. It is built in stock brick in
Middle Pointed style with a bellcote at the west end (44). Its most
interesting fixture is the Caen stone
high altar which came from Hales
Place, Canterbury and is probably
by E.W. Pugin (45, 46); this had
been made for the chapel of an
intended community of Carmelite
nuns on behalf of Miss Mary
Barbara Hales. The church suffered
bomb damage in 1944. The presbytery designed by Ninian Comper
for the Downside Benedictines who
ran the parish from 1892 to 1923
was destroyed.

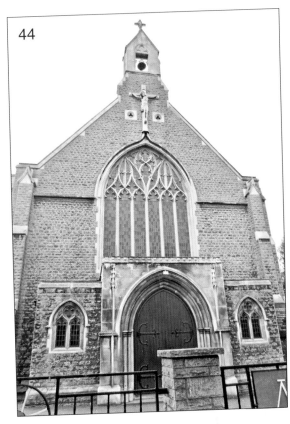

47

The Sacred Heart, Camberwell was built in 1952–3 by D. Plaskett Marshal to replace a bombed church of 1863 by Buckler. It is red brick, its shape determined by the nearby railway line (47). Its contemporary fittings survive.

The Most Holy Trinity, Dockhead and Jamaica Road, Bermondsey is by Goodhart-Rendel, a rebuilding of 1960 replacing a church of 1834–8 by Kempthorne, and is perhaps his best church, built in patterned brickwork (48) with its hexagonal towers and a barrel-vaulted interior (49). The sanctuary has polychromatic stone panels from the Forest of Dean, Portland and York (50).

48

49

Ecclesiastical grants in Southwark made by the Heritage of London Trust

1990 £500 for mosaic reredos at St George, Camberwell
1991 £9000 for restoration of parapet stones at St James, Bermondsey
1991 £7500 for work on railings at St Peter, Walworth
1994 £500 for restoration of altar at St George RC Cathedral
1996 £5000 for stained glass window at St Giles, Camberwell
2002 £2500 for regilding of weathervane and clockface at St Peter, Walworth
2006 £2000 for restoration of painting at St Jude, Southwark
2008 £2000 for restoration of stained glass window at St Augustine, Bermondsey
2010 £2000 to restore altar frontal at St Paul, Lorrimore Square
2011 £3000 to restore railings at St Peter, Walworth
2011 £2000 to restore tower stonework at St Augustine, Bermondsey

Part of the rich decoration of the Lady Chapel reredos at All Saints, Carshalton

SUTTON

The London Borough of Sutton was the result in 1965 of the merger of the Municipal Borough of Sutton and Cheam with the Municipal Borough of Bedington and Wallington to which was added Carshalton Urban District from Surrey. (For what it is worth, there is an old Surrey rhyme "Sutton for mutton, Carshalton for beeves, Epsom for whores and Ewell for thieves".)

It is bounded on the north by Merton, on the west by Kingston upon Thames and Surrey, on the south by Surrey and on the east by Croydon.

The borough is mainly 20th century suburban, especially in the north, which is pretty dreary. The towns were rural villages until well into the 19th century. There were a number of country retreats and early industry. The railway arrived in 1847.

Sutton was mentioned in Domesday Book as 'sudtone' (meaning south farm). The manor was purchased by the Abbey of Chertsey until the Reformation. It was eventually owned by the Carew family. The hammerbeam roof of their manor survives. Evelyn called it "a noble old structure, capacious and proper for Old English hospitality". The formal 17th century gardens with an orangery were famous in their time. It has subsequently had many owners including briefly the Duke of Portland of the time after the Restoration. Many coaching inns were built after the turnpike road to Brighton was opened in 1755; the pugilist 'Gentleman Jackson' for instance owned the Cock. George IV met his mistresses at Sutton Farm. Sutton was the recipient of 434 German bombs 1941–44 which caused 187 civilian casualties.

Cheam was known as 'Ceiham' in Domesday Book when it was again owned by the Abbey of Chertsey. The village was known for its potteries in the Middle Ages. Its chief claim to fame is as the site of Henry VIII's great palace of Nonsuch, built to rival the Chateau of Chambord in 1538–41. Because of its rich ornamentation it cost £24,000 (the equivalent of some £110m now). Charles II gave the palace to his mistress Barbara Castlemaine who demolished it in 1681–2.

Carshalton was called 'Aultone' in Domesday Book, an 'aul' apparently being a spring in Anglo-Saxon. It was then owned by Geoffrey de Mandeville. In the 17th century Thomas Fuller in his *History of the Worthies of England* praised Carshalton's walnuts and trout. It was subsequently known for its lavender fields. Carshalton House is an 18th century building of a certain architectural importance originally built for Sir John Fellowes. The 1st Earl of Hardwicke, Admiral Lord Anson and the Hon Thomas Walpole all lived there subsequently. In the last century it was owned by the Daughters of the Cross and is now St Philomena's Catholic School. It possesses a Vanbrughian water tower known as the 'Bagnio'. The centre of Carshalton with its lakes opposite the parish church remains a pleasant spot.

All Saints, Carshalton
has medieval arcades in the
nave but the church was
essentially built as a neo-
Perpendicular church by
Sir Arthur Blomfield and
his nephew, 1893–14 (1)
for the Reverend Lord Victor Seymour, son of the
Marquess of Hertford. The
riot of rich fittings (screen
(2,4,7), Lady Chapel reredos (3), organ case (8)
(decorated with somewhat
homoerotic angels),
gallery and glass (9) are essentially by Comper for the
Anglo-Papalist Father Cor-
bould who became Rector
in December 1919. A num-
ber of Baroque monuments
are in the south aisle including one to Sir William

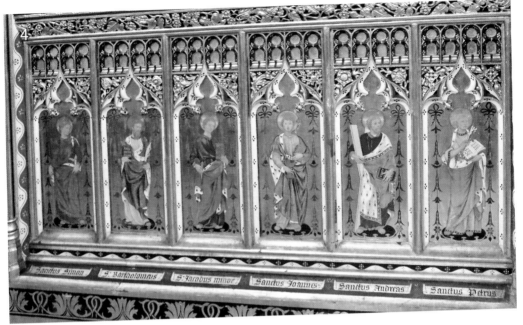

Sanctus Simon S. Bartholomeus S. Jacobus minor Sanctus Joannes Sanctus Andreas Sanctus Petrus

Scawen who died in 1722 (6).

Father looked a little grumpy during our visit (5).

St Mary, Church Road, Beddington (open Sunday, 5 – 6.30 pm) is mainly 14th–15th century. It has a handsome flint exterior (10). The roofs, chancel arch, etc were restored by Joseph Clarke 1867–9. The pulpit is 1611 and the organ case is by Morris and Co (11). The Carew Chapel contains monuments to the family. Sir Francis Carew died in 1611. His father having been executed by Henry VIII, he adopted a low profile throughout his life although he had to entertain Queen Elizabeth I for three days in 1599. His recumbent effigy is carved in alabaster, his children kneeling below (12). Glass by Clayton & Bell of 1878 can be found in the north aisle as can a copy of a 14th century 'doom' painting on the west wall of St Michael weighing the souls of the deceased (13).

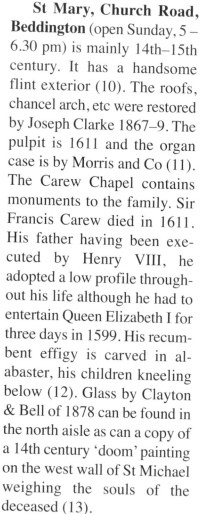

The Lumley Chapel, Cheam (key available from Whitehall House when open) is the flint chancel of the medieval church of St Dunstan (14) (now replaced by a not very interesting Victorian church). The chapel is now in the care of the Churches Conservation Trust. The white ceiling dates from 1592 (17). It has a number of monuments. Jane Lady Lumley died in 1578. She was the daughter of Henry Fitzalan, 19th Earl of Arundel and the first person to translate Euripides into English (16). The best monument is the recumbent effigy of Elizabeth, Lady Lumley obit 1603 (15). There are a number of interesting brasses.

All Saints, Benhilton, Sutton is a large and conspicuous church by Teulon. The parish was founded in 1863 when construction started. Charles Sumner, Bishop of Winchester, consecrated the church in 1866. It has a wide west tower (18). Good decorative details can be found inside including the screen of 1911 (19). The Willis organ was installed in 1870. The original stained glass was destroyed in the bombing of 1944. Modern glass was installed in 1965 including the east window by J. & M. Kettlewell (20) and that in the south aisle by John Hayward. This is a traditionalist Anglo-Catholic parish linked to Forward in Faith.

Christ Church, Christchurch Park, Sutton is 1888 by Newman & Jacques, built in red brick Early English (21, 22). The tower was never built. Its chief claim to fame is the spectacular rood screen (25). The church boasts a number of interesting decorative features. The baptistery and other work are later of 1910–12 (23, 24). There is some curiously chunky first world war memorial stained glass.

26

The Good Shepherd, Queen Mary's Avenue, Carshalton (open 9.30 am – 12 noon during term time) is a brick curiosity designed by Martin Travers in 1930 as a Spanish mission station (26). The interior is Baroque, dominated by the crucifix on the east wall (27). As can be seen by this print worship was Anglo-Catholic until c 1965 (28). It is now firmly Evangelical with Travers's stained glass of Our Lady and St Nicholas (29, 30) kept behind curtains so as not to corrupt the tender consciences of modern worshippers.

27

28

29

30

The only Catholic church of much architectural interest is **St Elphege, Stafford Road, South Bedddington.** The original church of 1908 (paid for by the convert Miss Frances Ellis) is now used as a church hall. The new church of 1971 is by Williams & Winkley (cf St Margaret, Twicken-

ham). The outside of the church, which is square, is in simple brick with the main altar near the entrance (31). There is a statue of St Elphege on the outside (32).

Ecclesiastical grants in Sutton made by the Heritage of London Trust

1989   £5000 for stonework at Holy Trinity, Sutton
1996   £5000 for various works at Carshalton Baptist Church

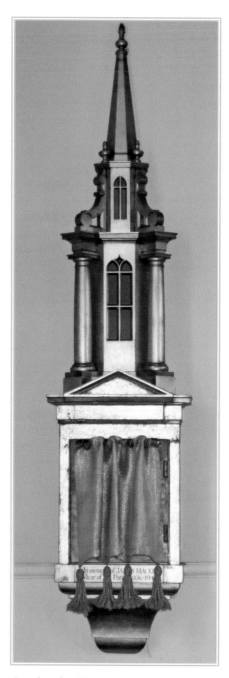

Aumbry by Martin Travers at St John, Bethnal Green

TOWER HAMLETS

The London Borough of Tower Hamlets was formed in 1965 out of the former boroughs of Bethnal Green, Poplar and Stepney.

It is bounded on the west by the City, on the north by Hackney, on the east by Newham and on the south by the River Thames.

It consists of flat, low lying land from the walls of the City to the River Lea. In the Middle Ages it was coterminous with the Bishop of London's large manor of Stepney. Originally agricultural land, certain noxious trades such as tanning came to be set up outside the City Walls. Various monastic settlements were also to be found. These included St Mary Graces, a Cistercian house. At the Dissolution these became tenements. Foreigners settled in the area from the earliest days as, being outside the walls of the City, they were free of guild restrictions. Tower Hamlets has seen successive waves of immigration – Huguenot, Irish, Jewish and Bengali.

The original 'tower hamlets' were a string of villages along the River Thames – Wapping, Shadwell, Limehouse. Stepney was Stibba's hythe or landing place. The Mile End and Commercial Roads made a fork with Whitechapel, historically a very poor area, inbetween. Poplar to the east was where the East India and West India Docks were built. The Isle of Dogs apparently gained its name from c. 1520 when Henry VIII's dogs at Greenwich were kept there. Bow lay to the north. Bethnal Green retained a degree of rurality for longer than the rest of what is now a highly urbanised borough. Victoria Park was opened in 1847.

The 'East End' during the 19th and early 20th century was pretty much 'terra incognita' to respectable inhabitants of the City and the West End, an overcrowded area regarded as being devoted to Lascars and opium dens. The development of Canary Wharf during the late 20th century as a financial and commercial centre has to a certain extent changed perceptions although one queries the extent to which the 'workers' there ever delve into the Isle of Dogs and Poplar.

The Royal Foundation of St Katharine was set up east of the Tower of London by Queen Matilda in 1147 to look after 13 infirm old men. Being under royal protection it rather remarkably survived the Reformation, albeit in a Protestantised state. In 1825 it moved to Regent's Park but returned to Limehouse in 1948. It was under the care of the Community of the Resurrection until 1993. The 1951 chapel retains the distinguished 14th century choir stalls from the earlier building.

Tower Hamlets has a number of buildings of interest. These include in chronological order the Royal Mint (1807–12), Wilton's Music Hall (1858–9), Tower Bridge (1886–94), the Whitechapel Art Gallery (1898–1901) and the East London Mosque (1982–5).

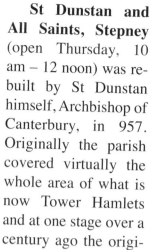

St Dunstan and All Saints, Stepney (open Thursday, 10 am – 12 noon) was rebuilt by St Dunstan himself, Archbishop of Canterbury, in 957. Originally the parish covered virtually the whole area of what is now Tower Hamlets and at one stage over a century ago the original area had been divided into 66 separate Anglican parishes. The church is in quiet surroundings, lying as it does in seven acres, with monuments to Georgian sailors and others. The chancel walls are 13th century, the rest 15th. The church was restored by the Victorians, and after bomb damage. Outside it is of Kentish rag with stone facings (1, 2). Internally it has a broad nave with aisles seven bays long. The church has a slightly shabby appearance with whitewashed walls. The east window by Hugh Easton shows a risen Christ above a war-damaged Stepney. The chief treasure of the church is a somewhat damaged Saxon rood (4). There is a tomb chest of Sir Henry Colet,

twice Lord Mayor of London, father of John Colet, rector here and subsequently Dean of St Paul's. A stone was brought to the church in 1663 from Carthage on which are inscribed inter alia the words "Time consumes all; it spareth none"; a cheering sentiment. An attractive Victorian triptych of the Annunciation is in the first chapel on the left (3).

St Mary, Stratford-Le-Bow (open 11am – 4 pm, first Saturday in month) was built as a chapel of ease to St Dunstan's in 1311. Isolated on an island site, it has a 15th century tower with the rest of the church somewhat later (5). It will be recalled of Chaucer's Prioress that "And Frensch she spak full faire and fetyshly after the schole of Stratford atte Bowe for Frensch of Parys was to her unknow". St Mary finally became an independent parish church in 1719. 17th and early 18th century monuments are in the church. Blomfield did some work on the sanctuary in 1881. It was well-restored by Goodhart-Rendel after war damage (6). George Lansbury, Leader of the Labour Party, is remembered here (7).

Various chapels of ease were also set up in the borough during the 17th century. In 1711 Parliament passed an "Act for the Building of Fifty New Churches in the Cities of London and Westminster or the Suburbs thereof". Nicholas Hawksmoor (1661–1736) built three churches in the borough under this Act.

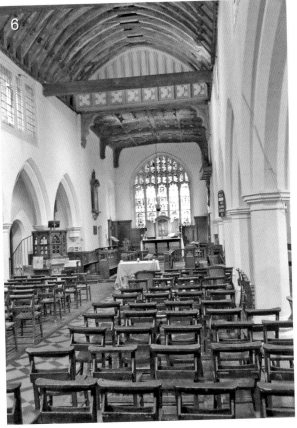

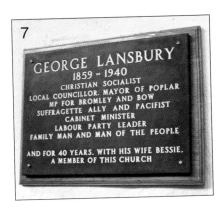

GEORGE LANSBURY
1859 - 1940
CHRISTIAN SOCIALIST
LOCAL COUNCILLOR. MAYOR OF POPLAR
MP FOR BROMLEY AND BOW
SUFFRAGETTE ALLY AND PACIFIST
CABINET MINISTER
LABOUR PARTY LEADER
FAMILY MAN AND MAN OF THE PEOPLE

AND FOR 40 YEARS. WITH HIS WIFE BESSIE.
A MEMBER OF THIS CHURCH

Christ Church, Spitalfields (open Monday to Friday 11 am – 4 pm and Sunday 1 pm – 4 pm) was constructed 1715–29 with a view particularly to combating Huguenot dissent in the neighbourhood. It has a dominating 225-foot high tower, rising up from a portico of four Tuscan columns (8). Inside it has a five-bay arcade, a chancel with a Venetian window, a magnificent organ and a classical rood surmounted by the Royal Arms (9). The church was heavily restored by Ewan Christian. It was closed as a church in 1958 but from 1976 was restored and revived by the admirable activities of the Friends of Christ Church, Spitalfields. A monument by Flaxman of Sir Robert Ladbroke, former Lord Mayor of London, who died in 1794, is to the right of the altar (10).

St George-in-the-East, Old Cannon Road
(open 8 am – 6 pm daily) was built between
1715 and 1723, and consecrated in 1729. It has
a west tower with an octagonal lantern, and
pepper pot towers (11, 12). It was bombed in
1941 although the exterior shell survived. In
1960–4 Ansell & Bailey inserted a small modern
church within the walls. 18th century plaster
work survives (in the apse) (14) as do some
mosaics of 1880 (13). In 1859 St George's
became notorious for anti-ritualist riots against
the activities of the Reverend Bryan King,
sometime Fellow of Brasenose College, Oxford,
who introduced such outrageously 'advanced'
practices as choral services, lighted candles on
the altar and coloured stoles.

The final church built by Hawksmoor is **St Anne, Limehouse**. It was built between 1712 and 1730 and named in honour of Queen Anne. It is in the shape of a Greek cross. The tower is in three stages, the top one surmounted by four pepper pots. As a landmark visible from the river, St Anne's was granted the right to fly the White Ensign (the flag of the Royal Navy) throughout the year. Stone vestibules are placed on either side of the west door which is surmounted by a dome above an apse (15). Four columns form a rectangle in the interior, inside of which is a circular ceiling (17). The church was gutted by fire in 1850 and restored by Philip Hardwick. The stained glass in the east window is of 1853 by Charles Clutterbuck and is of the Crucifixion (16). St Anne's now has an evangelical tradition.

A large and somewhat mysterious four-sided pyramid is situated in the churchyard.

St Matthew, Bethnal Green ("often open for private prayer") was built, in brick, in 1743 by George Dance (18, 19). It is situated in a large churchyard. The chancel was refitted by F.C. Eden but the interior of the church was destroyed in the Second World War. It was remodelled 1958–61 (21). The church has had an Anglo-Catholic tradition

since the Reverend Septimus Hansard in the late 19th century (20). His curate was the radical Christian socialist, Stewart Headlam, friend of Shaw and Chesterton. The church gained a certain notoriety when the burials of the three Kray brothers were conducted here. In the early 1990s the late Father Christopher Bedford took some 120 of the congregation "across the Tiber" to the Catholic Church.

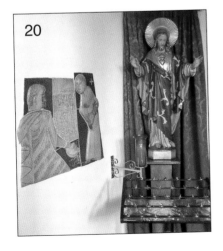

22

St John, Cambridge Heath Road, Bethnal Green was built by Sir John Soane in 1826 to 1828 as a Commissioners' church. Its tower has detached pillars and a cupola (22). The interior of the nave consists of Doric columns painted green and surmounted by galleries (23). The Bodley classical chancel of 1888 has a large Cecil Hare reredos of a statue of Christ standing with arms out-stretched of 1913 (24), as well as an organ case and aumbry in the form of a Wren spire by Travers (25). Four-teen Stations of the Cross by the painter Chris Gollon were installed in 2000.

23

24

25

Charles Blomfield, Bishop of London 1828–1856, embarked on a major church building campaign in Bethnal Green, naming churches after the twelve apostles. **St Peter, Bethnal Green** was built under this programme in 1840–41 by Vulliamy in neo-Norman style. The exterior is of flint and brick (26). The interior is of stucco and terra cotta. The west porch has an octagonal tower. The nave is long and rectangular with a complex exposed roof (29). The glass is by Heaton, Butler & Bayne (27). St Peter's is now a Holy Trinity, Brompton (qv) 'plant' but the early 20th century rood survives unaltered (28).

Holy Trinity, Brompton has also colonised **St Paul, Shadwell** ("open most of Sunday") designed as a classical church in yellow brick in 1817–20 (30). The tower is the most impressive feature of the building (31). Basil Clarke in 1966 noted "Little has been done to the church, and it keeps its old-fashioned Anglican parish church atmosphere very well". This is no longer true as the interior now resembles a recording music studio. Captain Cook was a parishioner here.

All Saints, Poplar (normally open 12 noon – 2pm, Mondays – Fridays) was built 1821–3 by Charles Hollis in Portland stone. It has a 18th century look with a steeple that could be by Gibbs and a massive Ionic portico (32). The inside of the

latter has four grooved columns. The interior was in fact remodelled in the 1950s by Cecil Brown to make it look 18th century with a baldacchino (33) and a western gallery. Martin Travers designed the tabernacle (34). The living historically belonged to Brasenose College, Oxford.

Tower Hamlets felt the full force of the Gothic Revival under Tractarian influences in the 19th century. Many churches of this persuasion (St Augustine, Stepney, St Philip, Stepney, St Faith, Poplar, St John, Isle of Dogs, etc.) are no longer extant as churches.

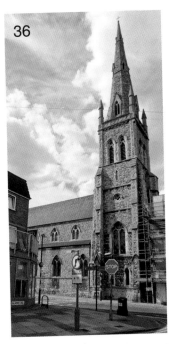

However three surviving churches exemplify this tradition. **St Mary, Cable Street** was designed by Frederick Francis in simple Middle Pointed style as a mission church for Lord Haddo, the eldest son of the Earl of Aberdeen. The tower and tall spire are later (36). The furnishings are simple (35).

Christ Church, Isle of Dogs was built 1852–4 by Frederick Johnstone for William Cubitt in an Early English style with stone from Old London Bridge (37). The land was given by the Countess of Glengall. The church has a long chancel. It has a collection of fittings, some from other vanished churches, e.g. Blomfield's St John, Roserton Street (38). In the 1950s the sanctuary was unfortunately redecorated with rather garish red and white wallpaper, replacing Victorian wall coverings.

St Peter, London Docks (open daily until 6.15 pm) was founded by the famous Father Charles Lowder of the Society of the Holy Cross (39) from St George-in-the-East in 1865 and built by Frederick H. Pownall. Shortly after the arrival of Father Lowder there was a bad outbreak of cholera in the wretched tenements of Wapping. He and his sisters of mercy tended the victims and established a profound reputation for charity.

He died in 1880. The saintly Father Wrainwright was a curate here from 1873 to 1929. The church is in a muscular French Gothic style, yellow brick outside (41) and red brick with black patterning inside (42). It has a courtyard entrance. It remains very atmospheric, full of Anglo-Catholic fittings (40). Some stained glass survived the bombing (43).

One 20th century Anglican church that should be mentioned is **St Paul, Bow Common**. The original 18th century church was bombed and a new church built as a brick square with glass lantern by Robert Maguire in 1958–60 (44). It exemplifies the ideals of the Liturgical Movement, which aimed to reduce the distance between the priest and the congregation through a central altar (46). Ian Nairn in 1964 wrote of it "The only modern building in the London Transport area to reflect any credit on the Church of England". Basil Clarke however said in his notebook "It looks like a seedy stable yard". The *Outraged Christ* (45) is by Charles Lutyens (great nephew of Edwin Lutyens).

Tower Hamlets is rich in Catholic churches (13 in all), built to service in the main the requirements of the Irish population working in the docks. **St Mary and St Michael, Commercial Road** was built by Wardell in 1852–6 with a stone-faced exterior of Kentish rag (47). It was opened by Cardinal Wiseman in 1856. The church has 11 continuous bays and reasonable fittings (48). When built it was the largest Catholic church in London. The intended tower and spire were never built. The sanctuary was reordered by Walters in 1898.

Gilbert Blount built **St Anne, Underwood Road** for the Marist Fathers in 1853–6. The exterior is again of Kentish rag (49). The sanctuary with its ribbed bay chancel and the side chapels were built in 1896 (50). Musical angels decorate the corbels. The church now mainly caters to the needs of a Brazilian congregation.

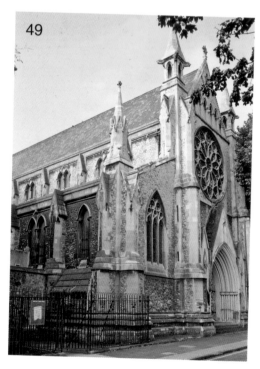

Our Lady and St Catherine of Siena, Bow was built in 1869–70, again by Gilbert Blount, for Dominican Nuns who eventually left in 1923 for Stone in Staffordshire (52). The church then became a parish church. The nave suffered damage in the war. The elaborate reredos is by Farmer & Brindley (51).

Edward Pugin built **The English Martyrs, Tower Hill** for the Missionary Oblates of Mary Immaculate in yellow stock brick on a constricted site in 1876 (54). The mosaics above the door of St John Fisher and St Thomas More are 20th century by Arthur Fleischmann. The church has a high altar of 1930 by Gilbert (55) and a fine interior with galleries. A statue of Our Lady of Graces by Boulton is in the north transept (53).

St Patrick, Wapping was built by F.W. Tasker in 1877–9 under the influence of Cardinal Manning (56). It has a grand basilican interior with large Ionic columns (58). The statue of St Peter is by Mayer of Munich. The painting on the high altar is by Greenwood (59). St Patrick overlooks the whole scene benevolently (57). The altar in the Lady Chapel is said to have come from Father Faber's first London Oratory in King William Street.

The Guardian Angels, Mile End Road was paid for by Lady Mary Fitzalan Howard as a memorial to Lady Margaret Fitzalan Howard, who had worked in the East End. They were both daughters of the 14th Duke of Norfolk. It is in red brick in Perpendicular style by Walters of c. 1902 (61). It has a tall rood (60). The traceried east window was given by the 15th Duke of Norfolk. A reordering of 1977 bequeathed a full immersion font.

Our Lady of the Assumption, Victoria Park Square, Bethnal Green was built in 1911–12 by Edward Goldie for the Augustinians of the Assumption who had been expelled from France in 1901. The exterior with its Decorated window over the porch is of brick (62). The inside has good fittings including a high altar by Earp and Hobbs with a gilded relief of the Last Supper (63, 64).

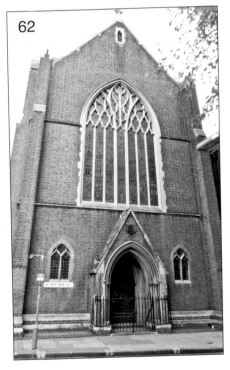

The **Lithuanian Church of St Casimir, The Oval, Hackney Road** is a curiosity. Built in 1911–12 by Father Benedict Williams it has an unpromising exterior (65) but the interior is dominated by a Tyrolean altar piece of 1851 with the Coronation of the Virgin (66) reputedly exhibited in the Great Exhibition. The church was reordered in 2004 and various furnishings have vanished.

St Mary and St Joseph, Poplar was built in 1951–4 by Adrian Gilbert Scott to replace the previous Wardell church bombed in 1940. It is a brick cruciform with stone dressings and a large octagonal tower surmounted by an open lantern (67). The interior is dominated by the striking baldacchino and pulpit (68). The Lady Chapel altar survives (69).

Ecclesiastical grants in Tower Hamlets made by the Heritage of London Trust

1981 £5000 for drawings for Christ Church, Spitalfield
1989 £5000 for clock repair at St Anne, Limehouse
1990 £10,000 for working drawings at Christ Church, Spitalfield
1991 £5000 for restoration of spire at Christ Church, Isle of Dogs
1992 £5000 for restoration of stencilling at St Anne, Underwood Road (R.C.)
1998 £1816 for Our Lady of the Assumption, Victoria Park Square (R.C.)
1999 £3000 to repair the tomb of Thomas Real at St Dunstan and All Saints, Stepney
2001 £4199 to restore wall paintings at Christ Church, Isle of Dogs
2005 £2000 for railings round tomb St Dunstan and All Saints, Stepney
2006 £4000 for St John, Bethnal Green
2006 £2000 for stone carving on the tower of St Dunstan and All Saints, Stepney
2008 £2000 for railings at St John, Bethnal Green
2009 £3500 for church of St Matthew, Bethnal Green
2011 £5000 for memorial plaques at St Mary, Stratford-le-Bow
2013 £3000 for organ case at Christ Church, Spitalfield
2013 £2000 for door frames at St John, Bethnal Green

Red brick Gothic by Caroe at St Barnabas, Walthamstow

Since 1965 the London Borough of Waltham Forest has consisted of the former boroughs of Chingford, Leyton and Walthamstow, all formerly in Essex. The name derives from Epping Forest which was owned by Waltham Abbey.

Newham lies to the south, Redbridge to the east, Essex to the north and Enfield, Haringey and Hackney to the west.

Chingford in the north is possibly named after the "shingly ford". It is on slightly higher ground that the rest of the borough. It retains a fairly green aspect, particularly in the north and west towards Epping Forest. On the edge of the forest remains Queen Elizabeth's Hunting Lodge. From 1608 until 1851 the top floor of the lodge functioned as a courtroom. William Morris talked of "a room hung with faded greenery ... and the impression of romance it made on me". In 1878 it was purchased by the Corporation of London. Highams is a late 18th century building, now the Woodford County High School for Girls. The Great Eastern Railway arrived in 1873 and "superior housing" followed.

Leyton is mentioned in Domesday Book and belonged to Westminster Abbey in the Middle Ages. In the 17th and 18th century it was "a pretty retiring place from London" for wealthy bankers and merchants. The arrival of the railway in the 19th century changed this and Leyton became a working class suburb. Industry led to zeppelin raids in the First World War with 1300 houses being damaged. The Temple Mills Railyard (originally a mill belonging to the Knights Templar/Hospitaller) was a particular target in the Blitz. Industrial decline followed the Second World War. Leyton is the home of Leyton Orient Football Club. Leytonstone boasts the so-called High Stone, an 18th century obelisk marking distances.

Walthamstow was known originally for its rural retreats. Pepys used to visit Sir William Batteh, Surveyor of the Navy there, whom he described rather enviously as "living like a prince". Walthamstow still has a number of elegant red brick Georgian houses. William Morris lived in the borough from 1848 when he was 14 until 1856. He described it as "all flat pasture except for a few gardens ... the wide green scene of the Essex marshes, with the great domed line of the sky, the sun shining down in one peaceful light over the long distance". There is little of this left now. The 18th century house in which he was brought up is now the William Morris Gallery. It was bought by the council in 1899 and opened as a museum in 1950. Benjamim Disraeli was educated in Walthamstow. After the arrival of the Eastern Railway Sir Thomas Courtenay Warner developed much of his estate into housing. The first mass production bus was built in Walthamstow by the company that subsequently became AEC, and the Avro Aircraft Company was also situated there.

All Saints, Old Church Road, Chingford (open 10 am, Saturday) is 12th–15th century. It was derelict from the 1840s until 1930, when it was restored by C.C.Winnill at the expense of Louisa Boothroyd Heathcote of Friday Hill. The churchyard is pleasantly rural (1, 4). The church has an attractive 16th century south porch (3). It has a south arcade of four bays and a 15th century chancel arch. Various Leigh, Boothroyd and Heathcote monuments are inside (2).

St Mary, Church Lane, Waltham-stow, again situated in a pleasantly rural churchyard, has a late medieval tower and a partly medieval interior including 16th century chapels (5). It suffered serious damage from a bomb in the Second World War. There is an Elizabethan monument to Margaret Stanley (7), a monument of 1633 by Nicholas Stone to Sir Thomas and Lady Merry and one to Sigismund Trafford of 1723 with him in Roman dress (6). He was MP for King's Lynn in 1689.

The chief ecclesiological interest of the borough is the agglomeration of high Anglican churches in Walthamstow and Leytonstone. In the late 19th century merchant bankers spent the proceeds of their profession on sensible matters such as funding churches. Richard Foster, a keen high churchman, was responsible for funding no less than three churches in Walthamstow, having also been busy in Haggerston.

The first was **St Saviour, Markhouse Road, Walthamstow** on land inherited from his uncle. The church was built by Francis T. Dolman in 1873–4. It has a huge broach spire visible from a distance (8) and an impressive interior. The original roof and fittings were lost in a fire in 1945. Much stained glass survives (9, 10).

The second church was **St Michael, Palmerston Road, Walthamstow**. This was built in 1885 for the first incumbent, Father William Ibbotson, by J.M. Bignall, a pupil of Scott's. It is built in yellow and red brick although without its planned tower and spire (11). It has lavish High Church fittings culminating in the tall reredos with prickly pinnacles by Zwinck

with painted saints on a gold background (12). Much of the glass is by Hardman including the great east window of 1915 showing St Michael defeating the Devil. Statues of saints abound including one of St Michael prodding a rather small dragon (13). A slightly more alarming dragon can be found in the stained glass (14).

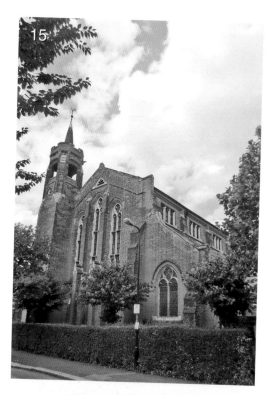

Last but by no means least comes **St Barnabas, St Barnabas Road, Walthamstow**. This was built by W.D. Caroe in 1902–3 in red brick with a small turret in Gothic (15). The interior (17) is full of excellent fittings, some original and some brought in more recently by Dr Julian Litten (16). The hanging rood (18) is by Caroe himself and was put in as a war memorial in 1921. Some stained glass by Clayton & Bell survives.

Leytonstone boasts **St Margaret of Antioch, Woodhouse Road, Harrow Green** in the same tradition. This huge basilica was built by J.T. Newman and W. Jacques in 1892–3 in yellow and red brick (19). It has a lofty interior with a rood of 1921 by Sir Charles Nicholson. The high altar of 1893, a memorial to the first bishop of St Alban's, has ornate carving by Sebastian Zwinck of Oberammergau, subsequently gilded (21, 22). St Margaret continues the good fight against dragons (20).

These last four churches have all seen the departure of priests and people to the Ordinariate of Our Lady of Walsingham.

The borough possesses one Catholic church of interest, **Our Lady of Grace and St Teresa of Avila, King's Road, Chingford**. This was built between 1930 and 1939 with the tower added later in 1956. The church was designed and built at cost by G.W. Martyn, a convert. It is Arts & Crafts Gothic brick with Perpendicular windows (23). It has a decent interior with good fittings (24) and glass by Veronica Whall of 1939. It was sensitively (an adverb for which there is often no call in these circumstances) reordered in 2002. The roof is particularly fine (25) as are carvings of angels carrying shields (26).

26

Ecclesiastical grants in Waltham Forest made by the Heritage of London Trust

1999 £1925 for the clock faces on the cupola of Leyton Parish Church
2002 £2000 for St Mary Walthamstow for the restoration of tombs in the churchyard
2002 £2300 for the restoration of tombs at All Saints, Chingford

The painted and polychromatic interior of All Saints, Lower Common, Putney

WANDSWORTH

The London Borough of Wandsworth remains essentially as it had been before 1965. It is bounded by the river Thames in the north, by Richmond upon Thames and Kingston upon Thames on the west, by Merton to the south and by Lambeth to the east.

Battersea appears in Domesday Book as 'Patricesy' with the manor belonging to Westminster Abbey. After the Reformation it was owned by the Crown and then from 1627 to 1777 by the St John Family who sold it to the Spencers, who pulled it down in 1793. The 17th century Old Battersea House still remains. In the 18th and early 19th century Battersea was known for market gardening (hence Lavender Hill) and pigs. In 1829, while Prime Minister, the Duke of Wellington fought a duel with the Earl of Winchilsea in Battersea Fields. In 1838 the London and Southampton Railway set up its depot in Nine Elms and Clapham Junction opened in 1863. Heavy industrialisation followed in the north of the borough – Price's Candle, the Plumbago Crucible Company, etc. Battersea Park with its 15-acre boating lake was opened in 1854. Battersea Power Station partly by Sir Giles Gilbert Scott was built 1929–35. Industry has now pretty much disappeared.

Putney Heath was mainly used for military reviews until the 19th century. William Pitt the Younger fought a duel there with William Tierney in 1798.

Roehampton has a number of substantial 18th century houses: Downshire House, Grove House (by James Wyatt for Sir Joshua Vanneck), Manresa House (by William Chambers for Lord Bessborough), Mount Clare (by Robert Taylor for George Clive) and Roehampton House (by Thomas Archer for Thomas Cary).

The south of the borough is leafier.

Tooting Bec was originally owned by the Abbey of Bec in Normandy and Tooting Graveney by Chertsey Abbey. In the 17th century Thorne described it as "a region for villas ... very pleasant and, apart from the common, very commonplace". Streatham Place was owned by Dr Johnson's brewer friends, the Thrales.

Wandsworth itself takes its name from the River Wandle whose then "fishful qualities" Izaak Walton described. The water led to the development of flour mills. In 1776 Harrison talked of "many handsome seats in the village belonging to the gentry and the citizens who have retired from the fatigues of industry". The railway and subsequent urbanisation arrived in 1846. Wandsworth Prison built in 1849 was originally the Surrey House of Correction. The Ram Brewery (subsequently owned by Young & Co) produced beer on the same site from 1581 to 2006.

St Mary, Putney Bridge (open daily) is situated on the banks of the Thames. The tower is mainly 15th century (1). Lapidge rebuilt most of the church in 1836–7. There was a bad fire caused by arson in 1973 and it was rebuilt in a very modern idiom 1980–2 (2). The fan-vaulted chantry chapel is medieval (3), and was built by Bishop West of Ely (educated at Eton and King's College, Canterbury, who died in 1533; few masses would have been said for his soul before the abolition of chantry chapels at the Reformation.) The 'Putney Debates' were held here between Oliver Cromwell and his generals in 1647; Colonel Rainsborough famously said "For really I think that the poorest he that is in England hath a life to live as the greatest he"; a dangerously radical sentiment for the time. Gibbon was baptised here.

All Saints, Wandsworth has a tower of 1680, a north aisle of 1724, and a nave of 1780 (4). The inside is barrel-vaulted with columns and a (classical) chancel of 1891 (5). The church contains a number of monuments including one of 1628 to Henry Smith (6).

The latter was born in 1549 and made a fortune in the City. He left his fortune (mainly in land) to found a Charity, which still exists. His trustees bought an estate in Kensington in 1640.

St Mary, Battersea is set by the river but now overhung by huge modern buildings. It was rebuilt by Joseph Dixon in 1775–6 as a brick rectangle. It is classical with a Tuscan portico and square tower with spire (7.) It has some 17th century glass. Its chief interest lies in the St John monuments in the gallery (8). The best are those to Oliver St John, Viscount Grandison, obit 1630 by Nicholas Stone, and to Henry St John, Viscount Bolingbroke, the politician (who died in 1751) by Roubiliac.

St Anne, St Ann's Hill, Wandsworth is a Commissioners' church of 1820–4 by Smirke. It is set high on the hill. It has a large Ionic portico surmounted by an even larger circular tower (described as "too phallic" by Elizabeth and Wayland Young) (9). It has a Victorian interior; the chancel (here seen in Advent) was added by Mountford in 1896 (10).

Battersea has a large number of Gothic Revival and other late 19th century churches.

St Mark, Battersea Rise is 1872–4 by William White in red and yellow brick with a Rhenish tower (11). It is now a HTB 'plant', but the interior is less wrecked than might be feared (12).

All Saints, Lower Common, Putney is by Street 1873–4. The land was donated by Earl Spencer and the foundation stone laid by HRH Princess Christina of Schleswig-Holstein. The exterior is yellow brick (14) and the interior red and black brick. The church has good furnishings and painted roofs (15). Its chief claim to fame however is the glass by Morris & Co (13), mainly designed by Burne-Jones.

The Ascension, Lavender Hill, very visible on the left as you go into Clapham Junction by rail from Waterloo, is in red brick by Brooks of 1876 and finished by Micklethwaite and Somers Clarke. It was financed by three aristocratic ladies and the foundation stone was laid by the Earl of Glasgow. The church has relatively recently been expensively restored (16, 20). It is firmly Tractarian tradition (18,19) and built like a Cistercian church with a narrow ambulatory round the chancel (17). It has no windows at aisle level but lancet windows in the clerestory. Kempe & Tower designed much of the glass.

St Paul, Augustus Road, Wimbledon Park is by Micklethwaite & Somers Clarke between 1877 and 1888. It is red brick and towerless (21). It has a spacious and light interior (22) with a satisfactory reredos (23). Again Kempe and Tower provided some stained glass.

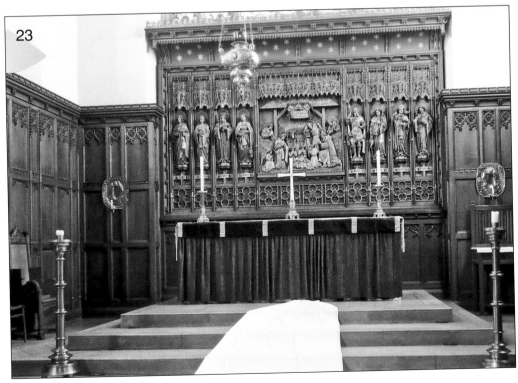

St Luke, Ramsden Road, Balham is a red brick Italian Romanesque church by F.W. Hunt of 1883–9 (24). The tower is 92 feet high and has a copper roof; it dates from 1892. It has wonderful furnishings. The marble screen, pulpit and lectern were designed by William White (25). Harry Hems was responsible for the stalls and sedila. The apse mosaic and glass are by Powell (26, 28). Martin Travers refitted the south Lady Chapel in 1924-7 (27) and was also responsible for the tall font cover. St Luke overlooks proceedings (29).

St Andrew, Garratt Lane, Wandsworth is by Mountford in red brick with twin turrets (31). The interior is red brick (30).

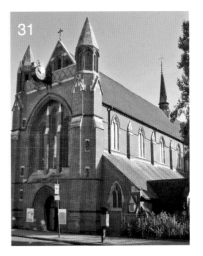

St Michael, Granville Road, Battersea is by Mountford in 1896–7, red brick, large and handsome (33). The interior has been re-ordered (34). A stained glass window of St Michael and All Angels can be found in the church (32).

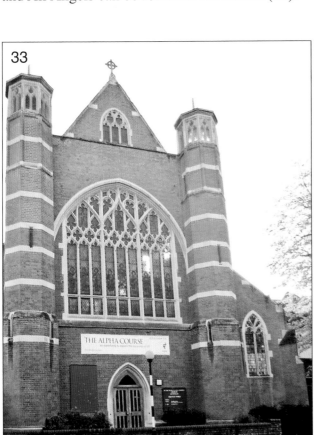

Started in the same year (1896) is **Holy Trinity, Roehampton Lane, Roehampton** by Fellowes Prynne. It has a stone exterior and a 200-foot high spire (35). The interior is dominated by the stone screen based on Great Bardfield in Essex (36). The church has excellent fittings including the reredos (37) and pulpit (38).

All Saints, Franciscan Road, Tooting was built in 1904–6 by Temple Moore for Lady Charles (Augusta) Brudenell-Bruce in memory of her husband (39). It is a large mainly brick church in late Decorated style. The church has a tower, a long nave and a choir of seven bays. It has double aisles. The

roofs are vaulted in timber. The furnishings (40) are Italian, collected by Canon John Stephens, the first vicar; Temple Moore disliked them and consequently resigned. He was replaced by Walter Tapper. The high altar is Baroque – here seen with Harvest Festival offerings (41). Iron screens are much in evidence (42).

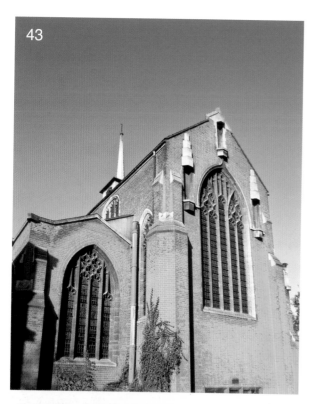

43

St Barnabas, Lavenham Road, Wandsworth is red brick with stone dressings, large and Perpendicular by C. Ford Whitcombe in 1906–8 (43). The interior is simple and spacious. An English altar survives (45). (The 'English altar' was promoted by Percy Dearmer. The altar has riddel posts (often surmounted by angels) with altar curtains to the left and the right and often behind as well. NB Betjeman "... before that divine baroque transformed our English altars and our ways".) Some modern glass adorns the church (44). The west end has been changed by the insertion of two meeting rooms.

44

45

St Mary, Keble Road Summerstown, Wandsworth is a remarkable red brick church by Godfrey Pinkerton in 1920 (46). The south east tower was never built. The church was built in a Roman basilica style with a long nave and chancel, a barrel roof, side aisles and a semicircular baptistery at the west end (50). The furnishings such as the pulpit (47) and the font (48) are attractive. Morris & Co. provided some of the glass, which was designed by Burne-Jones (49).

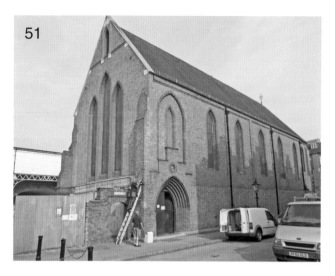

There are various Catholic churches of interest. **Our Lady of Mount Carmel and St Joseph, Battersea Park Road** is a Gothic building by Buckler of 1869, subsequently enlarged (51). It has a reasonably attractive interior (52), which is in some need of repainting.

    The Sacred Heart, Trott Street, Battersea is 1892 by F.A. Walters. The style is red brick late Norman and the church has a tall spire (53). It has another attractive interior (54).

St Thomas a Becket, Wandsworth was built in stages 1893–1912 by Edward Goldie. The tower was completed in 1926–7 by his son Joseph. It is built quite dramatically in red brick Perpendicular Gothic (55). The external statue shows the Blessed Virgin Mary being adored by angels. The church has good fittings (58).

Holy Ghost, Nightingale Square, Balham. It is 1897 by Leonard Stokes, not expensive, in yellow and red brick Arts and Crafts Gothic (56). It was originally built next to a convent of the Sisters of Perpetual Adoration. The foundation stone was laid by Bishop Bourne. The church has reasonable fittings (57, 59).

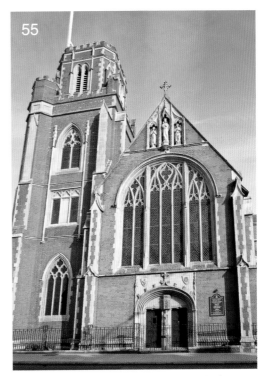

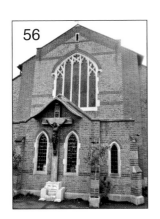

St Vincent de Paul, Altenburg Gardens, Clapham Common was built in 1903 by Kelly and is Italianate in inspiration (61). The interior is white (60).

St Mary Magdalen, East Hill, Wandsworth is an unremarkable design of 1905–6 by Lawrence Butler (63). Its claim to fame however is the internal decoration by the architect priest Father George Fayers (62, 64 – oppposite).

St Boniface, Mitcham Road, Tooting is 1906–7 by Benedict Williamson and is also Italianate. It has a north west campanile and a rose window (65). The interior is not unattractive (66) and the Stations of the Cross are interesting (67).

68

69

St Anselm, Tooting Bec is an extraordinary church of 1932–3 by J.B. Mendham in an eclectic mixture of styles – Byzantine, Romanesque, Gothic, Classical. Mendham (1851–1951) was brought up in Buenos Aires. Its north front on Balham High Street is red brick Mujedar (68); a statue of St Anselm stands under a canopy in the centre. The interior is dignified (69). The baldacchino of 1952 is early Christian in character, on grey columns with Romanesque capitals. The roof is barrel-vaulted. The benches are of plain oak.

Ecclesiastical grants in Wandsworth made by the Heritage of London Trust

1993 £5000 for pepper pot towers at St Anne, Wandsworth
1994 £5000 for railings at St Luke, Balham
2002 £2500 for pinnacles on façade of East Hill United Reform Church, Wandsworth
2002 £5000 for chancel ceiling and wall mosaics at St Mary, Balham
2002 £3000 for wall restoration at St Mary, Battersea
2005 £4000 for fleche of St Andrew, Wandsworth
2008 £3000 for St Michael, Battersea
2010 £4000 for restoration of spire and pinnacles, Holy Trinity, Roehampton
2011 £2900 towards altar at Our Lady of Mount Carmel & St Joseph (RC)
2014 £3000 for windows for Putney Community Church

The Corinthian portico of St Martin-in-the-Fields, Trafalgar Square

WESTMINSTER

In 1965 the City of Westminster assumed its present shape with the addition of the former boroughs of St Marylebone and Paddington. Westminster is bounded in the east by the City of London and Camden, in the north by Brent, in the west by Kensington and Chelsea and in the south by the River Thames.

Westminster Abbey was on its present site on Thorney Island by the late 10th century. Henry III was responsible for most of the building, with the western towers designed by Hawksmoor in the late 17th century. The Strand became known for its secular palaces (such as the Savoy) during the 12th and 13th centuries. At the Reformation Henry VIII built Whitehall Palace and set up the various royal parks. Inigo Jones built the Banqueting House 1619–22. The 18th century saw the construction of such edifices as the Admiralty, Horse Guards and the Scottish Office (Dover House). Buckingham House was transformed by Nash into Buckingham Palace after 1825. In the mid 19th century Barry and Pugin rebuilt the Palace of Westminster after a fire. Scott was the architect of the Foreign Office (1862–75).

Covent Garden was developed by the Earls of Bedford from the 1630s onwards. Somerset House in the Strand was built by Sir William Chambers in 1776–1801, the National Gallery in 1833-8 by William Wilkins, the Royal Opera House in 1857-8 by E.M.Barry and the Royal Courts of Justice in 1871–2 by Street.

St James's, Mayfair and Soho were developed from the 1670s. St James's Palace was built 1531–4 on the site of a leper hospital. Inigo Jones was responsible for the Queen's Chapel in 1623. The surviving great houses in St James's include Marlborough House (Wren), Spencer House (Vardy), Clarence House (Nash), Lancaster House (Benjamin Dean Wyatt and Philip Wyatt) and Bridgewater House (Sir Charles Barry). Of clubs Brooks's (Henry Holland), Boodle's and White's all date architecturally from the 18th century. Nash built Regent Street etc from Carlton House to Regent's Park in the early 19th century. The 'May Fair' moved Haymarket to Mayfair in the 1680s. The Grosvenor, Burlington, Berkeley and other estates developed the area from the 1720s. Many good Georgian houses remain. Most of the large aristocratic houses such as Devonshire House have gone.

Tothill Fields to the south and west of the Abbey was marshy and development was delayed. The Catholic neo-Byzantine red brick Westminster Cathedral is 1895–1903 by John Francis Bentley. Belgravia came to the Grosvenors through marriage in 1677. It was developed after 1820 by Thomas Cubitt as was Pimlico. Marylebone became part of the West End during the 18th century. Paddington was a village until the 19th century, when it was covered with stucco villas in the south and slums in the north.

St Margaret (of Antioch), Parliament Square, Westminster (open daily 9.30 – 3.30) is the only medieval parish church surviving in Westminster, being rebuilt from roughly 1482 to 1523 (1). The tower was reconstructed by John James in 1734, and Pearson was responsible for the porches in the 1890s. Scott heavily restored the nave in 1877–8, and Walter Tower was responsible for extending the chancel in 1905–6 (2). The church is eight bays long with graceful aisles. Much stained glass survives, the most interesting piece being the east window of the Crucifixion, of Dutch manufacture, part of the dowry of Katharine of Aragon (7) as does also work by Kempe, Holiday,

Piper, etc. (8). The church has a large collection of fairly small monuments (4). The furnishings are good (3, 5). Raleigh's body was brought here after his execution (6). Pepys, Milton and Churchill were all married here.

Inigo Jones in 1631–5 built **St Paul, Covent Garden** (open Monday to Friday, 8.30–5) for the 4th Earl of Bedford, to whom he is reputed to have promised "the handsomest barn in England". It is a plain oblong with a deep east portico with Tuscan columns and a pediment and overhanging eaves (9). It was damaged by fire in 1795 and restored by Thomas Hardwick. Most of the fittings are 19th century (10). It is known as the Actors' Church and many thespians have memorials on the walls (11). Grinling Gibbons, Sir Peter Lely, Thomas Arne, Dame Ellen Terry and Dame Edith Evans are all buried here.

The 17th century saw two other churches built in Westminster, both by Wren.

The first in 1676–84 was **St James, Piccadilly** (open daily). Damaged in 1940–1 it was restored by Sir Albert Richardson. It has a red brick exterior with green copper roof, tower and steeple (12). The outside pulpit in the north churchyard is by Temple Moore. The interior is light, spacious and galleried, five bays with Corinthian columns (13). The wood reredos (14) (much praised by John Evelyn) and the font with Adam and Eve are by Grinling Gibbons. The organ case came from the then Roman Catholic Chapel Royal in Whitehall (15). William Pitt the Younger and William Blake were both baptised in the church. Gillray and the 4th Duke of Queensberry ("Old Q") are buried here. Wren wrote "The churches must therefore be large. The Romanists, indeed, may build larger churches, indeed it is enough if they hear the murmur of Mass and see the elevation of the host but ours are to be fitted for Auditories ... I endeavoured to offer this in building St James, Westminster."

16

17

The second in 1680–2 was **St Clement Danes, Strand** (open daily 9 am to 4 pm) (now the RAF church) (16). It is a five-bayed classical building with a curved Baroque apse (17). The steeple of the tower was built by Gibbs in 1719–20. The church was gutted in 1941 but was successfully restored. The nave is barrel-vaulted and has Corinthian columns. The only 17th century fitting surviving is the pulpit. Dr Johnson worshipped in the church.

In 1711 the Act for Fifty New Churches was passed, and Westminster was an inevitable beneficiary with four good churches built under the Act.

18

St John, Smith Square (open for performances) was built 1713–28 by Thomas Archer at the then astronomic cost of £40,875. Situated on an island site, with four baroque towers, on a Greek-cross plan, each entrance presents a different temple-like termination to the adjacent streets (18). It is built in Portland stone. Lord Chesterfield thought the towers made the church look like an elephant on its back. The church was gutted in 1941 and restored by Marshall Sisson. The interior (now a concert hall) is dominated by giant Corinthian columns of 1742.

St Mary-Le-Strand (open Monday to Saturday, 11 am to 4 pm) was built by James Gibbs in 1714–17 and is also on an island site (19, 20). It is seven bays long, two storeyed with Corinthian over Ionic columns. The tower was an afterthought. The interior is aisleless with the orders outside repeated. The vaulted ceiling is richly decorated with squares and lozenges and the apse with cherubs' heads (21). The windows are high to block out noise, and the interior is fairly dark. St Mary-le-Strand is one of the oldest parishes in London. The original church was dedicated to the Nativity of the Blessed Virgin Mary. In 1548 it was demolished by Protector Somerset to provide stone for his new palace at Somerset House. For the next 175 years the parishioners took refuge at the Savoy Chapel but paid for their own vicars. The most famous of these was the 17th century church historian, Thomas Fuller. In 1711 the 50 New Churches Act was passed and St Mary-le-Strand applied for a new church to replace the demolished one.

22

St Martin-in-the-Fields, Trafalgar Square (open daily) is also by Gibbs, in 1721–6. It was another expensive church, costing £33,661. The 192-ft stone steeple rather clumsily surmounts the Corinthian portico (22). The interior of the portico has galleries, and four tall columns either side supporting the vaulted ceiling with its elegant plaster work (23). Equally elegant plaster work can be found inside (25). A large Venetian window dominates the east end. In January 2006 a £36 million restoration project was initiated by the then vicar, Nicholas Holtam, now Bishop of Salisbury; the glass in the east window, in particular, has been mildly controversial (24). Nell Gwynne, Hogarth and Reynolds were all buried in the church. George Herbert worshipped here when young.

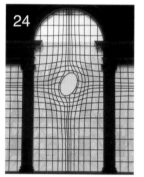

24

23

25

St George, Hanover Square
(open Monday to Friday, 8 am –
4 pm) (quintessentially a church
of the rich – see the wonderful
list of aristocratic church wardens in the church) was built
1720–5 by John James under the
Fifty New Churches Act on land
donated by General William
Steuart. The church has a
massive portico on Corinthian
columns surmounted by a steeple
(26). The interior is satisfying.
Corinthian columns support the
galleries (27). The fittings are
contemporaneous. The reredos
picture is by Willam Kent (29).
The east window has beautiful
16th century Flemish glass of the
Tree of Jesse, brought over in the
1840s (28). Henry Holland, John
Nash, Benjamin Disraeli,
Theodore Roosevelt and Herbert
Asquith were all married, and
Lawrence Sterne buried, here.

Two more classical churches were built later in the 18th century.

The Grosvenor Chapel, South Audley Street (open Monday to Friday, 9.30 am – 1 pm) (beloved of Rose Macaulay and John Betjeman in the 1950s) was built in 1730–1 as a proprietary chapel for Sir Richard Grosvenor, 4th Baronet. It is of colonial appearance, brick, with spire and porch (30). The interior is light and white, with galleries and vaulted ceilings (32). Ninian Comper restored the church in 1912–13; he was responsible for the screen, some glass and the decorative scheme (31). John Wilkes "a friend of liberty" has a tablet here. The American Armed Forces used the chapel during the Second World War.

St Mary, Paddington Green was built in 1788–91 by John Plaw. The West Way now roars past. It is built on a Greek-cross plan and surmounted by a belfry (33). The walls are made of yellow brick with porches of Portland stone on three sides and a Venetian window on the fourth. It is full of white-painted pews (35) and galleries, augmented by high church fittings (36). The church

was sensitively restored by Quinlan Terry and Raymond Erith in the 1970s; this fresco can be found adorning a building in the churchyard (34). Nollekens and Sarah Siddons are buried in the church.

The classical tradition continued into the first few decades of the 19th century.

St Mary, Marylebone Road (open Monday to Friday, 10 am – 4 pm) was built in 1813–17 by Thomas Hardwick on land given by the Duke of Portland. A portico with six Corinthian columns faces Marylebone Road (37), surmounted by a steeple with gilded angel-caryatids (38) and a belfry in stone. The galleried interior is Victorianised, the new apse being erected in 1882 (39, 40). James Gibbs and John Wesley were buried here. Nelson was a worshipper in the earlier church. Lord Byron was christened and married in the church.

All Souls, Langham Place (open daily) (an Evangelical stronghold) is a Commissioners' Church of 1822–4, built by John Nash. The church has a circular columned portico crowned by a colonnaded sharp, rather Gothic spike, designed to complete the design of Regent Street (41). Inside the church is a Corinthian hall with a flat ceiling but the earlier

furnishings with the exception of a painting of Christ before the Crucifixion went in the 1970s (42).

St Peter, Eaton Square (open Monday to Friday, except Wednesday afternoon, 7.30 am – 5 pm) was built between 1824 and 1827 by Henry Hakewill. Its dominant feature is the six-columned Ionic portico and steeple (45). Blomfield added a Romanesque chancel in 1875. An arsonist set fire to the church in 1987 under the mistaken impression that it was a (Roman) Catholic church and the interior is now modern with high church fittings (44).

St Mark, North Audley Street is now sadly an "events venue" known as "Mayfair One". It was built 1824–8 by Gandy Deering and has a large Grecian front with Ionic columns surmounted by an octagonal tower (43). The interior was almost totally reconstructed by Blomfield in 1878–9 and the furnishings remained pretty intact until recently. The reredos by Westlake and Bentley appears from the publicity photographs to survive. The church closed for regular worship in 1974.

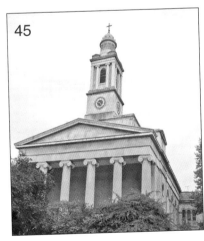

The Gothic Revival and the Tractarian movement has left Westminster with many churches, some by the greatest of Victorian architects.

The first Gothic church to be built was **St Paul, Wilton Place** (open daily, 9 am – 6.30 pm), built on the Grosvenor Estate by Thomas Cundy II in 1840–3 for the ritualist vicar, William Bennett. The building itself is yellow brick, pre-Puginian and undistinguished (46). The furnishings are however glorious, with the screen, reredos and organ case by Bodley in 1892 (47, 48, 49). He was also responsible for the design of the east window of the Tree of Jesse. The walls were decorated by Daniel Bell (50). Lavers, Westlake and Wailes provided the stained glass. Thomas Cundy II went on to build a number of other churches (below) in Westminster.

St Mark, Hamilton Terrace, St John's Wood was built in 1846–7, with a later spire (51). The church has excellent later fittings (52, 54). The pulpit is decorated with the four Evangelists flanking Saints Peter and Paul. The middle mosaic commemorates the death of the Reverend Charles Erskine from tuberculosis in the Alps (53).

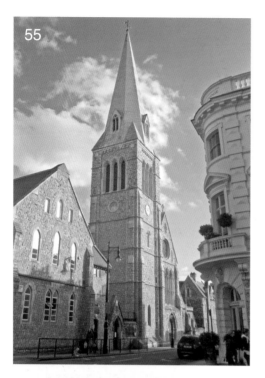

St Barnabas, Pimlico (usually open Wednesday, 12 noon to 2pm) was built in ragstone in 1847–50 for Father Bennett (cf above) in a then poor quarter, hence the ensemble of church, clergy house and school. *The Ecclesiologist* described it as "the most sumptuous church which has been dedicated to the use of the Anglican communion since the revival". It has a tower and spire at the north west (55). The evangelical Lord Shaftesbury said he "would rather worship with Lydia on the banks of the

river rather than with a hundred surpliced priests in the gorgeous temple of St Barnabas". It has wonderful late Victorian fittings – the reredos (58) and screen (56) by Bodley, the statue of Our Lady (60), the sacrament house, the chancel decoration and much sculpture by Comper (59) and stained glass by Kempe and his successors.

St Gabriel, Warwick Square was built in 1851–53 in middle pointed style. It is built in ragstone on land donated by the Second Marquess of Westminster with a 160-foot spire (61). Again it has beautiful late Victorian fittings (62, 63, 64) particularly the high altar by J.F. Bentley and the east window by Kempe (57) of Christ in Glory. A bomb in the Second War blew out the rest of the glass. Lord Edward Pelham-Clinton installed the alabaster and opus sectile work in the chancel.

Ferrey built **St Stephen, Rochester Row, Westminster** (normally open weekday mornings until 2 pm except for school terms when the local school uses the church 10.00 am – 11.30 am Wednesday and 11.00 am – 11.30 am Thursday) in 1847–50 in Middle Pointed style (65). The building is dominated by its tower and spire, the top half of which is a carbon fibre reconstruction of 1994. The church was the gift of Baroness Burdett Coutts. It has a long chancel. Most of the original fittings remain (66–69). Richard Chartres was vicar here from 1984 to 1992, becoming Bishop of Stepney in the latter year and 132nd Bishop of London three years later.

The prolific G.G. Scott was not so busy in Westminster as elsewhere and was responsible for only one surviving church – **St Matthew, Great Peter Street, Westminster** (open daily) in 1849–51. The church suffered a bad fire in 1977 but was rebuilt by Donald Buttress for Father Gerard Irvine. Scott's solid tower survives (70). The interior has been re-oriented. The reredos is by Tower (72, 73) and there is also work by Travers and Kempe. The upstairs Lady Chapel is by Comper and boasts the first ever English altar.

At the entrance to the church there is a memorial to the "extreme colonial bishop" Frank Weston of Zanzibar (71). He was a curate here as was Eric Mascall, the latter in the 1930s.

74

William Butterfield was responsible for **All Saints, Margaret Street** (open 7 am to 7 pm) in 1850–9, under the aegis of Beresford Hope and the Cambridge Camden Society (later the Ecclesiological Society). The Margaret Chapel had been a Tractarian oasis since 1839. Its successor remains an Anglo-Catholic shrine. The 227-foot red and brick tower and slate broach spire overshadow the church, clergy house and choir school.

75

(74, 75). The nave is short leading the eye to the lofty chancel arch (76) and reredos (77). The interior is however dazzling with frescoes, mosaics, gilding wherever the eye can look (80). The marbled pulpit is by Butterfield (78). The reredoses (79) and much

76

77

of the statuary is by Comper (83). Some of the stained glass is by Alexander Gibbs (81, 82). The church is undergoing a process of gradual restoration which is revealing its hidden beauty. David Hope, subsequently Archbishop of York, was once vicar here. The church has always prided itself on a certain loyalty to the Book of Common Prayer; Cyril Tomkinson, Vicar 1943–51, once famously said "The rule here is music by Mozart, choreography by Fortescue, decor by Comper but libretto by Cranmer".

84

George Edmund Street was responsible for three churches in Westminster.

The first is **St James-the-Less, Vauxhall Bridge Road** (normally open lunchtime Monday to Friday), built in 1859–61. It is one of his most significant churches, built at the expense of three daughters of Bishop Monk of Gloucester in his memory in a poor neighbourhood as a "lily among weeds". It is constructed in red and black brick, lying back from the street. The detached Italianate tower with its heavy spire rises from the porch, ending in a central spike surrounded by four spirelets (84). The inside is wide, with red granite columns (85). The pulpit by Thomas Earp (88) and capitals (86) are well-carved. Watts painted the Doom over the chancel arch, and much glass is by Clayton & Bell (87). Worship at the church was 'high' until c. 1960 by when it had become 'broad'; it has been evangelical since the 1990s.

85

86

88

87

St James-the-Less, Sussex Gardens, Paddington (open daily) is a more conventional church, flint-faced with a tall spire, built after 1882 (89). Street preserved the chancel of the previous (1841–3) church. It has much Victorian glass (90) by Clayton & Bell in the chancel and by Heaton, Butler & Bayne in the nave, and also later stained

glass (91). The church has been re-ordered and a modern altar is situated in the centre (92). Oscar Wilde was married here.

93

St Mary Magdalene, Woodchester Square, Paddington (normally open 9.30 am – 5.30 pm on Thursdays during school term) is a more remarkable church, situated in what was a poor area near the canal. Much of the original housing went in the 1960s. The church has a tall thin spire with alternating brick and stone bands (93). The interior is tall and dark (95), and much decorated with statues, etc. (94, 96). The Victorian glass is good. In the crypt beneath the south aisle lies the later chapel of St Sepulchre by Comper with the attractively decorated organ case lit by his stained glass and a star-spangled vault. After considerable deterioration from damp it is now finally being restored.

94

95

96

St Saviour, Pimlico (usually open during the week during Parish Office hours) is a later church built by Thomas Cundy II for the Marquess of Westminster, being completed in 1863–4. It is a six-bay Gothic church built in ragstone (97). The 170-foot spire was the highest in London when originally constructed. High church fittings (98, 99) can be found, some from the 1860s and others (e.g. the statue of the Madonna and Child and the Stations of the Cross) from Oberammergau in the 1930s. Victorian glass adorns the windows, some by Clayton & Bell (including the east window of Christ in Glory), and some by others. Some war damage was sustained. Laurence Olivier's father was curate here, and the actor himself was a choir boy and altar server. Sir Compton Mackenzie (subsequently a Catholic) was married here.

John Loughborough Pearson was responsible for building **St Augustine, Kilburn Park Road** (open Saturday 10 am to noon) for a high church incumbent (Dr Richard Kirkpatrick) in 1870–80. It is externally one of the most dramatic churches in England with its striking 254-feet high stone Normandy Gothic spire and eastern pinnacles rising above a red brick church (100). The west front has a gothic rose window. The interior is vaulted in brick with stone ribs with a stone screen (101). The triforium goes all round the church and the chancel is three-bayed (104). Clayton & Bell decoration can be found up to the gallery level. The high church fittings are lavish (102). The statue of the Madonna is apparently modelled on Lady Diana Cooper. A moving crucifix adorns the churchyard (103).

Very different is **St Mary, Bourne Street** to the south in Pimlico. This was built in 1873–4 as a chapel of ease to St Paul Wilton Place by Withers. It is essentially a small red brick mission church (106). Goodhart-Rendel built the north-west polygonal porch in 1925–8 (105); this leads into a chapel and then the original church through a grey arcade. Numerous fittings from the 1920s associated with the Society of St Peter and St Paul survive (109). The high altar (108) was classicised in 1921 by Martin Travers who also was responsible for the beautiful statue of the Our Lady in the north aisle. Colin Gill painted the reredos of the Seven Sorrows in the north chapel. Roderick Gradidge built the columbarium in 1999, and his ashes now lie there. The 2nd Viscount Halifax, who died in 1934, for many years the leader of the English Church Union, has a monument by Goodhart-Rendel which states he "spent his life in defence of the Catholic truth and in labour for the re-union of Christendom" (107). St Mary's remains a traditionalist Anglo-Catholic shrine.

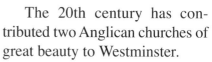

The 20th century has contributed two Anglican churches of great beauty to Westminster.

The first is **St Cyprian, Clarence Gate, Glentworth Street** (open Thursday 11 am – 2 pm) by Sir Ninian Comper, his only complete church in the Diocese of London, an attempt to build an East Anglian church in the capital. The exterior is brick-buttressed and towerless (110). The windows are Perpendicular with bottle glass panes. This all contrasts with the sumptuous interior. The nave is wide with graceful arcaded piers. The white plastered walls set off the lavishly gilded furnishings including the lacy and golden screen of 1903 (111, 112) and the English altar. Comper also provided much decoration (114) and glass (115). Pevsner famously remarked of this church "There is no reason for the excesses of praise lavished on Comper's church furnishings by those who confound aesthetic with religious emotions".

The second is **The Annunciation, Old Quebec Street** (open Monday to Saturday (10.30 am – 5.00 pm) built in 1912–14 by Sir Walter Tapper. The buttressed brick exterior (116, 117) fails to prepare one for the tall interior (119). The excellent fittings include a huge reredos and screen with curved rood beam high above the church, setting off the vaulted ceiling (118).

There are also a number of interesting Catholic churches in Westminster.

Our Lady of the Assumption and St Gregory, Warwick Street (open daily) is the only physical survivor of the 18th century Roman Catholic chapels of London attached to embassies. It began life as the Portuguese Chapel but in 1747 became the Bavarian Chapel. The present church was built by Joseph Bonomi in 1789–90. For reasons of safety at the time it has a modest brick front to the street (120). The classical inside is divided into two parts. The west is 18th century, while Bentley made the east end Byzantine with much mosaic work (121). The altar is Italian dating from the early 19th century. Mrs Fitzherbert, wife of the Prince Regent, worshipped, and Sir Richard Burton married, here. The Royal Stuart Society has erected a monument to the late Crown Prince Rupert of Bavaria (122). The church is now under the care of the Personal Ordinariate of Our Lady of Walsingham.

Catholics were not exempt from the Gothic Revival.

The Immaculate Conception, Farm Street (open daily 7 am to 7.30 pm) was built for the Jesuits as their English headquarters by Scoles in 1844–9 in an extravagant mid to late Gothic style. The west front is based on a transept of Beauvais Cathedral (123). The nave is lofty and the later side chapels very ornate. The roof is attractively painted (124). The furnishings are magnificent and somewhat surprisingly have survived the aftermath of Vatican II intact (125, 126). The high altar is by Pugin in 1848; he would have loathed the free-standing altar in front, a fibre glass copy of the bottom of his high altar. The statue of the Virgin is by Mayer of Munich. Both Evelyn Waugh and Edith Sitwell were received into the Catholic Church here.

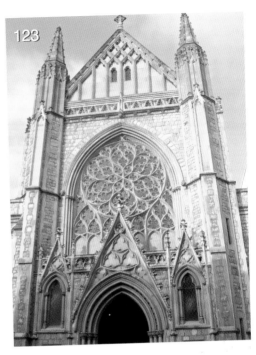

St Mary of the Angels, Moorhouse Road, Paddington was built for the then Father Henry Manning and the Oblates of St Charles in ragstone, mainly by Clutton, and completed in 1857 (127). Bentley provided later additions. The interior is ornate and has been recently restored (128). Father Michael Hollings was parish priest here 1978–97.

St Charles Borromeo, Ogle Street was built in 1862 by Nicholl in a Gothic Early English style and consecrated by Cardinal Wiseman (131). The high altar, large reredos (with painted panels by Westlake) (130) and chancel stalls are by Bentley. The church has recently received the benefit of a full immersion font (129), courtesy of the late Father Fudge.

Corpus Christi, Maiden Lane (open daily) is situated opposite Rule's Restaurant in Covent Garden although its inconspicuous entrance can be easily missed (132). It was built in 1873 by Frederick Pownall (whose son was to become parish priest of the The Assumption, Warwick Street). It is entered by steps down to the Early English interior (134). The high altar is by Thomas Earp (133). Father Francis Stanfield, writer of the well known hymn "Sweet Sacrament Divine" was parish priest here in the 1880s. The church is currently undergoing refurbishment at the hands of Anthony Delarue.

St James, Spanish Place (open daily) started life as the Spanish Embassy Chapel. It was rebuilt by Edward Goldie in Kentish ragstone on a slightly different site between 1890 and 1918 (135, 136). It is a tall vaulted stone Gothic building and has lavish decorations by Bentley and by Garner (137–9).

Thereafter the Catholics reverted to classicism. **St Patrick, Soho Square** (open daily) was rebuilt 1891–3 by John Kelly of Leeds. It is red brick and classical with a campanile on the square (140, 142). It has an imposing Italian interior with side chapels (141, 143). All has recently been expensively restored at a cost of some £3 million by Father Alexander Sherbrooke.

Notre Dame de France, Leicester Place, off Leicester Square (open daily), is a curiosity. It was rebuilt for Fr Deguerry after the War in 1951–5 by Professor Hector Corviato. The church is now run by the Marist Fathers. The concave front (144) merges into the adjacent flats and has a relief of Our Lady of Mercy by Georges-Laurent Saupique (146). Steps lead up to the interior rotunda (145). Much modern sacred art can be found inside, including wall paintings in a side chapel by Jean Cocteau (147), mosaics by Boris Anrep and the tapestry by Dom Robert de Chaunac-Lanzac.

Ecclesiastical grants in Westminster made by the Heritage of London Trust

1983 £2500 for the restoration of the church clock at St Paul, Covent Garden

1983 £1000 for cleaning work at St Mary-le-Strand

1985 £8125 for the restoration of the orb and weather vane at St Martin-in-the Fields

1989 £5000 for repair of clock stonework etc at All Souls, Langham Place

1990 £5272 for tower brickwork at St James-the-Less, Vauxhall Bridge Road

1990 £5000 for wall paintings at St Augustine, Kilburn

1991 £4950 for spire cross and clock face at St Saviour, Pimlico

1991 £5000 for the clock tower of St Anne, Soho

1991 £1000 for timber spiral staircase at St John, Smith Square

1992 £5000 for caryatids at St Marylebone Parish Church

1992 £1500 for turret clock at St John, St John's Wood

1993 £5000 for restoration of Burne-Jones windows at St Peter, Vere Street

1995 £2500 for regilding of chancel screen at St Paul, Knightsbridge

1997 £5000 for replacing terra cotta tiles at All Saints, Margaret Street

1998 £4000 for stonework repair at St John, Smith Square

2000 £3000 for statue at St Stephen, Rochester Row

2000 £3161 for porch of St Barnabas, Pimlico

2006 £4000 for restoration of west window at St Mary Magdalene, Paddington

2005 £4000 for sgraffito work at Russian Orthodox Church, Ennismore Gardens

2006 £4000 for restencilling at St Patrick R.C., Soho Square

2007 £2350 for portico of St.Martin-in-the-Fields

2008 £2000 for altar frontal and dossal at St Cyprian, Clarence Gate

2008 £5000 for stonework at St Gabriel, Warwick Square

2009 £1300 for restoration of two panels at St Martin-in-the-Fields

2010 £3000 for restoration of the clock at St George, Hanover Square

(continued)

Ecclesiastical grants in Westminster made by the Heritage of London Trust (continued)

2010 £3000 to conserve pulpit at St James-the-Less, Vauxhall Bridge Road

2011 £2000 for east window of St Mary Magdalene, Paddington

2011 £2000 for stonework at St Gabriel, Warwick Square

2013 £2000 for stone cross finial at St John the Evangelist, Kensal Green

2013 £2000 for stained glass at St Mary, Bourne Street

2014 £3000 for tower and spire at St Mark, Hamilton Terrace

St George, Camberwell (Southwark), 326
St George, Hanover Square (Westminster), 407
St George RC, Sudbury (Brent), 61
St George, Woolwich (Greenwich), 128
St George-in-the-East, Old Cannon Road (Tower Hamlets), 353
St Giles, Camberwell (Southwark), 328
St Giles, Ickenham (Hillingdon), 192
St Giles-in-the-Fields (Camden), 76
Good Shepherd, Carshalton Beeches (Sutton), 346
Grosvenor Chapel, South Audley Street (Westminster), 408
Guardian Angels RC, Mile End Road (Tower Hamlets), 365

St Helen, Kensington (Kensington & Chelsea), 235
St Helen and St Giles, Rainham (Havering), 181
St Hilda, Stondon Park (Lewisham), 278
Holy Cross, Cromer Street (Camden), 84
Holy Cross, Greenford (Ealing), 107
Holy Ghost RC, Balham (Wandsworth), 393
Holy Innocents, Hammersmith (Hammersmith & Fulham), 155
Holy Redeemer, Exmouth Market (Islington), 216
Holy Redeemer, Streatham Vale (Lambeth), 264
Holy Spirit, Narbonne Avenue (Lambeth), 263
Holy Trinity, Brompton (Kensington & Chelsea), 225
Holy Trinity RC, Brook Green (Hammersmith & Fulham), 157
Holy Trinity, Clapham Common (Lambeth), 251
Holy Trinity, Cloudesley Square (Islington), 213
Holy Trinity, Dalston (Hackney), 143
Holy Trinity, Eltham (Greenwich), 128
Holy Trinity, Hoxton (Hackney), 139
Holy Trinity, Northwood (Hillingdon), 195
Holy Trinity, Prince Consort Road (Kensington & Chelsea), 234
Holy Trinity, Roehampton (Wandsworth), 388
Holy Trinity, Sloane Street (Kensington & Chelsea), 233

St Ignatius RC, Tottenham High Road (Haringey), 165
Immaculate Conception RC, Farm Street (Westminster), 429
Immaculate Heart of Mary RC, Hayes (Hillingdon), 196

St James, Bermondsey (Southwark), 327
St James, Clapham Park (Lambeth), 265
St James, Clerkenwell Close (Islington), 212
St James, Piccadilly (Westminster), 403
St James, Spanish Place RC (Westminster), 432
St James-the-Less, Sussex Gardens (Westminster), 421
St James-the-Less, Vauxhall Bridge Road (Westminster), 420
John Keble Memorial Church (Barnet), 48

St Luke, Charlton, Greenwich (Greenwich), 125
St Luke, Eltham (Greenwich), 129
St Luke, Kidderpore Avenue (Camden), 86
St Luke, Old Street (Islington), 211
St Luke RC, Pinner (Harrow), 177
St Luke, Ramsden Road (Wandsworth), 386
St Luke, Sydney Street (Kensington & Chelsea), 224
St Luke, West Norwood (Lambeth), 254
Lumley Chapel, Cheam (Sutton), 343

St Margaret, Lee (Lewisham), 275
St Margaret RC, East Twickenham (Richmond upon Thames), 321
St Margaret, Streatham (Lambeth), 262
St Margaret, Westminster (Westminster), 400
St Margaret and All Saints RC, Canning Town (Newham), 297
St Margaret of Antioch, Barking (Barking & Dagenham), 36
St Margaret of Antioch, Leytonstone (Waltham Forest), 375
St Mark, Battersea Rise (Wandsworth), 383
St Mark, Dalston (Hackney), 142
St Mark, Hamilton Terrace (Westminster), 413
St Mark, Kennington (Lambeth), 254
St Mark, North Audley Street (Westminster), 411
St Mark, Regent Park (Camden), 81
St Mark, Silvertown (Newham), 295
St Martin, Gospel Oak (Camden), 87
St Martin, Ruislip (Hillingdon), 191
St Martin-in-the Fields (Westminster), 406
St Martin of Tours, Chelsfield (Bromley), 64
St Mary Abbots, Kensington (Kensington & Chelsea), 223
St Mary, Addington (Croydon), 96
St Mary, Battersea (Wandsworth), 382
St Mary, Beddington (Sutton), 342
St Mary, Bexley (Bexley), 52
St Mary, Bourne Street (Westminster), 425
St Mary, Cable Street (Tower Hamlets), 359
St Mary RC, Cadogan Street (Kensington & Chelsea), 236
St Mary RC, Chislehurst (Bromley), 70
St Mary, Dartmouth Park Hill (Camden), 83
St Mary, Ealing (Ealing), 109
St Mary, East Barnet (Barnet), 42
St Mary, East Bedfont (Hounslow), 200
St Mary, Grafton Road (Barking & Dagenham), 38
St Mary, Hampton (Richmond upon Thames), 315
St Mary, Harefield (Hillingdon), 193
St Mary, Harmondsworth (Hillingdon), 188
St Mary, Harrow (Harrow), 168

St Mary Magdalene, Woolwich (Greenwich), 127
St Matthew, Bethnal Green (Tower Hamlets), 355
St Matthew, Brixton (Lambeth), 255
St Matthew, Westminster (Westminster), 417
St Matthias, Richmond (Richmond upon Thames), 316
St Matthias, Stoke Newington (Hackney), 140
St Michael, Blackheath (Greenwich), 127
St Michael, Chiswick (Hounslow), 204
St Michael, Camden Road (Camden), 84
St Michael, Croydon (Croydon), 101
St Michael, Granville Road (Wandsworth), 387
St Michael, Highgate (Camden), 79
St Michael, Mark Street (Hackney), 143
St Michael, Walthamstow (Waltham Forest), 373
St Michael and All Angels, Bedford Park (Hounslow), 203
St Michael and All Angels, London Fields (Hackney), 146
St Mildred, Addiscombe (Croydon), 102
St Monica RC, Hoxton (Hackney), 148
St Monica RC, Palmers Green (Enfield), 121
Most Holy Redeemer and St Thomas More RC, Cheyne Row (Kensington & Chelsea), 238
Most Holy Trinity RC, Dockhead Road (Bermondsey), 336
Most Precious Blood RC, O'Meara Street (Southwark), 333
Most Precious Blood and St Edmund RC, Edmonton (Enfield), 121

St Nicholas, Chislehurst (Bromley), 65
St Nicholas, Chiswick (Hounslow), 202
St Nicholas, Deptford (Lewisham), 273
St Nicholas, Plumstead (Greenwich), 124
Notre Dame de France RC, Leicester Square (Westminster), 434

Our Lady of the Assumption RC, Victoria Park Square (Tower Hamlets), 365
Our Lady of the Assumption and St Gregory RC, Warwick Street (Westminster), 428
Our Lady and St Catherine of Siena RC, Bow (Tower Hamlets), 363
Our Lady of Grace RC, Charlton (Greenwich), 132
Our Lady of Grace and St Teresa of Avila RC, Chingford (Waltham Forest), 376
Our Lady Help of Christians RC, Blackheath (Greenwich), 132
Our Lady of the Holy Souls RC, Kensal Town (Kensington & Chelsea), 238
Our Lady of La Salette RC, Bermondsey (Southwark), 332
Our Lady of Mount Carmel RC, Kensington Church Street (Kensington & Chelsea), 240
Our Lady of Mount Carmel and St Joseph RC, Battersea Park Road (Wandsworth), 392
Our Lady of the Rosary and St Dominic RC, Haverstock Hill (Camden), 91
Our Lady of Sorrows RC, Peckham (Southwark), 332
Our Ladye Star of the Sea RC, Croom's Hill (Greenwich), 131
Our Lady and St Thomas of Canterbury RC, Roxborough Park (Harrow), 176
Our Lady of Victories RC, Clapham Park Road (Lambeth), 265

St Saviour, Aberdeen Park (Islington), 215
St Saviour, Eltham (Greenwich), 129
St Saviour RC, Lewisham High Street (Lewisham), 279
St Saviour, Pimlico (Westminster), 423
St Saviour, Walthamstow (Waltham Forest), 372
St Silas, Kentish Town (Camden), 87
St Silas, Pentonville (Islington), 217
St Simon Zelotes, Moore Street (Kensington & Chelsea), 235
St Stephen, Dulwich (Southwark), 330
St Stephen, Gloucester Road (Kensington & Chelsea), 229
St Stephen, Hounslow (Hounslow), 203
St Stephen, Lewisham High Street (Lewisham), 277
St Stephen, Rochester Row (Westminster), 416
St Stephen, Rosslyn Hill (Camden), 88

St Thomas, Clapton Common (Hackney), 137
St Thomas, Hanwell (Ealing), 111
St Thomas a Becket RC, Wandsworth (Wandsworth), 393
St Thomas of Canterbury RC, Rylston Road (Hammersmith & Fulham), 156
St Thomas of Canterbury RC, Woodford (Redbridge), 306
St Thomas More RC, Dulwich (Southwark), 335
Transfiguration RC, Kensal Rise (Kensington & Chelsea), 239

St Vincent de Paul RC, Clapham (Wandsworth), 394

St Wilfrid RC, Lorrimore Road RC (Southwark), 334
St Winefride RC, Latimer Road, Wimbledon (Merton), 287